SINK
THE
FRENCH

Sink the French

The French Navy
after the Fall of France 1940

David Wragg

Pen & Sword
MARITIME

First published in Great Britain in 2007 by
Pen & Sword Maritime
an imprint of
Pen & Sword Books Ltd

ISBN 978 1 84415 522 4

A CIP catalogue record for this book is
available from the British Library

Typeset in Palatino by
Phoenix Typesetting, Auldgirth, Dumfriesshire

Printed and bound in England by
CPI UK

Pen & Sword Books Ltd incorporates the Imprints of Pen & Sword Aviation,
Pen & Sword Maritime, Pen & Sword Military, Wharncliffe Local History,
Pen & Sword Select, Pen & Sword Military Classics and Leo Cooper.

For a complete list of Pen & Sword titles please contact
PEN & SWORD BOOKS LIMITED
47 Church Street, Barnsley, South Yorkshire, S70 2AS, England
E-mail: enquiries@pen-and-sword.co.uk
Website: www.pen-and-sword.co.uk

Contents

	Acknowledgements	vii
	Introduction	ix
1	Entente after Enmity	1
2	Distant Wars	6
3	Germany Strikes East	25
4	The Marine Nationale in 1940	34
5	The Balance of Power at Sea	44
6	Germany Strikes North	65
7	The Battle of France	74
8	Surrender and the French Forces	92
9	Vichy France	119
10	Stand Off at Alexandria	128
11	Conflict in North Africa	136
12	The Cross of Lorraine	150
13	Madagascar	175
14	Syria	182
15	Operation Torch	188
16	Scuttle!	204
17	The French Fleet at War	211
	Appendix I – The French Fleet in 1940	221
	Appendix II – Comparison of French and British naval ranks.	232
	Bibliography	234
	Index	235

Acknowledgements

In researching and writing any book like this, the author is always grateful to those who have helped to ease his way, and especially the team at the Imperial War Museum Photograph Archive and Sound Archive, an invaluable source of original material.

David Wragg
Edinburgh
December 2006

Introduction

One of the essential truths of warfare is that, at the outset, it is the aggressor who scores the victories, whereas the ultimate victor takes successive defeats while preparations are put in hand for the build-up of forces and the preparation of strategies that will ultimately lead to victory. That was the fate of the United Kingdom during the Second World War. Later, when war was joined in the Pacific, that was the fate of the United States, and again of the United Kingdom.

The exception to the above comes when the defenders are swept aside and their country occupied. That was the fate of Czechoslovakia, then Poland, Denmark, Norway, the Netherlands and then Belgium during the Second World War. The French lived in an awkward limbo, defeated, but not wholly conquered, and with substantial forces left in unoccupied Vichy and in the French colonies, many of which were within easy reach of Europe.

Those citizens of the territories occupied by Germany had two choices, remain and live under occupation, or escape and continue the war fighting with an ally. The French had a third choice, neutrality, with the initially unoccupied Vichy France having an uneasy subjugate relationship with Germany, and at the same time harbouring resentment against the British, whom they firmly believed had betrayed them. Vichy France was in fact very much a German satellite, with its workers encouraged to volunteer for work in German war industry. The degree of control exercised by the Vichy authorities over French forces outside France was variable and uncertain, but these forces were substantial, especially in North Africa and the Near East, bordering the Mediterranean and where, before French surrender, French forces in the air, on the ground and at sea, were larger than those deployed by the British. This was hardly surprising, as the French territories along the Mediterranean were far larger than those of the British Empire: Morocco, Algeria, Tunisia and Syria individually, let alone collectively, were larger than Gibraltar or Malta, and also had populations to match.

Elsewhere, in the Far East, French Indo-China was soon pulled into the Japanese empire, but Madagascar remained as a thorn in the side of the Allies. The island was in a position to provide bases from which domination of the Indian Ocean would be challenged. Once Axis air superiority and advances on the ground in North Africa, with Greece, Albania and Yugoslavia occupied, closed the Mediterranean to British shipping, supplies for forces defending the Suez Canal in Egypt had to be sent via the Cape route, and Madagascar sat astride the route north from the Cape to the Red Sea.

The mistake at the outset was that British and French military planners thought that any future war in Europe would follow the pattern set during the First World War, still spoken of as the Great War. Belgium would be invaded and most likely suppressed and occupied, while German forces would invade France but be held there. Thus the French had built the Maginot Line, although with the earlier experience in mind, had failed to continue this to the Channel Coast, but instead had relied on German forces being held in Belgium. No one considered the invasion of the Netherlands, still less the distraction caused by the invasion of Denmark and Norway.

This was as nothing compared with the lack of preparation before the German forces started to move. Belgium knew that in any future war, salvation once again would lie in the intervention of the United Kingdom and France, but there were no joint plans, still less exercises. Belgium was not one of the Allies at the outset of the war. The Dutch could be excused for believing that once again their neutrality would be respected, but this was a shade over-optimistic. Hitler's Germany was not that of the Kaiser. It is much easier to understand the Danish and Norwegian attitudes, although again, the dependence of German industry, short of home-produced raw materials, on Swedish iron ore should have been a warning. After all, the Gulf of Bothnia froze in winter, so the only all-year route between Sweden and Germany lay through Norway and Norwegian coastal waters. Even so, perhaps this was discounted in Oslo, and possibly they believed that it would be all over by Christmas, despite the experience of the Great War.

The real danger signal for Denmark and Norway lay in the success of the British maritime blockade of Germany during the Great War. This would be more difficult to enforce with Germany holding Danish and Norwegian territory. This was a lesson overlooked. When British and German forces took the war into Norwegian coastal waters, showing that neutrality was no longer an option, it was too late. Invasion was already imminent.

The mistake made by those who draft alliances and sell them to the parliamentarians and, ultimately, to the electorates of the democracies, is that all parties are believed to share the same interests and fears. This has always been nonsense. Alliances between nations are not marriages. They are subject to interpretation and only work when there is sufficient overlap in objectives and in common interest, and when this lasts long enough for the alliance to be effective. Indeed, the Allied intervention in the Russian Civil War failed because of differences between the Allies, and differences between them and the forces engaged by those territories fighting for their own independence from Russia, and nothing more, such as the Poles, the Finns and the Ukrainians. It was even a problem with the North Atlantic Treaty Organisation, NATO, for while most of the participants in the most successful and enduring alliance of all time saw Soviet expansion as the threat, for Greece and Turkey, mutual antipathy and distrust was the main reason for maintaining a high defensive profile.

In fact, here too is a comparison with the situation leading up to the outbreak of the Second World War, and the period between the declaration of war and the start of the Battle of France. The British wanted an Inter-Allied War Council with the French so that the overall strategy could be kept under constant review, but the French authorities resisted this. The same streak of independence became apparent during Charles de Gaulle's second term of office as president, beginning in 1958. Difficulties between de Gaulle and the North Atlantic Treaty Organisation, NATO, meant that while France remained nominally part of the alliance, it eventually left the NATO Council and did not take part in joint exercises or joint ventures such as the NATO Standing Force Atlantic.

As the Battle of France went against the Allies, the British were concerned about their own survival and husbanding resources to prevent a German invasion and eventual defeat. The French wanted everything that both countries possessed put into the battle, even if it meant a double victory for Germany. Earlier, the French had resisted British plans to bomb German cities and lines of communication for fear that their own cities would be bombed in retaliation. The fear was realistic, as until it had bases in the Low Countries and France, the Luftwaffe, lacking long-range heavy bombers, would only have been able to strike at French targets and those on the East Coast of Scotland. On the other hand, it meant that the Germans had a free hand and enjoyed a victory with relatively light losses and with the civil population spared the horrors of the war. More important, it meant that the Germans began to suspect that the Allies had no real stomach for war. Such a delusion might seem odd with hindsight, but until the invasion of Norway, the Germans faced little real opposition, for while the Poles had fought, their armed forces were ill-equipped.

Effective and broadly-based alliances with a consolidated command and well organised exercises at the outset would have sent different signals to Germany. Yet, while the Allies were unprepared for war, so too was the German Navy, the Kriegsmarine, which had not expected war until 1944 or 1945, with a major fleet action unlikely before 1948. The Kriegsmarine had little more than a tenth of the planned force of submarines, few of the battleships and none of the minimum of four aircraft carriers envisaged in Plan Z, its plan for war. After Czecho-slovakia, Hitler did not believe that the British and French would stand by Poland. Even before that, Abyssinia had shown the international community to be reluctant to take a firm stand. Once war had been declared, some form of compromise or negotiated peace was still considered possible. Even once fighting broke out, considerations of German retaliation inhib-ited French, and by implication British, strategy.

CHAPTER ONE

Entente after Enmity

Anglo-French rivalry and enmity pre-dates the creation of the United Kingdom itself. The Norman conquest in 1066 was the result of the frustrated ambitions of William, Duke of Normandy, who was convinced that Edward I of England, more usually known as Edward the Confessor, had promised him the throne on his death, and that his successor, Harold, was a usurper. William's success in England created not so much Anglo-French tensions as a rift in society, with an overwhelmingly French-speaking aristocracy ruling over Anglo-Saxon peasants, while the church was reformed with a similar influx of French bishops.

The true tensions between England and France arose as a result of William's success, with the King of France and the Counts of both Anjou and Flanders alarmed by his growing power. By 1086, the King of France, and William of Normandy, King of England, were at war, with William finally dying the following year as a result of wounds received during the campaign. Just as the Normans, descendants of the Norsemen who had occupied the territory that became known as Normandy, had been fully assimilated into French society, so too did they eventually become assimilated into English society. The new English royal dynasty retained their French territories, leaving the French with the uneasy situation that a substantial and prosperous part of France owed allegiance not to the King of France, but the King of England. This was the situation that led to repeated wars between England and France over the centuries that followed, and it was not until the Hundred Years' War, which lasted from 1337 to 1453, that the English were finally expelled from France, retaining just one foothold, the port and town of Calais, eventually lost by that most unpopular of the Tudor monarchs, Mary I in 1558.

Nevertheless, the eviction of the English from French soil did not lead to any significant improvement in relations between the two countries. Wherever their interests clashed, conflict followed. The French provided a haven for the Stuarts during the period of the Commonwealth, and later supported Scottish attempts to re-establish the Stuart monarchy in Scotland against Hanoverian rule from London. The two powers clashed as a result of an aggressive French foreign policy that succeeded in uniting most of the rest of Europe against them, so that by 1763, France had lost its colonies in both Canada and India.

Revolution in France changed little, other than that many of the French nobility fled to England to escape the guillotine. The foreign wars that followed the revolution, led by Napoleon Bonaparte, the French emperor or dictator, saw some of the most famous British victories, including the great naval battles of the Glorious First of June, 1794, the Nile, 1798, and Trafalgar, 1805, between which the British evicted the French from Malta, and with their continental allies, won a decisive military victory in 1815 at Waterloo.

While it would be misleading to suggest that the end of the Napoleonic era and the restoration of the monarchy in France in 1815 marked a sea change in Anglo-French relations, the two countries did at least stop fighting. The absence of open hostilities between what was by this time the United Kingdom and France even survived the second revolution and overthrow of the French monarchy in 1848, and Napoleon III, nephew of Napoleon I, becoming emperor in 1852. Napoleon III once again embarked on an expansionist foreign policy, provoking the

Franco-Prussian War of 1870–1871 and the siege of Paris.

French defeat at the hands of the Prussians resulted in the loss of Alsace and Lorraine to Prussia, as well as further change within France itself. The foundation of the Third Republic saw expansion once again, but this time through establishing much of North Africa as French colonial possessions, with further colonies established in the South Pacific and France taking over what became known as French Indo-China.

Prussia had emerged as one of the leading European powers and with the unification of Germany that followed, threatened to dominate the continent. Even so, it was not until 1904 that a formal alliance between the United Kingdom and France emerged with the signing of the 'Entente Cordiale' in 1904. The term perhaps says it all, in that this was not an alliance in the sense that it would be understood after the Second World War, but instead simply, as the French would have it in translation, a 'friendly understanding'. The specific benefits to both countries were that the British recognised and accepted French interests in Morocco and the French did the same for British interests in Egypt. With the exception of Spanish territory in Morocco, most of North Africa from the border between Tunisia and present-day Libya to the Moroccan shores of the Atlantic Ocean became French territory, with large scale settlement by French colonists especially significant in Algeria. Although never formally a British colony, Egypt effectively became subservient to British interests.

Nevertheless, the Entente did at least mean that two of the most powerful nations in Europe were at peace and a balance to the rising power of Germany in the years before the First World War. It also marked the basis for an alliance with France as the threat of war in Europe loomed. The Entente almost coincided with the start of an Anglo-German naval race. The laying down of the first all-big-gun battleship, HMS *Dreadnought*, in 1905, overnight made all other battleships obsolescent when she joined the fleet in 1906, having taken just a year to build. In one stride, the Royal Navy had left all other navies behind, but in doing so, it had, paradoxically, also thrown away its own overwhelming numerical superiority over its rivals. The race to build the largest fleet of Dreadnought battleships and battle-cruisers was open to anyone with the necessary shipbuilding capacity, and the Royal Navy could be said to have been starting from scratch once again. On paper, the Royal Navy was still the equal of any two navies it was likely to engage in combat, but at sea, the gap had closed dramatically, especially when the Imperial German Navy received its first Dreadnought-type battleship as early as 1907. The United Kingdom still had a superior naval shipbuilding capacity compared to that of Germany, but the parsimony of the pre-war Liberal government meant that money rather than productive capacity was the limiting factor in re-equipping the Royal Navy, while for the Germans it was a simple matter of industrial capacity.

The spark that ignited the First World War was the assassination of the heir to the Austrian throne at Sarajevo, Bosnia, on 28 June 1914. After recriminations had flown back and forth, Austria declared war on Serbia on 28 July, leading Russia to mobilise in support of their Slav cousins, while Germany declared war on both France and Russia, and demanded that Belgium allow 700,000 troops to cross its territory to attack France. This last move meant that British involvement was inevitable as the UK was the guarantor of Belgian sovereignty. In anticipation of war, a Triple Entente consisting of the United Kingdom, with its empire, France and Russia was in place, to which Italy and Japan later became allied. Germany and Austria-Hungary comprised the Central Powers, and also gained allies of their own, of which Turkey was possibly the most strategically significant. Both Austria-Hungary and Turkey were concerned to retain their empires, while a war aim of Russia was to free the Slavonic peoples from Austro-Hungarian dominance.

'Entente' rather 'alliance' meant that British and French co-operation was far from smooth. The British were unprepared for a major European land war, and had not experienced such for almost a hundred years. The French probably had not antici-pated Germany moving through Belgium, even though this was a far easier route than attacking directly from Alsace and Lorraine. Neither country had exercised with the other, and it seems little short of a miracle that in due course they cooperated as well as they did. Pre-war exercises may well have been considered as being provocative, but it is unlikely that they were even considered. Even within the two nations, the armies were ill-prepared, although the French did at least have sufficient reservists ready to call up, while the British, with their history of small, professional armies, had fewer trained or partly-trained men amongst the civilian population, and it was to take a massive mobilisation to remedy the shortfall in numbers.

Cooperation was not confined to the Western Front. French troops and warships were present at Gallipoli, landing on the coast of Anatolia to create a diversion.

While the conflict devastated Belgium and much of France, and at one time Paris itself was threatened, total defeat never seemed likely with most of France still unoccupied; even a small part of Belgium around the port of Ostend never fell to the Germans. French forces were even able to join those of the United Kingdom, the United States and Japan, as the war ended in an attempt to influence the outcome of the Russian Civil War.

The First World War, or Great War as it was known at the time and for more than two decades afterwards, left both Britain and France financially exhausted and with a massive loss of manpower. Friendly relations remained, but neither had learnt the true lesson of combat: to be prepared.

CHAPTER TWO

Distant Wars

The end of the First World War was marked in the western democracies with a mixture of relief and anxiety. There was relief that this 'war to end all wars' was over and that the massive toll of casualties had come to an end. This was balanced by concern over events in Russia.

Allied intervention in the Russian Civil War that followed the revolution had been a failure, largely because the makeshift alliance that had been put in place had fallen apart. First, the Poles and other nationalities fighting for independence had given up as soon as their objectives had been attained. Second, this tendency was also reflected in the fact that many foreign forces, such as the Czechoslovaks, simply wanted to return home once their own country had been freed from Austro-Hungarian domination. Third, the wartime allies themselves had different objectives, which meant that equipment was not always sent quickly towards the front, especially in Siberia, where the Americans had different objectives from the British and the French, and the Japanese were playing a different game altogether, with more than a hint of their future policy in the Far East. The Americans in particular saw no reason for the re-instatement of the Romanov dynasty, and later were to be slow to appreciate the threat posed by what was then known as

Bolshevism, and only later became more usually known as Communism.

Even the White Russian anti-Bolshevik forces suffered from fragmentation and indecision, while the leaders played power games with no single undisputed leader to rally behind.

The shock waves that passed through the European democracies in particular surpassed those that had followed the French Revolution. As earlier, the fear was that revolution could be exported. This concern dissipated fairly quickly after the French Revolution, but persisted following the Bolshevik Revolution. Coming at the end of an exhausting war, society itself lacked the cohesiveness that would have enabled the democracies to shrug off events in Russia. In Germany, in particular, returning soldiers and others soon made their presence felt, and in several cities, but especially Munich, attempts were made at revolutionary activity.

Such nervousness should not be under estimated. The initial momentum behind the rise of National Socialism in Germany was inspired almost as much by anti-Soviet feeling as by anti-Semitism. Industrialists and others looked for signs of Bolshevik tendencies. One railway manager, appointed to a self-contained operating area of the Southern Railway, on the Isle of Wight, was warned that men in one workshop were suspected of harbouring 'Bolshevik tendencies'. The deteriorating industrial situation in the United Kingdom, which culminated in the General Strike of 1926, only fuelled these fears. In the United States, the Wall Street Crash was seen as a very real crisis of capitalism.

In the United States, initially the Russian Revolution was taken less seriously than in Europe. After all, the new Soviet Union was to be a republic, and wasn't the United States also a republic? This went beyond naivety. Parts of Soviet industry were rescued, even created, with the assistance of American industrialists, especially the motor industry. Given subsequent events, it is also strange that the Soviet aircraft industry benefited to some extent from German involvement, as the Treaty of Versailles forbade German aircraft manufacture, amongst other activities, and Soviet Russia was one of the 'offshore' locations where German designers could continue to develop their ideas.

American attitudes also had their counterparts in Western Europe, where apologists for the Soviet regime soon appeared.

The negotiations that led to the Treaty of Versailles were not only attempts to redraw European boundaries and create a better post-war world, they were also an attempt to seek full retribution from Germany for the damage inflicted by the war. British and, especially, French demands for reparations seriously undermined the Germany economy, creating resentment and hardship. On the other hand, American insistence that aid given to the United Kingdom and France during the war years be repaid in full, meant that neither country could afford to be overcome with concern for their former foe. To some extent, reparations offset the debt to the United States.

Nevertheless, the situation became so acute with the German economy suffering first from hyperinflation and then massive unemployment, that action was necessary. In 1931, the American president, Hoover, imposed an emergency moratorium on British and French war debts, which gave both countries the freedom to ease the burden of reparations on Germany. In 1932, both countries finally ended reparations from Germany. Hoover, meanwhile, turned to the difficult task of persuading Congress to cancel the British and French war debts.

The truth was that the state of the world economy in the aftermath of the First World War had been such that generosity was in short supply. Governments could not afford welfare reform for their own people, let alone for their allies, and certainly not for a former foe. Yet, such problems were largely in the West. In the Far East, Japan had been remarkably unaffected by the war years, and indeed, despite being one of the allies, had contributed relatively little to the war effort. Mention has already been made of Japanese duplicity during the Russian Civil War, but Japan had already indicated its intentions as early as the Russo-Japanese War of 1904–05.

The Americans, for their part, did not want to see the cancellation of war debt as a means of releasing funds for British and French re-armament. The result was that, in 1932, the United States launched two conferences, one for disarmament in Geneva and the other in Lausanne for international debts. These followed on from earlier attempts to impose limitations on armaments, such as the Washington Naval Treaty of 1922, which imposed limits on the size of the major navies, including restricting the total tonnage of ships, the maximum size of warship in each category and limits for the total tonnage of each category of warship. For Germany, the Treaty of Versailles had banned aircraft manufacturing, an air force and even, at first, commercial aviation, while the Germany army was limited to 100,000 men and the navy became simply a coastal defence force. The treaty also imposed tight restrictions within Germany, so that the Rhineland was demilitarized.

From the German point of view, the outcome of the war had been one of constant injustice. Apart from the burden of reparations, the country had also lost its few colonies. Hitler, and others, were amongst those who saw colonial possessions as providing a captive market, and also space or *Lebensraum* into which expanding populations could move. Indeed, not only Germany but also both Italy and Japan were inspired by the need to establish empires, having missed their share of the colonial expansion of the nineteenth century, largely because Italy itself had been fragmented and because Japan had been isolationist. Another factor that all three countries had in common was a paucity of natural resources, with Germany having massive reserves of coal, but nothing else, while Italy and Japan didn't even have this to any appreciable extent.

So it was that markets were not the sole driving force behind German and Japanese expansionism. Both countries lacked natural resources, although Germany at least had coal. Nor were German intentions aimed mainly at securing the return of her colonies, such as South West Africa and German East Africa. Germany was looking east, but within Europe, but at first such intentions were kept from the world at large and simply mentioned within the National Socialist Party and the core of the future German armed forces.

The poor financial outlook had another side effect: the democracies sought to curtail expenditure wherever they could, and with peace firmly established, or so they liked to believe, disarmament was on the agenda. The problem with disarmament was, and has always been, that only the democracies remained true to their word, so American insistence on disarmament; while never complete, did further undermine the future defence capabilities of the European democracies. The British government in particular was to attempt to set an example by making a gesture in scuttling a cruiser at sea, while also attempting to reduce the maximum tonnage permitted for any single warship type and reducing the calibre of armaments.

HITLER TAKES POWER

Hitler became Chancellor, effectively prime minister, of Germany on 30 January 1933. Seldom has anyone been projected into such high office in a major country with so little experience of political life and of government. The former didn't matter, for inter-war Germany had had its taste of democracy, and it was nothing more than a taste as the new national diet was to be dictatorship rather than monarchy. Hitler and his supporters were effectively a militant protest movement rather than a constructive political party, yet they had become the party of government.

Today, the fact that on 1 February, Hitler was to make the first radio broadcast of his life would be regarded as amazing for a prominent politician, but radio had only been available for a decade or so, something reflected in the fact that only a small minority of the population had radios in their homes. Nevertheless, he not only had to make his first broadcast, he had to deliver a decisive policy address that would set the tone of his government. What is more, he had to gain the support of the vast majority of Germans at a time when popular support for his political party had passed its peak, and also encourage his own followers. While Germany was still militarily and financially weak, he also had to avoid alarming the democracies. Only a minority of Germans had radio receivers at the time, but the medium was already important, and his address would be taken seriously by listeners both within, and without, Germany at the time. Perhaps it was as well that television wasn't available, for Hitler has been described as sweating with anticipation.

Despite the wide interest in what he had to say, Hitler's speech concentrated on domestic issues. The recurring theme of his speech was the need for national unity. He harked back to Germany's surrender in November 1918, and to the Communist revolutionaries that had come to the fore in the period immediately following the armistice. In the speech, and in the years that followed, the trauma of German surrender in 1918 became a recurring theme, an obsession with defeat.

Relieving unemployment and the poverty of the German peasant farmers were two specific objectives promised by Hitler, as well as reforming the relationship between the central government or the state, usually referred to as the *Reich*, the provinces or states, known as the *Länder*, and local government. Given the traumatic impact of hyperinflation on the population during the 1920s, his promise to promote efficiency and economy in public services, but to maintain health care and pensions must have reassured many sceptics, as well as promising to protect the Germany currency. All of this was innocuous, very much a case of 'motherhood and apple pie', and for domestic consumption.

On foreign policy, in many respects it was what Hitler did not say that mattered more than his actual words. Doubtless aware that his words would be considered carefully by the former wartime allies, Hitler gave conditional support to the Geneva disarmament negotiations. He even went as far as to stress that he would even accept the abolition of the German army, if every other country also disarmed completely. Yet, he laid equal stress on the fact that the state's primary duty was protection of society and 'the restoration of the freedom of our *Volk*'. Few would argue that the first duty of government is the defence of the people, but as the German people were at this time still free, the stress on restoring freedom implied a hidden meaning. Many believe that by 'freedom', Hitler meant the freedom for Germany to do much as it pleased, placing national self-interest above all other considerations.

Inevitably, the generalized message for the world at large differed somewhat from the specific message intended for a more sympathetic audience. On 3 February, the new Defence Minister, General Blomberg, invited Hitler to address the country's senior military officers. The message was much clearer to this select and loyal audience. At home, Hitler's new administration would destroy Marxism and reconstruct the economy, while preparations would be made for a rearmament programme. Rearmament was essential because Hitler was anxious lest the former wartime allies might re-intervene whenever they felt like it, while he also saw Germany as vulnerable to attack from Poland and France, being squeezed between these two powers. The fact that Poland lacked the financial, industrial and military strength to do very much, and attacking Germany was far beyond its capacity, was conveniently overlooked.

The real meat of Hitler's address to the high command lay in his foreign policy ambitions. The concept of *Lebensraum*, 'living space', was to the forefront of his ambitions. He also called for new 'export opportunities', which was Hitler-speak for new colonies. By colonies, Hitler did not mean looking for tracts of Africa or Asia, but expansion to the east, followed by a ruthless and single-minded Germanization of the occupied territories that could be incorporated into the *Reich* and thus provide the *Lebensraum* that was so necessary. This was colonization with a continental twist.

An even clearer indication of the way in which the new regime was to evolve followed on 9 February, when Hitler chaired a cabinet committee on job creation. The sole theme of the work creation programme was to be rearmament, whatever the country's representatives might say at Geneva. 'The future of Germany depends exclusively and only on the reconstruction of the Wehrmacht,' demanded Hitler. 'All other tasks must cede precedence to the task of rearmament . . . the interests of the Wehrmacht must in every case have priority.' [1]

Hitler still had to fight a general election, set for 5 March 1933. While doubtless the National Socialists had high hopes, the results were a disappointment. Support for them had peaked far too early, and despite widespread and often brutal intimidation, they failed to sweep the board. Nevertheless, what has been described as 'massive pressure', was applied to the Catholic Centre party, and after no doubt considerable arm twisting, their support was gained and Hitler had a two thirds majority that enabled him to force through the Reichstag the all-embracing Enabling Law of 23 March 1933, which effectively cancelled parliamentary debate and control, so that the road to dictatorship was opened wide. This piece of legislation meant that, from that time on, Hitler's government could rule by decree rather than by considered legislation.

The nature of the new Germany was soon apparent. A good example was that, doubtless noting the promises to relieve unemployment and rural poverty, the socialist trade unions convinced themselves that they could work with the new government. For the first time in Germany, 1 May 1933 became a public holiday, with Hitler, Goebbels and the trade union leaders joining in a celebration of national labour. The day after, the trade union leaders faced reality. On 2 May 1933, large squads of brownshirt militia stormed the trade union offices and closed them, while trade union funds and property were confiscated. At works level, there were also Nazi activists on the shop floor, but their activities were getting out of hand and becoming an embarrassment for the party, so the National Socialist Party launched a German Labour Front, which acted as a controlling organization for a regional network of 'trustees' of labour.

Meanwhile, members of the other political parties, including the Communists and Social Democrats, were subjected to violent attacks, as were members of the Jewish minority, whose homes and businesses were attacked.

Gradually, Hitler's ambitions started to become apparent to a wider audience. In June 1933, Hitler told the Hungarian prime minister, Julius Goemboes, in private, that he intended to crush France. Before that, the German government had imposed a moratorium on all of Germany's foreign debts, to take effect from 30 June, and at the same time a massive programme of rearmament was initiated that would account for up to 10 per cent of the gross national product for the future. The initial debt moratorium was to be short-lived due to the volume of protests from the wartime allies, and payments at the rate of half the interest and capital due soon restarted, but in December these rates were reduced to 30 per cent.

Meanwhile, in response to a British initiative calling for a further round of reductions in national armed forces, and British rejection of German plans for limited rearmament, Hitler withdrew from both the Geneva disarmament talks and membership of the League of Nations on the grounds that he could not accept Germany's second class status. It seems that if not Hitler himself, then several of his close associates, expected intervention, especially from France and Poland. The two countries could have acted together and possibly succeeded, but France suffered from internal civil unrest at the time aroused by its own fascists, and Poland was placated in early 1934 by a combination of economic concessions and a treaty of friendship.

The initial plans for reconstruction of the armed forces had included plans for a secret air force. Already, German manufacturers had continued their work abroad while gliding schools in Germany ensured that young pilots were being nurtured. In 1932, the air force was planned to have 200 aircraft, but in September 1933, this was raised to 2,000 combat aircraft, due to be operational by 1935. For the army, there were two four year plans at the end of the first, in 1937, it was to have 300,000 men in twenty-one divisions, with adequate reserves to expand to sixty-three divisions on the outbreak of hostilities. This required conscription, forbidden by the Treaty of Versailles. Plans were laid to re-occupy the Rhineland by 1937.

By April 1934, with a German military budget that forced the French to withdraw from discussing military issues with

Germany, it was clear that the country was embarked on a course of military expansion of a degree that had not been seen for some years. Until 1934, most foreign observers could remain blissfully unaware of German intentions, but from that time onwards, the course was set. Individual projects could be hidden or their full extent disguised, as when one new battle-cruiser was laid down officially, but two, *Scharnhorst* and *Gneisenau*, were actually built. Airliners were developed that had a concealed military role, with the Junkers Ju52 trimotor originally being intended to double up as a transport, although it was obsolescent by the time the opportunity came. Until the mid-1930s, this means of aircraft development was none too difficult to sustain or conceal, as it was not until the late 1930s that the basic designs of bomber and transport aircraft began to diverge significantly, and many air forces, including the Royal Air Force, had operated bomber-transports. As the bombers became slimmer and leaner, some of the Dornier airliners produced during the 1930s must have been extremely un-comfortable for the passengers of Deutsches Luft Hansa (not Lufthansa, as today), the national airline, so cramped and slender were their 'bomber' fuselages.

WAR IN PEACE

The period between the two world wars was far from peaceful, and the signs that peace was threatened were there for those who cared to notice. The British armed forces had been heavily involved in low level conflicts in the Middle East during the 1920s. As the 1930s passed, initially the leading protagonists were Italy and Japan, and it was not until later in the decade that Germany felt confident enough to attempt to impose territorial demands on her neighbours.

Despite having only a limited involvement in the First World War, Japan felt the effects of the post-war recession. The country had suffered from a banking crisis in 1927, followed by a collapse in the market for agricultural goods and complaints that the country was too densely populated, echoing the demands for *Lebensraum* being heard from Germany. International trade was affected by the world depression during 1930–1932. Despite the isolation practised by Japan until the late nineteenth century, the country had developed a sophisticated free market economy by the early twentieth century, but throughout the 1930s, the economy began to become militarised with increasing state control. As in Germany and, for that matter the Soviet Union, state control and planning became the dominant feature in Japan, with electricity supplies and oil brought under state control during the mid-1930s, followed by rice production in 1936. As in Germany, the requirements of the military received priority over everything else as the country began to prepare for war.

Japan had been the first to show its hand, although the conquest of Korea at the beginning of the twentieth century was evidence enough of Japanese expansionist intentions. Mainland China was the obvious area for Japanese expansion, a task made more tempting by the weak control exercised by the Chinese government in Peking. After Korea had been occupied, attention focused on the Chinese province of Manchuria, which had long been claimed not only by Japan and China, but also by Russia. The Japanese had maintained a presence on the Chinese mainland since their victory in the Russo-Japanese War of 1904–05, policing the area with the Kwantung Army, supposedly independent of the Imperial Japanese Army. Using allegations of sabotage on the important Port Arthur-Mukden line of the Japanese-owned and operated South Manchurian Railway Company as an excuse, the Japanese Kwantung Army occupied Manchuria in September 1931. It seems that the Japanese government in Tokyo was itself surprised by this development as the Kwantung Army was out of control by this time, having staged the railway incident of its own accord, planting the explosives, and then overran Manchuria contrary to the orders of its own commanding officer and of the Japanese authorities in Tokyo.

The Japanese at first euphemistically referred to their assaults on China as 'incidents', so first there was the 'Mukden incident', referring to the railway line, followed by the 'Manchurian incident' as the entire territory was overrun. The term 'incident' avoided the legal complications of formally declaring war, and was suggestive of a localised punitive action, and some maintain that it was also intended to indicate that the Chinese would accept blame and seek a compromise.

Manchuria was then given the name of Manchukuo, the state of the Manchus, and a puppet state under the emperor Pu-Yi was established. The Kwantung Army followed up its conquest of Manchuria with the occupation of the Jehol region of Inner Mongolia. Not content with this, it also fostered independence movements in neighbouring areas, conducted experiments in biological warfare and prepared for ultimate combat with the Soviet Union, which it regarded as the real threat in the Far East. Because the Soviet Union did not declare war on Japan until the last days of the Second World War, this effort was wasted, and when the Kwantung Army eventually engaged with Soviet forces during August 1945, despite having more than 500,000 men, it had so little equipment, including just fifty combat aircraft, and was so short of fuel, that a rout occurred with heavy casualties and the survivors taken prisoner.

Although Manchukuo was established in March 1932, it was not formally recognized by Tokyo until September, and few other countries did so.

The occupation of Manchuria was followed by an uneasy period during which there were many minor clashes between Japanese and Chinese forces, usually being settled by negotiation, and that inevitably seemed to entail further concessions by the Chinese.

THE CHINA INCIDENT

During the night of 7/8 July 1937, shots were fired at a Japanese detachment engaged in manoeuvres not far from Peking. While one Japanese soldier went missing, he was later found and returned to his unit. There were no casualties. Many believe that the shots were fired by Japanese troops to create yet another 'incident', and while this has never been confirmed, the fact the events were far less serious than many earlier encounters between Japanese and Chinese forces, yet led to war with China, suggests that the Japanese were anxious to contrive a *casus belli*. This was the 'China incident', although some senior Japanese officers, anxious to play down the increasing militancy towards China, which some of them saw as a costly and unnecessary distraction, referred to its as the 'North China incident'.

Initially, the local authorities in the areas close to the 'incident' seemed anxious to placate Japanese wrath, but in Nanking, the nationalist leader, Chiang Kai-Shek, decided to take a stand. From this time on, the 'incident' developed, often in a haphazard way, into what was nothing less than total war between the two countries. Further clashes took place not in north China, but in the region around Shanghai, where Japan had long had considerable business interests. Japanese warships sent to the area, possibly as a show of strength to discourage nationalist attacks on Japanese citizens and businesses, were attacked by Chinese aircraft on 14 August 1937. An immediate response by the Japanese resulted in intensive fighting in and around Shanghai, while further north, Japanese forces began to advance through northern China.

This was effectively the beginning of the Sino-Japanese War. The West was thoroughly aware of what was happening, not only because of press and newsreel footage, but because Shanghai had the largest concentration of European and United States citizens and business houses. Japanese brutality, culminating in the 'rape of Nanking' when the nationalist capital was taken on 13 December, was hard to ignore, although the western democracies continued to be slow to react. Japan continued to have a free hand in China for a few years longer until 1940, when the United States applied severe economic sanctions which were eventually to prompt the Japanese to attack the US Pacific Fleet's forward base at Pearl Harbor in Hawaii, without a prior declaration of war.

The Far East was distant enough for public opinion to be

complacent, although both the United Kingdom and France had extensive interests in the area, and the UK had made considerable promises of strong support to its important dominions of Australia and New Zealand. Of the British colonies in the region, Singapore and Hong Kong were important as bases and as trading stations, while Malaya has been described by some historians as being the only British colony worth having, with its output of tin and strategically vital rubber.

London was anxious to allay Australian and New Zealand fears, and promised that in the event of war in the Far East, a strong fleet would be sent to Singapore. By the time the threat erupted, the 'strong fleet' was heavily engaged elsewhere and British forces in Malaya and Singapore were singularly ill-equipped to repulse a Japanese invasion.

ABYSSINIA

Less easy to ignore in Europe were the expansionist policies of Italy. As with Japan, Italy was a former First World War ally, and unlike Japan, had become involved to some extent, not least by helping to confine the Austro-Hungarian fleet to the Adriatic.

Italy had been a democracy from unification in 1861 until Benito Mussolini became the first fascist dictator in 1922. Although Italy had unified too late to take part in the scramble for colonial possessions, it did have a small number of colonies, including Libya in North Africa, Eritrea and Italian Somaliland in East Africa or the 'Horn of Africa', and the Dodecanese Islands in the eastern Mediterranean.

This was not enough. In October 1935, Abyssinia, present-day Ethiopia, was invaded by Italian forces based in Eritrea and Italian Somaliland. The outrage was condemned by the League of Nations and war was anticipated, with the British Mediterranean Fleet preparing plans to block the Suez Canal to Italian shipping and mount an attack on the major Italian naval base at Taranto, in the instep of the 'foot' of Italy. French reluctance to become embroiled in another war meant that had the

British been determined to act, they would have had to do so alone. Despite the League of Nations having been one of the American President Woodrow Wilson's plans for a lasting peace, the fundamental weakness of the organization was that the United States never became a member. Certainly, the commander-in-chief of the British Mediterranean Fleet at the time of the crisis fully expected war to break out. If it had done so, a British blockade of the Suez Canal would have been relatively easy to enforce and would have had an almost immediate impact on Italian forces in East Africa.

Following the invasion of Abyssinia, Italy and Germany signed the Axis Treaty in June 1936, despite the international opprobrium being suffered by the Italians and the imposition of economic sanctions against Italy, albeit barely enforced. That was also the year that Hitler sent German troops into the Rhineland, marching through the towns and cities to the cheers and applause of the population, almost as if they were a liberating army. The Rhineland had been demilitarized under the Treaty of Versailles, but yet again, the wartime allies did nothing.

It was clear that Germany, Italy and Japan were doing as they thought fit, and discounted the attitudes of the rest of the world. For the dictatorships, international opinion didn't matter.

As it was, the Abyssinian Campaign was far more one-sided even than the war in China. Cinema audiences were treated to the sight of tribesmen armed with nothing more potent than rifles being attacked by Italian bombers and mechanised forces. Almost overnight, the country's sovereign, Haile Selassie, became a popular figure for Western audiences.

The next step was the Spanish Civil War, which started in 1936 and lasted until early 1939. While the conflict, between Republicans and Nationalists did not fit the pattern of territorial gain sought by the Japanese and the Italians, it did enable both the Soviet Union and the Germans and Italians to become involved, causing considerable disquiet in the democracies. The Republicans were supported by the Soviet Union, which supplied manpower and weapons, while the Axis powers supported the Nationalists, led by General Franco. It was the use of German-built Junkers Ju52 trimotor transports to lift the Spanish Foreign Legion from the Spanish enclaves in North Africa to mainland Spain that enabled the Nationalist offensive to gain momentum.

The war enabled the Germans to try out tactics and evaluate their latest aircraft, although the aircraft initially provided were obsolescent. German forces involved in the campaign were known as the Condor Legion. The Nationalists won, but the conflict left Spain bankrupt and exhausted, divided and as backward as ever. Nevertheless, as in Abyssinia and China, the overpowering impact of the bomber was there to be seen.

Hitler had been an early admirer and protégé of Benito Mussolini, and although their friendship was to suffer under the stresses of wartime, when Hitler felt that his southern ally was not always fully committed, it was the Führer who was behind the successful rescue of Mussolini when he was first imprisoned after his downfall.

AUSTRIA

Outside of Germany, the biggest single group of Germans were the Austrians. In fact, when Austria emerged as an independent state after the collapse of the Austro-Hungarian Empire in 1918, the name chosen at first was *Deutsch-Österreich*, and union with the new post-war German republic was planned. The Treaty of Versailles, anxious to avoid creating a new power group having just seen the two main protagonists in the war crippled, forbade both moves. In addition, the new Austria lost much of its pre-war territory to neighbouring Czechoslovakia, Hungary, Italy and Yugoslavia, including areas such as the South Tyrol, ceded to Italy, which were German-speaking.

The post-Versailles history of Austria was difficult. In addition to the economic difficulties suffered by most countries between the wars, the political situation was unstable with violent clashes between opposing groups. Amongst such groups were National Socialists and others advocating union with

Germany. So violent was the situation that many political parties maintained their own private armies, known as *Wehrverbande*, almost as if their leaders were warlords.

While the Austrian government sponsored a non-party coalition, the *Vaterlandische* Front, after the National Socialists took power in Germany in 1933, it failed to gain credibility, and increasingly Germany felt free to interfere in Austrian politics and sponsor those parties that favoured union with Germany. A counter to such moves had come from Italy, but as Italy and Germany formed the Axis, Italian efforts in supporting Austrian independence became much weaker. Seeking a compromise, the Austrians signed an agreement with Germany in 1936 that gave Germany control over foreign policy in return for Germany respecting Austrian independence!

In March 1938, the *Anschluss* was declared after German troops marched into Austria, and the Austrian government decided not to oppose these overwhelming forces. The *Anschluss*, meaning coming together, was at first very popular with the majority of Austrians.

In contrast to other German occupations, the Germans were anxious to make the whole affair seem as unmilitary as possible, but the 100,000 German troops initially stationed in Austria were under strict orders to suppress any opposition.

Austria not only provided Germany with additional territory and manpower, with a population of some 6.7 million, it also brought additional industrial capacity, energy and raw materials for the increasingly hungry German industrialization.

MUNICH

By this time, German confidence was growing. They had not only supported Mussolini and Franco, they had seen that the rest of the world seemed to lack the will to intervene. Now was the time for Hitler to demonstrate what he meant when he described the German people as *ein Volk*, one people. He had his eyes on those Germans living beyond the country's borders, of whom the most obvious were the Sudeten Germans, living in the west of Czechoslovakia. The Sudetenland had been ceded to Czechoslovakia, a new state created from the ruins of the Austro-Hungarian Empire, by the treaty of Versailles. The German population of 3 million was a substantial minority of the 14 million people living in Czechoslovakia.

Hitler's demands for the Sudetenland to be incorporated into Germany became increasingly strident, and Europe appeared to be on the verge of all out war. Nevertheless, the British and French were anxious to avoid another war if at all possible, and in the Munich Agreement of September 1938, signed by the United Kingdom, France, Germany and Italy, Czechoslovakia was effectively compelled to cede the territory to Germany.

Often criticised, usually with the benefit of hindsight, the Munich Agreement bought the democracies time in which to continue their rearmament, and the evidence suggests that the United Kingdom in particular put this time to good use, indeed, far more so than Germany, suffering from an acute shortage of foreign exchange and unable to meet the equipment demands of all three branches of the armed forces simultaneously. On the other hand, it signalled to Hitler that an aggressive tone could win the day. Significantly, Mass Observation, the early survey of the attitudes of the British public that started its work during the period immediately before the outbreak of war, noted that a leadership that desired appeasement was in tune with the mood of a public determined not to fight another war if at all possible.

Slovakia, by far the poorer end of the country, began to come under the sway of the Germans, while Hungary annexed part of its territory. In the north, the Poles seized their chance and annexed the main area occupied by the 60,000 people of Polish descent living in Czechoslovakia. Despite the original German demands having been met, in March 1939, Germany occupied most of what remained of Czechoslovakia.

If further evidence was required that Italy and Germany were embarked on a course that could only ultimately lead to war, it came on 7 April 1939, Good Friday, when Italy invaded Albania, a poor, mountainous country on the other side of the Adriatic.

Colonel Abas Kupi took two battalions of the small army and with some tribal levies, managed to resist the Italian forces for seventy-two hours, giving King Zog time to escape. Once again, the United Kingdom and France did nothing, with the UK recognizing the annexation in an attempt to discourage Italy from allying itself with Germany in the future conflict that was increasingly being seen as inevitable.

Once again, appeasement had been the preferred option.

Notes
1 Minutes of meeting of work creation committee, 9 February 1933.

CHAPTER THREE

Germany Strikes East

Poland had been governed by Tsarist Russia, and had fought and gained its independence during the Russian Civil War. Essentially landlocked at the time (the borders were changed in the aftermath of the Second World War), access to the Baltic Sea was by means of a narrow strip of land that cut through German territory and was known to the Germans and both the UK and the USA as the 'Polish Corridor'. The 'corridor', although it didn't look like one on the map, was sizeable, about 6,000 square miles (15,000 square kilometres), roughly the size of Northern Ireland. The Germans saw the corridor as cutting off East Prussia from the rest of the country, while, to the Poles, it was more than a simple link with the sea, it was territory that had been seized from Poland by the Prussians in 1772, and therefore theirs by right.

Having finally taken the whole of Czechoslovakia in March 1939, it was only a matter of time before Hitler moved against the Poles. German diplomats demanded that the port of Danzig, at the head of the corridor, be incorporated into the Reich, while Germany should have complete control over the road and rail links between the fatherland and East Prussia. Anxious to put an end to German expansion, the United Kingdom offered Poland an alliance, while at home the prime minister, Neville

Chamberlain, declared that the UK would guarantee Poland's independence and promised military aid. This was followed up by a mutual assistance pact, signed on 25 August 1939.

INVASION

The promise of British assistance infuriated Hitler. He denounced the 1934 non-aggression pact with Poland, and as early as late May had outlined his plans for an invasion to his service commanders. A bizarre twist was then applied to the plans, with an offer of Polish territory to the Soviet leader, Joseph Stalin, which led to the secret Nazi-Soviet Pact signed in Moscow on 23 August. The two opposing ideologies had buried their differences to ensure that Hitler could conclude his plans for Poland without fear of Soviet intervention, and that Stalin could regain what he still regarded as his rightful territory. Perhaps this twist of fate was not so surprising, since rather than Hitler being 'right' and Stalin 'left', both National Socialism and Communism should be seen as variations on extremist politics. Although the pact between the two dictatorships was styled as a 'non-aggression pact', the 'non-aggression' only applied between themselves, and it was a vehicle for aggression against other countries, with a substantial division of Poland at the top of the agenda. The value placed upon such pacts by Stalin can be gauged from the fact that the Soviet Union had also signed a non-aggression pact as far back as 1932 with Poland, and this too was worthless. In fact, it was probably intended to prevent Poland providing a base for anti-Bolshevik counter-revolutionaries rather than ensuring that the two nations did not go to war.

Stalin was subjected to diplomatic approaches by both the British and the French as war drew closer. Both saw salvation in an eastern front that would force Hitler to divide his forces and make the prosecution of the war difficult and costly. In this, as in other respects, all the evidence is that both allies saw the Second World War following the pattern of the earlier global conflict, although, of course, neither Italy nor Japan could be counted on as allies by this time.

Recalling the international situation during that last summer of peace, Admiral (later Admiral of the Fleet) Sir Andrew Cunningham commented that it continued to be tense.

'Hitler was pursuing his now well-known technique over Danzig, and it seemed only a matter of time before he made a move against Poland,' wrote Cunningham in his memoirs. 'It appeared there were many indications of preparedness in Germany for a coup after August 15th, probably connected with Danzig. As it was evident that words alone carried no conviction with Hitler, it had been decided to commission the Reserve Fleet on July 31st for two months. At the same time an idea had got about that Hitler would not rush things, and that a state of tension might last for two years or more.'[1]

In planning the assault on Poland, the Germans adopted the Japanese tactic of staging an 'incident', in this case faking an attack by Polish forces on a German radio station close to the border between Poland and Germany during the evening of 31 August. The refinement was that all of the nine-man assault force were dressed in Polish army uniforms. The radio station personnel were locked up and those tuned in to the radio station heard shots and then an announcement by the 'Poles' that it was time to attack Germany. The attackers had also brought a concentration camp inmate with them, whom they shot before leaving so that the corpse could be shown to war correspondents as an innocent German civilian slaughtered by the brutal Poles.

POLAND'S DEFENCES

That any Poles would have attempted to provoke war with Germany beggared belief as there was no way by 1939 that Poland would have been in a position to pose a military threat to Germany. While the Germans had modernized their armed forces within the limitations of finance, industrial capacity,

manpower, the balance of payments and scarce natural
resources, the Poles had failed to do so. It has been pointed out
that Germany between the two wars had a weaker economy
than the United Kingdom or France, with a poorer standard of
living for the population, but Poland was worse off still.

In terms of population, Poland had 35 million people in 1939
compared with 79.5 million in Germany. The Polish armed
forces were inferior in numbers and equipment to those of
Germany, with much of their equipment obsolete, with just one
motorized division and even included mounted cavalry. The
Polish Air Force, *Polski Lotnictwo Wojskowe*, which had become
autonomous only in 1938, having originally been part of the
army, was still primarily designed to serve the needs of the
army, but not in the concept of *blitzkrieg* as the German would
have it since the force of more than 250 aircraft attached to the
army was there for aerial observation post, AOP, and liaison
duties. Combat aircraft included just 55 fighters and 76 bombers.
While the country had an indigenous aircraft industry and plans
to modernize its armed forces, the only modern aircraft in
service was the PZL P-37 twin-engined bomber. A small navy
was maintained, and there was a Polish merchant fleet, but this
was no maritime power.

The German attack followed early on the morning of 1
September, 1939. By any objective measure this was a very rapid
response indeed to a provocation by a neighbouring power!
Normally such an action would have been followed by diplomatic protests, perhaps punitive measures, but not by all out
warfare. This was the first example of the *blitzkrieg* assault with
air force and armour operating in close coordination, so that it
was indeed a lightning war and furthermore was applied along
a broad front. Despite fighting valiantly, the Poles were overwhelmed. There was considerable skill exercised in planning the
German assault. None of the German armed forces was at its
planned strength, the navy least of all, but by concentrating the
Panzer divisions and providing overwhelming force at strategic
points, the advance was rapid. The element of surprise was such
that most of the Polish Air Force's aircraft were destroyed on the

ground, although a few did manage to get into the air to challenge the Luftwaffe.

A joint British and French ultimatum to Germany to withdraw from Poland was ignored. The Germans knew that there was little either country could do to relieve the plight of the Poles. Poland was beyond the range of the aircraft of the day flying from British or French territory, and sending warships into the Baltic would have been suicidal, even leaving aside the navigational difficulties of passing through the relatively shallow waters of the Kattegat. Of course, as many have argued, the United Kingdom and France could have attacked those areas of Germany within easy reach of aircraft based in France, including the industrial areas of the Saarland, but even during the Battle of France, the French resisted proposals to bomb Germany for fear of reprisals upon their territory. In the event, British forces based in France were not present in sufficient strength early enough to ease the pressure on the Poles. There was also the curious state of mind that accepted Germany applying maximum force to Poland and the Poles, but had the British and French concerned about causing civilian casualties in Germany. Neither of the Allies had the truly heavy bomber that was to inflict so much damage on Germany later in the war, with the RAF's heaviest aircraft being the Vickers Wellington, later to be downgraded to a medium bomber; but the Handley Page Hampden was no better than a medium bomber and the Fairey Battle light bomber was useless.

In the end, any opportunity to affect events in Poland was lost and, after signing their new treaty, both Germany and the Soviet Union warned the two western allies not to remain at war with Germany.

ALLIES UNPREPARED

Perhaps the worst aspect of the relationship between the two allies at this early stage of the war was that the French repeatedly resisted British proposals for an Inter-Allied War Council with the French so that the overall strategy could be kept under constant review.

'Meetings on a lower level between local British and French commanders were taking place and were undoubtedly a step in the right direction,' wrote Cunningham later. 'But it by no means followed that the action proposed had the approval of the respective governments.'[2]

While German forces made good progress across Poland, fighting continued until, early on the morning of 17 September, Soviet forces invaded the country from the east. Thereafter, continued resistance was pointless as Polish forces had been concentrated on the front against the German invaders. The Soviet Union tried to hide its aggression by claiming that it was invading Poland to safeguard the Slavonic population, the Belorussians and Ukrainians who, for the most part, were the majority in the region taken by Soviet troops.

After the second invasion, Germany and Russia had to decide how to administer Poland. Neither side wanted a Polish puppet state, and instead both kept their separate parts of the country. The one big change was that instead of the boundary between German-occupied territory and that of the Soviet Union running along the River Vistula, it was moved 93 miles east to run along the line of the River Bug. Stalin was prepared to concede a large area of Poland in return for German agreement to the Soviet seizure of the Baltic states of Estonia, Latvia and Lithuania. Once again, a pact was entered into by the two countries, signed in Moscow on 28 September as the German-Soviet Treaty of Friendship, Co-operation and Demarcation.

Poland was effectively divided into three. There was a Soviet zone of occupation, really a buffer zone, and in the west of the country, a large area was annexed to Germany, marking the start of the territorial expansion to give the German people their *Lebensraum*, or living space, at the cost of the inhabitants. In between these two areas was a zone that was occupied by Germany but not annexed, known as the General Government.

For the Poles, what mattered was continuing the fight against the invaders. Many Polish servicemen escaped to join the

Western Allies, and prominent amongst these were the officers and men of the Polish Navy and the Polish merchant fleet. This did not mark a substantial increment to Allied strength as the naval forces consisted of just four destroyers, three of which managed to join the Royal Navy, but one of which was sunk by the Germans, five torpedo boats, and two gunboats, while a minelayer was sunk by the Germans. Of the small flotilla of six submarines, one was interned at Tallin in Estonia, and two others in Sweden, with only one reaching the UK. There were also four minesweepers, some river craft, a surveying ship and a submarine depot ship.

Many believe that Hitler genuinely expected peace, and believed that, as at Munich, appeasement would again become Anglo-French policy. On the other hand, German industrial and economic success in the years following the Second World War have allowed many to overlook the dire state of the German economy during the 1930s. Few countries escaped the impact of the years of depression, and Germany, with scant natural resources, found exporting difficult; therefore the balance of payments situation became difficult with insufficient funds to buy such essentials as fertilizer and animal feed, iron ore, non-ferrous metals and oil. Every means was tried to ease the situation, including authorizing officials to raid homes where gold and foreign currency might have been kept, taxing Jewish emigrants, subsidizing exports and developing synthetic oil and rubber production. In the case of synthetics, oil and petrol were both possible, produced from coal, the one natural resource that was abundant in Germany, although at almost four times the price of refined petrol. Rubber was much more difficult to produce in the necessary quantities at the desired quality.

Many of Germany's trading rivals had taken their currencies off the gold standard, effectively devaluation of the currencies. Such a move had been considered in Germany, as it would have made German exports so much cheaper and more competitive, but it would also have made imports much more expensive. The standard of living of the average German at the time was well below that of their British and French counterparts. Worse still, the biggest demand for imports came from the armaments industries.

It has been said of the United Kingdom on the outbreak of war on 3 September 1939, that the country could only hope to win a long war, but could only afford a short one. In fact, the pressures on the German economy of re-armament and the expansion of its armed forces had been such that it had effectively tipped the country into bankruptcy. Plans for a German field army of 3.6 million men on mobilization were matched by plans for a Luftwaffe of 21,000 aircraft, something that the United States Army Air Force and United States Navy combined only approached in the later stages of war, despite having more than three times the population of 1940s Germany and enormous natural resources of its own. At sea, one plan had succeeded another to create a massive German Navy, but again realism was lacking.

The truth was that Germany had given itself four years from 1934 to rebuild its armed forces to create a viable defensive capacity and a further four years to establish a significant offensive capability, which meant that the country's armed forces would not be ready for war until 1942. Given the priority accorded the army and air force, the navy in fact would not have been ready for war for two or three years later than the 1942 deadline for the other armed forces. Yet, the cost of re-armament had been such that by 1939, time had run out. Germany's economy had been on a war footing for some time, with defence expenditure running at up to 30 per cent of GNP, and in 1939, the authorities had weakened their resolve and started to print money, effectively devaluing the currency and taking it on the road to inflation. The bounty that had come with the *Anchluss*, Austria's gold and foreign currency reserves, had been spent.

In short, when the Anglo-French ultimatum expired on 3 September 1939, it was 'now or never' for Germany. Even if the funds, including foreign exchange, had been available, allowing war to be postponed, any progress in finishing the re-armament and rebuilding of the German armed forces would have been at least matched and, more likely, exceeded by progress in the

United Kingdom and France, and in the United States as well, given their superior industrial capacity.

It was factors such as these that led many to believe that had British and French forces attacked Germany in the west during the autumn of 1939, Germany could not have managed to continue its occupation of Poland, having to fight the war on two fronts. Yet, neither ally possessed the strength or the will to engage in aggressive warfare at this early stage. The strength of the armed forces of both countries was in fact variable, good in parts, less so in others.

After the initial declaration of war, many were in doubt over what might follow.

Notes
1 and 2 *A Sailor's Odyssey*, Admiral (later Admiral of the Fleet) Sir Andrew Cunningham, RN, Hutchinson, London, 1951

CHAPTER FOUR

The Marine Nationale
in 1940

K nown officially to the French as the 'Marine Nationale', and generally referred to simply as the 'Marine' by the man in the street, in common with most major navies the French Navy had expanded far beyond its Washington Treaty limits during the 1930s as a naval race began with neighbouring Italy. While in 1939, both the British and the French expected a re-run of the First World War, between the wars French naval planners had worked on the basis that the most likely opponent in a future conflict would be Italy, initially as a reaction to the bellicose stance of the Italian dictator, Benito Mussolini, and then as his aggressive intentions became clearer during the late 1930s. Parts of the South of France had been Italian territory in the past and given the arguments advanced by Hitler, similar moves by Mussolini could not be ruled out.

Like the Royal Navy, the Marine Nationale had to wield a worldwide presence. But being considerably smaller it operated large squadrons rather than fleets, so the Atlantic Squadron equated to the British Atlantic, later Home, Fleet, and the same relationship could be applied to the Mediterranean Squadron and the British Mediterranean Fleet. The main bases in France were at Brest on the Atlantic coast and Toulon on the Mediterranean, but there were other smaller bases and just as the British had Gibraltar and Malta, the French had Oran and Mers-el-Kebir in Algeria, Bizerte in Tunisia, Casablanca in French Morocco and Dakar in West Africa. At the time, Dakar had the only dry dock between Gibraltar and Cape Town, so it was of immense strategic value.

There were also ships stationed in the Caribbean, in the Indian Ocean at Madagascar, and in French Indo-China, as well as at Beirut in the Lebanon.

'Honour', 'country', 'valour' and 'discipline' were the words displayed on the quarterdecks of all French warships in large gilded letters. These qualities were meant to be imbedded within every French seaman, regular, conscript or reservist, and regardless of rank. Despite animosity between many French officers, including such senior figures as Admiral Darlan, who made little attempt to disguise his Anglophobia, honour was meant to be important above all else. This was something that was perhaps not to be fully appreciated later by the British when they doubted whether Vichy France would abide by its commitment to scuttle its fleet rather than allow it to be taken over by the Axis powers, which effectively meant Germany and Italy since the third member of the triumvirate, Japan, was half a world away.

In 1939, the French had the fourth largest navy in the world. While the Marine Nationale had been limited to 175,000 tons of shipping by the Washington Naval Treaty, it had gone well beyond this by 1940, when it had a total tonnage well in excess of 600,000 tons. Even by the standards of the day, it was not a balanced fleet. It was strong in battleships and cruisers, and far stronger than Germany in 1939 and 1940 in terms of submarines and destroyers, but it was weak in aircraft carriers, with just one elderly ship, the converted battleship *Béarn*, 22,000 tons, and a seaplane tender, although two carriers of modern design were under construction. Part of the problem had been that, since between the wars France had expected its most likely adversary to be Italy, the need for aircraft carriers was not so obvious. As the Italians viewed the French in the same light, as already mentioned, a naval race had developed between the two countries, and the fleets tended to reflect this.

It is worth noting that Italy also had a far stronger submarine fleet in 1939 and 1940 than the German Kriegsmarine, and had neglected naval aviation even more than the French, with the Regia Aeronautica, the Italian air force, keeping a tight grip on all forms of service aviation. By contrast, the three strongest navies, the British, Japanese and American, all had strong air components, although the British were hampered by a lack of high performance fighter aircraft, and were in 1939 and early 1940, still waiting for the first of six new fast armoured carriers.

For the French, the lack of a carrier fleet was a weakness as the nation found itself at war with Germany rather than Italy; carriers would also have been very useful during the Norwegian campaign, and indeed for a nation with a far flung empire. Yet, for as long as Italy had appeared to be the likely foe, the case for aircraft carriers was much harder to sustain. The bulk of Italian heavy industry was in northern Italy and so comfortably within reach of land-based bombers operating from bases in the South of France. In some ways, the Italian and French fleets were almost mirror-images of one another, except for the single French aircraft carrier and a seaplane carrier, while the French had also tended to produce a very distinctive ship type of their own in the *contre-torpilleur*, a large destroyer, almost of light cruiser dimensions and armament.

Fully mobilized during August 1939, the Marine Nationale had 160,000 men. Like the other services, there were no joint exercises with the British before the war, or even during the months of the 'phoney war', although Franco-British signal codes did exist and were re-issued, while liaison officers were exchanged.

THE FLEET

Although the Italians had done most to create a strong submarine arm between the wars, France was not that far behind and certainly ahead of Germany. Given the permitted tonnage, the Marine Nationale had preferred to spend the 1920s building submarines and fast torpedo craft rather than exercising its right to build large battleships or a fleet of aircraft carriers, although two battleships were under construction when war broke out and the fleet included two fine modern battlecruisers. Nevertheless, in the naval race that developed between France and her old ally Italy as the new Mussolini regime took the lead in re-armament, some significant differences developed in the ships chosen. The Italians favoured large and elegant cruisers with a high speed, against which the French developed the large super destroyer, usually referred to as the *contre-torpilleur*, which were fast, but short on range.

Nevertheless, the French were one of just four countries to build aircraft carriers between the wars, although the one French ship, the *Béarn*, a converted battleship, was slow and obsolete by the time war arrived. Belatedly, the French had resumed building battleships, but in 1939, the fleet consisted of:

1 elderly aircraft carrier
3 modernised battleships
4 old battleships
2 battlecruisers
7 heavy cruisers
12 light cruisers
32 large *contre-torpilleur* destroyers
38 other destroyers
1 seaplane tender
77 submarines

Ashore, while some naval air squadrons had been transferred to the new autonomous air force, the *Armée de l'Air*, the French Navy had never, unlike the British, lost control of naval aviation between the wars, and even shore-based maritime reconnaissance aircraft remained in naval hands.

In fact, the official tonnage figures gave an exaggerated impression of the size of the Marine Nationale, or at least of its wartime fighting potential. Four old battleships were counted in the official figures, but these were beyond combat. *Condorcet* was a training ship, which was just as well as she dated from 1909. She was not alone, as three other ships were also of pre-First World War vintage. These were the *Courbet*, which started the war as an anti-aircraft battery and later simply became a breakwater. *Ocean* was a target ship. *Paris* was an accommodation ship, although it seems that she was spared the indignity of being classified as an accommodation hulk.

Three other battleships that had been completed in the years immediately following the earlier conflict had been extensively modernized between the wars, just as the British had started modernizing their Queen Elizabeth-class ships (although the programme was not completed before war broke out). The French ships were not only refitted, but given new boilers and their armament increased, with additional emphasis on anti-aircraft protection. These were *Bretagne*, *Lorraine* and *Provence*, all of 22,000 tons, which was not especially heavy for a capital ship of the day, and they were also slow, at 21 knots. Like many French ships, their armament was decidedly individualistic, with 340mm guns, which equated to 13.4-in, with *Bretagne* and *Paris* having ten in four turrets, but *Lorraine* having just eight. Naming a battleship *Lorraine* must have been like a red rag to a bull as far as the Germans were concerned, as this disputed province, along with neighbouring Alsace, had been part of the booty of the Franco-Prussian War, but was returned to France under the Treaty of Versailles.

Two new battleships were under construction in 1940. The first of these, *Richelieu*, was completing and was to be moved to Mers-el-Kebir as French surrender became inevitable. Her sister ship, *Jean Bart*, was not completed until the end of the war. These were ships worthy of their type, being much larger and faster than the three older ships, at 35,000 tons and capable of

30 knots. In some ways they were similar to the British battle-ships *Rodney* and *Nelson*, with their main armament all forward in 'A' and 'B' turrets, but unlike the three triple 16-in turrets of the British ships, and for once the French chose a more conventional calibre, with two quadruple 15-in turrets. The secondary armament was also conventional, with 6-in guns in five triple turrets.

Of the fleet actually operational in 1940, the two best ships were the battlecruisers, *Dunkerque* and *Strasbourg*, rivals to the German *Scharnhorst* and *Gneisenau*, which had been built as Germany's answer to the French ships. These battlecruisers were in fact heavier than the older French battleships, at 26,500 tons displacement, and like the new generation of battleships, had their main armament forward in two quadruple turrets, but here the comparison ended, as the guns were of 330mm calibre, 13-in, and so compatible with neither the older nor the new French battleships. These two ships outgunned the German battle-cruisers, and would have made light work of the German *Panzerschiffe*, which were, as was already known in 1940, capable of being sunk by British cruisers.

The French Navy in 1940 had twenty-two cruisers, but most of these were elderly vessels, and again many had non-standard calibre guns, including some with 5-in which made their status as cruisers somewhat doubtful as the Washington Naval Treaty had stipulated 6-in guns for light cruisers and 8-in for heavy cruisers. Again, the more modern vessels did conform, with the *Algerie*, a heavy cruiser displacing 10,000 tons dating from 1933, having eight 8-in guns in four turrets arranged conventionally fore and aft. Six other cruisers, including the *Emile Bertin*, 5,886 tons, also dated from the later 1930s and had 6-in guns.

As already mentioned, a French peculiarity, some might suggest a speciality, were the *contre-torpilleur* 'super' destroyers, developed in response to Italy's light cruisers. These varied between 2,000 and almost 3,000 tons in size, and had 5.5-in guns as opposed to the 6-in of a light cruiser. The two newest and largest were *Mogador* and *Volta*, at almost 3,000 tons and with eight 5.5-in guns in four turrets. They were capable of up to 43 knots – probably not in the open Atlantic but achievable in the calmer waters of the Mediterranean. Another six *contre-torpilleurs* had been completed in 1934 and 1936, and were *L'Audacieux*, *Le Fantasque*, *L'Indomptable*, *Le Malin*, *Le Terrible* and *Le Triomphant*. These were slightly smaller, at 2,600 tons, and slightly slower as well. There were another twenty-four *contre-torpilleurs*, of 2,000 tons and 2,300 tons, as well as thirty-eight standard destroyers.

At the other end of the scale, in common with the Germans, the French had some torpedo boats that were almost of destroyer standard at 1,000 tons. The French had also not neglected motor torpedo boats and small gunboats, unlike the British, and again, like the Germans.

The oddity in the submarine fleet was the *Surcouf*, a corsair submarine similar to the British M-class, also referred to some-times as a cruiser submarine, with two 8-in guns forward and a small aircraft hangar for a floatplane after of the conning tower. Many commentators have pointed out that this type of vessel would have been ideal for Germany's warfare against merchant vessels, as U-boat commanders preferred to use their deck arma-ment rather than their limited number of more expensive torpedoes. On the other hand, surfacing in the middle of a heavily escorted convoy was hardly calculated to ensure a long and successful career, so torpedoes were often best. At 2,880 tons, *Surcouf* was the world's largest submarine at the time.

Brief details of the main warships operational with the Marine Nationale in 1939–1940 are given in Appendix I on page 221.

In 1936, as war in Europe became increasingly likely, a new warship building programme was agreed, while the fleet had already exceeded the Washington limits, by this time now widely ignored, especially by the Axis future belligerents. The programme showed that even if the German Navy had the extra years needed to achieve the full potential of Plan Z, its projected wartime strength, it would still not have matched the French fleet, let alone that of the United Kingdom. The Marine Nationale's building programme included:

2 aircraft carriers
4 battleships
3 light cruisers
4 large *contre-torpilleur* destroyers
12 destroyers
40 submarines

Of these, the most interesting ships were the two 18,000 ton aircraft carriers, the *Joffre* and *Painlevé*, which, while dated in outline with their hull not plated up to flight deck level, in plan view showed the flight deck and hangar offset to port to balance the large superstructure island. Some have suggested that this was an early version of the angled flight deck, but this was not so. Reputedly, a third hull was ordered before the German invasion.

THE MEN

While the French army was largely based on conscription, the Marine Nationale was primarily based on volunteers, although ratings could sign up for as little as five years, which was less than the minimum period for a volunteer in the Royal Navy, where new recruits at the time signed on for an initial twelve years. The minimum age for recruits was seventeen years as against eighteen years in the Royal Navy, although the latter also had the concept of 'boy service' and British ratings did not sign on until their initial training had been completed.

Jean-Pierre Gauthier, from Lyons, who had worked in a bakery, decided to volunteer and signed up for his initial five years on 28 April 1939. While he knew that the war was coming, he was also attracted by a change in routine and travel, since Lyons was far from the sea. His recollection of his training was that it was enjoyable, with the petty officers acting more like friends, while the food was good. He trained as a gunner, handling one of the 5.1-in guns on the destroyer *Casque*, lead-ship of her class, 1,800 tons. He recalled conditions on board being very good.

We had good food and wine. There would be a quarter (litre) of wine at lunchtime with a three course meal, and a quarter again in the evening, but sometimes we got a double ration if our work was good or there was a celebration. I remember one week, we had chicken for lunch four times. Aboard, we had coffee on getting up, and breakfast around 10.00. Aboard destroyers, we slept in hammocks, but the submarines had bunks.

The *Casque*'s home port was Toulon, but we spent a lot of time in Algiers.[1]

Another volunteer for the French navy before war broke out was Arsene Le Poittevin, who had been born and brought up in Normandy. When he left school, he went to Cherbourg, hoping to join the Marine Nationale, but he was too young and was turned away. He spent most of the next two years working on a line fishing boat, part of a team using long-pole rods to catch fish such as conger eels, and where, apparently, the money was very good. When war broke out, he volunteered to help unload supplies for the British Expeditionary Force and made several friends amongst the British troops. The supplies consisted mainly of ammunition and light weapons, including machine guns.

He finally was old enough to join at the end of 1939, but it was perhaps an indication of the pace at this stage of the war, that Christmas and the New Year intervened, so the recruitment office could not see him until January 1940. Having joined at Cherbourg, he was given his initial basic training, which included such matters as saluting and marching, before being told that he would be sent to Brest to train as a gunner. He protested that he wanted to be a wireless operator, and was told that the course had already started. Nevertheless, when he persisted, he was allowed to take the examination for wireless operator, and passed with full marks. He was then posted to the wireless school at L'Orient. He recalled

I had to catch up, but a friend helped me with the early stages of the course and with the Morse, so that by June, I had caught up. Then, as the Germans advanced, they called for volunteers to help stop them. About forty or fifty of us went and set up a road block, waiting for the Panzers. We were strafed by Stuka dive-bombers, but no one was hurt.

Then one of the officers decided after a couple of days that we wouldn't be able to stop a Panzer, so we went back to our barracks, passing L'Orient, which was in flames with the oil storage tanks and the harbour out of action.

We found three small fishing boats that had just arrived and we commandeered them, still full of fish, with about twenty of us to each boat. We left harbour, and to avoid the German air force, one went north, one went straight ahead and was sunk, and we went south, eventually reaching the River Gironde near Bordeaux.[2]

They were eventually taken aboard a liner that was waiting to evacuate the French government, including Paul Reynaud and Charles de Gaulle, but they never turned up as de Gaulle had been hurried out of France by the RAF. They went to North Africa, and while *en passage* heard the news about the armistice. On arrival, Le Poittevin resumed his wireless operator's training at Mogador.

Notes
1 IWM Accession No 19773
2 IWM Accession No 19864

CHAPTER FIVE

The Balance of Power
at Sea

I f the outbreak of the Second World War found the United Kingdom and France ill-prepared, the German Navy, the Kriegsmarine, was also caught wrong-footed. In contrast to the period prior to the outbreak of the First World War, there had been no naval construction race during the 1930s between the Royal Navy and the Kriegsmarine, as Hitler had re-named the Reichsmarine. Germany undoubtedly wanted a far larger navy than that allowed by the Treaty of Versailles, or even by the Anglo-German Naval Agreement of 1935, but this was still some time away. The senior officers and planners of the Kriegsmarine did not see war with the British Empire until 1944–45, while Grandadmiral Raeder foresaw a major battle with the Royal Navy, one that would settle the issues left unresolved at Jutland, in 1948. This was not just wishful thinking, even Hitler had assured Raeder that there would be no war with England before 1943.

In September 1939, the Kriegsmarine had:

> 2 elderly battleships plus 2 building
> 2 battlecruisers

3 armoured cruisers
3 heavy cruisers
6 light cruisers
22 destroyers
20 torpedo boats and small destroyers
59 submarines

At its best, this was a modern navy, but it lacked what was to prove to be essential for any blue water navy in the war that lay ahead, aircraft carriers and naval aviation. Priority had been given in the period immediately before the outbreak of war to the development of the air force, the Luftwaffe, and while the army had massively expanded, it was not without its weaknesses, with artillery and most supplies still depending upon horses. The Kriegsmarine was third in the queue for modernization and expansion behind the army and the air force.

REBUILDING THE GERMAN FLEET

While the Treaty of Versailles had banned the Germans from the skies, it had allowed them a 'brown water' navy, meaning that what amounted to a coastal defence force was permitted. The largest ships were elderly coastal battleships, but for the most part the fleet was tasked with nothing more important than fisheries protection. A small army, just 100,000 strong, and even smaller navy were all that the victorious allies would allow. Under the terms of the Treaty of Versailles, there was no German air force and even aircraft manufacture was forbidden in Germany.

On the other hand, the Washington Naval Treaty of 1922 had ensured that no longer would the United Kingdom be able to boast a fleet twice the size of any it was likely to engage in combat, even if it could afford it. In this way, even the victors were cut down to size. The United States and United Kingdom were limited to fleets of 525,000 tons each, with Japan being permitted 315,000 tons while France and Italy were each allowed fleets of 175,000 tons. Within these limits, the maximum tonnage of a capital ship was limited to 35,000 tons, cruisers to 10,000 tons, aircraft carriers to 27,000 tons, although the United States and United Kingdom enjoyed certain exceptions to these limits, and certain ships could be classified as 'experimental' and be excluded from the limits.

The treaty was also prescriptive in the maximum tonnage allowed for each type of vessel. The USA and UK had to limit their total carrier tonnage to 135,000 tons, while Japan was limited to 81,000 tons of aircraft carriers, and again France and Italy had the same lower total limit, in this case of 60,000 tons. The United States Navy and the Royal Navy were both allowed to build two aircraft carriers of 33,000 tons apiece, while the USS *Langley*, the first American aircraft carrier, was treated as an experimental vessel, outside the treaty limits, which was fair given that she was a converted collier of no great speed, although her displacement of 12,700 tons was somewhat greater than the British HMS *Hermes*, the first aircraft carrier designed as such from the keel upwards rather than as a conversion.

These limits upset the Japanese, who argued unsuccessfully that they were entitled to the same limits as the two major naval powers. The matter was academic, since as the years passed, the Japanese built whatever ships they wanted and soon had one of the world's strongest navies, including a strong carrier force, although its giant battleship programme was not complete when war reached Japan in late 1941.

While the Washington Treaty clearly took aircraft carriers seriously, given the substantial tonnages allowed, this type of vessel was still in its infancy. The treaty dealt with some of the existing types more harshly, leaving the three largest treaty navies with an excess of battlecruisers over and above their permitted total tonnages, and so, not surprisingly, these ships were earmarked to be converted to aircraft carriers.

Armaments were also covered by the treaty, which for the first time laid down that a light cruiser would have nothing heavier than 6-in guns, while a heavy cruiser would be limited to 8-in guns – the actual tonnage had nothing to do with whether a 'cruiser' was classified as 'heavy' or 'light'. In fact, as the Second World war approached, the British 'Town' class cruisers with twelve 6-in guns in four turrets would have been considered as light cruisers under the terms of the treaty, but the British Admiralty classified them as heavy cruisers. This was an interesting point – as twelve 6-in guns packed a powerful punch when a full broadside was fired, but individual shells inflicted less damage than an 8-in shell would have done and, very much to the point, the range of 6-in guns was considerably less than that of 8-in guns.

The attitude of the treaty powers varied considerably. As already mentioned, the Japanese were furious. The Italians did not bother with aircraft carriers, although they had plans later for a converted liner, while the French contented themselves with a single ship, the *Béarn*, although two more were ordered as war approached. The British spent their time trying to lower the treaty limits. They even built heavy cruisers with three twin turrets to prove that cruiser tonnages could be lowered – in fact the reduced top weight improved sea keeping, so all was not lost! They also attempted to reduce the tonnage of individual aircraft carriers, and the result was *Ark Royal*, a ship with a flight deck so thin that even a 20-lb practice bomb could, and on one occasion did, burst through it.

The British even interfered with battleship construction, building a new class with 14-in guns rather than the 15-in or 16-in guns of earlier ships. Again, it was not only the amount of explosive that made a 15-in or 16-in gun better than a 14-in, it was also the greater range of the heavier projectile.

The Germans, of course, had no tonnage to speak of. It was not until 1935 that the question of rebuilding the German navy came to the fore. The service changed its name from Reichsmarine, 'State Navy', to Kriegsmarine, 'War Navy', suggesting a more aggressive role. More important, the Anglo-German Naval Treaty, also of 1935, laid the foundation for the reconstruction of the German fleet, with a surface fleet of up to 35 per cent of that of the Royal Navy, based once again on tonnage rather than warship numbers, and up to 45 per cent of the Royal Navy's submarine strength. Given the impact of the German U-boat fleet on the United Kingdom during the First World War, what was surprising was that the negotiators allowed the Kriegsmarine to have parity in submarines with the Royal Navy if the extra submarine tonnage was subtracted from the tonnage allowed for surface vessels. While hindsight is generally credited with perfect 20:20 vision, in this case it seems that the negotiators were blind to the potential of the submarine and ignored the lessons of what was at the time the still recent history of the First World War.

Many believe that Hitler took the British position at the negotiations as a clear indication that Germany and the United Kingdom would not be at war, and that any future conflict would be with France or the Soviet Union. It was not until 1938 that war between Britain and Germany became inevitable in the eyes of the Führer.

The ultimate objective of German naval planning was to have a fleet that was the equivalent of the Royal Navy or the United States Navy. The head of the navy, Grand Admiral Raeder, believed that a substantial surface fleet, pre-positioned in foreign waters, would be able to deal with the Royal Navy. The weakness in this argument was that suitable foreign bases would be a problem for Germany which had lost its small number of colonies in the defeat of 1918, and the ships would be heavily reliant on a good fleet train for re-supply.

At senior level, there was considerable disagreement over the future shape of the German navy. Raeder's logic was that the increasingly widespread use of ASDIC, as sonar was known during the war, meant that submarines were obsolete and vulnerable, and that surface raiders would be more important. The commander of the U-boat arm, Admiral Doenitz, was a fervent supporter of the submarine, and believed that unrestricted submarine warfare against British merchant shipping would bring the United Kingdom to starvation and its armed forces would be unable to fight for want of fuel and munitions.

Looking ahead, the German plans to create a navy that would be able to match that of the United Kingdom started with Plan

X, which was then superseded by Plan Y, and finally emerged as Plan Z. This called for:

6 battleships
8 heavy cruisers
4 aircraft carriers
17 light cruisers
223 U-boats

Plan Z was approved by Hitler in January 1939, not quite the eve of war, but far too late for the targets to be attained. In fact, Plan Z was not intended to come to fruition until 1944, meaning that the Kriegsmarine was the least prepared of all the German services when war came in September 1939.

Despite the differences between Donitz and Raeder, Donitz's request that the submarine arm should have 300 boats was granted by his superior. In any case, as the war advanced, Hitler became increasingly disillusioned by the surface fleet and effectively committed this to the dustbin in 1943, concentrating most of the country's shipbuilding resources on the U-boat programme.

Plan Z is often referred to by naval historians, but does not seem to have received serious consideration. Several have written it off on the grounds that Germany could not produce sufficient fuel for such a large fleet, and would have difficulty with the raw materials, but these were problems that Hitler tried to address in his thrust eastwards, seeking to guarantee Germany's war machine adequate fuel and the raw materials necessary both for armaments and ammunition.

Yet, despite a modern fleet being the stated objective, German aircraft carrier design was badly dated, while operational questions over naval air power had not been resolved by the Germans even while Plan Z was being progressed. Plan Z also seemed to overlook the resumption of naval construction by the British and French, which would have rendered the proposed surface fleet inadequate. The real questions over Plan Z have to be:

- How realistic would the plan have been given Germany's other military goals and the consequent knock-on effect on armaments production?
- How long could Britain and France have held back from war as Germany flexed her muscles?
- How would the ships have compared with those operated by the British and French navies?
- Could the Germans have made use of Japanese expertise?
- How long could Germany have afforded the manpower, materials and money that her massive arms build-up was already costing?

In fact, by late 1938, the Germans could not afford the materials or the foreign exchange for their existing plans for the army and air force, let alone the additional burden of the naval ship-building targets. Japanese expertise was also problematic at this time as Japan's main concern was conflict with the Soviet Union over Manchuria, while Germany sought some form of rapprochement with the USSR to ease the conquest of Poland and also ensure adequate supplies of food, fuel and other raw materials once Anglo-French naval action made obtaining these supplies from overseas sources difficult, and even impossible.

Despite the Kriegsmarine being promised priority over all other services for its Plan Z in January 1939, as the crisis in raw materials and fuel grew, Hitler took a series of decisions late in 1939 that meant that only those ships that were almost completed, such as the great battleships *Bismarck* and *Tirpitz*, could continue, while work on the remainder was halted. The size of the Kriegsmarine's surface fleet was effectively frozen, and from this time onwards the only new construction would be U-boats. Rather than receive a substantial share of armaments production, the Kriegsmarine was reduced to no more than 15 per cent. Shipyards were quickly turned over to U-boat produc-tion, initially using the standardized Type VII design, although later some innovation was allowed. The die was cast – Hitler was following the policies advocated by Donitz. He could do nothing else, the industrial and economic situation did not permit it.

Gloomily, on the outbreak of war, Raeder noted that:

> As far as the navy is concerned, it is . . . not at all adequately armed for the great struggle . . . assuming it is fully committed in action, it can only demonstrate that it knows how to go down with dignity.[1]

While much of German naval design was brilliant, the plans for the first aircraft carrier would have resulted in a ship that would have been several years out-of-date on commissioning. It owed more to ships such as the British *Courageous* and *Glorious* than to the later *Ark Royal*, and could not compare with the *Illustrious*, the first of a class of six fast armoured carriers, which themselves included a sub-class that was even more potent.

HITLER'S NAVAL POWER

In fact, the Kriegsmarine started the war in 1939 with:

> 2 old battleships
> 2 battlecruisers
> 3 pocket battleships or armoured cruisers
> 3 heavy cruisers
> 6 light cruisers
> 22 destroyers
> 20 torpedo boats/small destroyers
> 59 submarines

The two new battleships, *Bismarck* and *Tirpitz*, were still under construction. The so-called pocket battleships were known to the Germans as *Panzerschiffe*, armoured ships, and their designation of 'pocket battleships' was a creation of the British media. They were soon re-designated armoured cruisers by the Germans, although the six 11-in guns in two turrets meant that they were considerably above even the 8-ins of a heavy cruiser. Their role in war was as commerce raiders as they would have stood little chance against a British battleship with guns of 14-in, 15-in or even 16-in. In December 1939, one of these ships, the *Admiral Graf Spee*, fell prey to a British heavy cruiser supported by two light cruisers in the Battle of the River Plate. The *Panzerschiffe* had been built to replace the old coastal battleships, but their diesel engines gave them a global range.

The Germans had also been forced to compromise. The two battlecruisers, *Scharnhorst* and *Gneisenau*, were intended to have 15-in guns, but these were not available and so the two ships were commissioned with 11-in guns.

Also still awaited on the outbreak of war was Germany's first aircraft carrier, the *Graf Zeppelin*, ordered in 1935 and launched in December 1938. Unlike her British, American and Japanese counterparts, the *Graf Zeppelin* was conceived not for engaging in major fleet actions, but instead to provide air cover for commerce raiders and also to take part in commerce raiding. The ship was built without any experience of carrier construction, and included a heavy surface armament which not only consumed weight, but was unlikely ever to be needed. The anti-aircraft armament was heavy, but concentrated on just one side. The ship was also short on range, and would have been a liability for the other ships engaged in commerce raiding.

All of this was to prove to be academic, as the *Graf Spee* never entered service and work was soon abandoned in favour of more important naval assets as inter-service rivalry broke out. The Kriegsmarine wanted control of the ship's aircraft, but this incensed the air minister, Hermann Goering who fought against the formation of a separate naval air service and demanded that all German service aviation be part of the Luftwaffe. Even when the Kriegsmarine backed down, the Luftwaffe did not want to spare any of its precious aircraft for service at sea.

It is interesting to speculate here on what might have happened. Carrier variants of both the Messerschmitt Bf 109 fighter and the Junkers Ju 87 Stuka dive-bomber were indeed developed, but never entered service. The Bf 109 was known to have a weak tail section and would have been ill-suited to the stresses and strains of landing on a carrier, with the sharp jerk of the tail hook catching the arrester wires and the aircraft thumping down onto the carrier deck. Converting a landplane design to carrier operation was no easy task, and even the much admired Supermarine Spitfire did not convert easily to carrier operations, with its naval variant, the Seafire, being inclined to bounce on landing and topple forward onto its nose. On the other hand, the sturdy Stuka could well have been an outstanding carrier strike aircraft early in the war, although dated even by the middle years. In fact, the Japanese Naval Air Force at Pearl Harbor included the Aichi D3A1, which had been influenced in its design by German work on dive-bombers and was similar in many ways to the Stuka, even to the fixed spatted undercarriage.

Given the short range of the *Graf Spee*, and the lack of suitable refuelling bases, it is hard to see just where she could have been of use. Certainly, she would have been an additional problem for the Arctic convoys, but the Germans had air bases along the Norwegian coast. The one naval engagement where she could have made a difference would have been the Battle of the North Cape, while earlier, had she been ready in time, she could have provided air cover for the *Bismarck*.

THE ROYAL NAVY

Despite the conditions of the Washington Naval Treaty, in 1939 the Royal Navy was the world's largest, albeit by a small and decreasing margin as US and Japanese naval expansion plans continued. Many of its ships were obsolete or obsolescent, with many of its capital ships and light cruisers dating from the First World War, although some at least, including the battleship HMS *Warspite*, had been extensively modernized between the two wars. Even one of its aircraft carriers, the converted battlecruiser HMS *Furious*, had seen service during the previous conflict, while another two had been converted from First World War battlecruisers (or to be completely correct, 'light battle-cruisers', another from a liner of around the same vintage, which had entered service as a carrier just before the war ended, and yet one more from a battleship on which work had been suspended during the war years.

The problem for the Royal Navy was one of overstretch, while like the Germans and the French, some of its best ships were yet to come on the outbreak of war. In September 1939, the Royal Navy had:

15 capital ships, including battlecruisers
7 aircraft carriers
15 heavy cruisers
46 light cruisers
181 destroyers
59 submarines
54 small escorts

Areas of weakness included the lack of torpedo boats and gunboats able to counter the German E-boats, but at the beginning of the war, with no German naval presence on the English Channel or the Bay of Biscay, this did not appear to be too serious. Of the ships on order, the six fast armoured aircraft carriers were to set a standard for others to follow, but, even if they had been in service, the Royal Navy's Fleet Air Arm lacked high performance aircraft, and most especially high performance fighters with which to defend the fleet from air attack.

While much has been made of the British possession of radar, most of the ships lacked this essential aid to modern warfare in 1939. Even the older carriers, the ships best able to make use of this asset, were without radar.

By modern standards, these ships may seem like a strong fleet, but the Royal Navy was not only present in home waters and on the North Atlantic, it was also committed in the Caribbean, the South Atlantic, the Mediterranean, India and the Far East. On the outbreak of war, the Atlantic Fleet was renamed the Home Fleet, while the other major fleet was in the Mediterranean, with all other ships being attached to 'stations'.

THE ITALIAN NAVY

On paper, major units of the Italian fleet sounded impressive enough. The Andrea Doria class of battleships, which included the *Conte di Cavour* and the *Caio Duilo*, were vessels from the First World War, reconstructed between the wars, as indeed were a number of units in the British fleet, including the much heavier battleship *Warspite*. These ships had a tonnage of 22,964 tons, were capable of 27 knots, and had a main armament of ten 12.6-in guns, with a secondary armament of twelve 5.2-in, ten 3.5-in and nineteen 37mm, the last being primarily for anti-aircraft protection.

More modern and more impressive were the Impero-class, under construction just before the outbreak of war and intended to make full use of the maximum dimensions permitted by the Washington Treaty. The four ships included the *Littorio*. These were ships of 35,000 tons, capable of 30.5 knots. Their main armament consisted of nine 15-in guns, with a secondary arma-ment of twelve 6-in and four 4.7-in, twelve 3.5-in, twenty 37mm and thirty-two 20mm. For comparison, the British *Prince of Wales* also weighed in at 35,000 tons, but was only capable of 28.5 knots. Her main armament was ten 14-in guns, with a secondary armament of sixteen 5.25-in, forty-eight 2-pounder pom-poms, a single 40mm and twenty 20mm.

Domination on paper was not the same as domination in reality. The Italian Navy had not been engaged in a fleet action since the creation of modern Italy in the nineteenth century. Italy's naval history, such as it was, was that of pre-unification Genoa and Venice, the latter state having played a major role in the important Battle of Lepanto in 1571. The 'leg of Italy' created that unusual phenomenon of a country virtually surrounded by the sea, and yet not a maritime power in the true sense. There was a sense that Italy had a navy because it was expected, rather than out of necessity, as in the case of the British and the French, or even smaller countries such as the Netherlands, since the Dutch have always been a seafaring race. Italy's unification came so late in the country's history that it had no opportunity to create a substantial empire, and so it was that the country that had ruled so much of the known world at the start of the first millennium had little overseas territory in the closing decades of the second.

Apart from the deficiencies in their ships, there was that of the ships' companies. Training was poor, and so too was the study of naval warfare by the officers. Britain's naval commander in the 'Med', Admiral Sir Andrew Cunningham, recorded: 'They had not visualised a night action between heavy ships and did not keep their heavy guns manned . . .' The gap between officers and men was far greater even than that of the pre-war Royal Navy, in which progress between the decks had been so difficult between the two wars as to be virtually unknown. This, combined with poor training meant that good morale and the sense, as Nelson would put it, 'of all being of one company', was hard to achieve. The older officers were aristocratic, the younger officers who had joined the service during the period of Mussolini, *Il Duce*, were described as being boorish, while the ratings were peasants, and looked down upon by their officers. Political infiltration of the Regia Navale by the Fascists was resented by the older officers, of a predominantly royalist state of mind. German interference was later to make this situation much worse, undermining morale still further.

On the other hand, it would be wrong to overlook the fact that the Italian Navy, and the other Italian armed forces, did excel in using small specialized forces, such as the two-man crews of the human torpedoes. Skill, courage and imagination meant such teams a potent threat, but a wider *esprit de corps* was usually lacking. Instances of Italian ships being well fought during the war in the Mediterranean were rare, although Cunningham's autobiography does mention one outstanding destroyer action.

While Italy had a major shipbuilding industry, and in many ways was far better equipped for this task than Germany, the other problem faced by the Italian armed forces was the shortage of fuel. Britain possessed the fuel resources of the Middle East and, at times, North America, even after the loss of those in the Dutch East Indies. Italy depended on the Balkans, and on whatever Germany would offer her increasingly despised ally. Fuel was to be one of the objectives in Germany's ill-judged thrust eastward into the Soviet Union, and later in the war, as this failed, so the Italian war machine also suffered and eventually faltered.

Cunningham's autobiography relates how, in 1938, the two Italian battleships, *Giulio Cesare* and the *Conte di Cavour*, under the command of Admiral Riccardi, paid a courtesy visit to Malta. The nature of such visits was that the hosts and guests embarked on a round of entertaining and inspections. In return for British hospitality, Cunningham and his senior officers were invited aboard.

> We lunched on board the *Conte di Cavour* with Admiral Riccardi, and came to the conclusion that he must have embarked the whole catering staff and band from one of the best hotels in Rome, so distinguished was his entertainment. Afterwards he took us round his palatial and highly decorated private apartments, and took some pride in pointing out a book, *The Life of Nelson*, which always lay on a table by his bedside. His subsequent actions during the war showed that he had not greatly profited by his nightly reading.[2]

There it was, in a nutshell. Despite the impressive armament, the *Conte di Cavour* was really an admiral's yacht. By the outbreak of war Riccardi had become Chief of the Italian Naval Staff, based in Rome at the Italian Admiralty, or Supermarina. No British naval officer would have boasted of *The Life of Nelson* by the side of his bunk, indeed, it would have earmarked him as at best a poser, and at worst, an amateur. A true naval officer did not need to display knowledge of Nelson's life, since this was taken 'as read', and whereas Nelson's example of leadership remained important, strategy had moved on in 135 years.

While the Italian Navy must have understood that war was likely, and that the United Kingdom would be the most likely opponent from the start of the Abyssinian adventure in the mid-1930s, no official indication was given to the armed forces until April 1940, that Italy would expect to fight alongside the Germans. Mussolini listened to and consulted the army, who dominated the Supreme Command, leaving the sailors and airmen to do as they were told.

The Chief of the Italian Naval Staff, Admiral Domenico Cavagnari, also held the political post of Under Secretary of State for the Navy, and should have wielded great influence. Like his German counterpart, Raeder, he viewed the prospect of a naval war with the Royal Navy with strong misgivings. He wrote to Mussolini, effectively complaining that entering a war once it had already started, meant that any chance of surprise had gone. In the circumstances, Italy was in a weak position. Cavagnari thought that Britain and France could block the Mediterranean at both ends and starve Italy of the fuel and raw materials needed to survive, let alone prosecute a war, or seek combat, in which case both sides could expect heavy losses. He stressed the difficulties inherent in being dependent on the co-operation and goodwill of the Regia Aeronautica.

This was a pessimistic forecast, but in many ways very realistic, certainly more so than that of the Italian Army. That the Army had not properly considered the impact of maritime strategy in wartime soon became apparent. On the eve of war, the Italian Army maintained that it had six months' supplies in Libya. Once fighting started, and especially after Marshal Graziani, Italy's commander in North Africa, began his push towards Egypt on 13 September, the demand for supplies of all kinds soared. A convoy system had to be hastily initiated, but here the lack of Italian preparation was soon to be felt, as often just one or two small warships would guard a number of merchantmen.

There were a number of elderly cruisers still in service during the late 1930s, but the more modern ships had 8-in main armament in the case of the heavy cruisers, and 6-in for the light cruisers. Italian destroyers used 4.7-in guns.

Many commentators have taken the view that although it was a modern fleet, the Regia Navale suffered from many shortcomings. Their warship designers had placed more emphasis on style and speed than on effective armament and armour protection, but, more important still, they lacked radar. According to Britain's naval commander in the Mediterranean, the Italians 'were no further advanced than we had been at Jutland twenty-five years before'. Although an aircraft carrier was under construction, this was never finished. The one big success lay with the human torpedoes, known officially as the *Siluro a Lenta Corsa*, or 'slow running torpedo', but to their two-man crews as the *Maiale*, or 'pig'. These were ridden by their operators who sat on top, and once inside an enemy harbour and under the target ship, detached the warhead and fastened it to the hull. The intrepid crew could then make their escape on the torpedo. Apart from the obvious dangers and difficulties of penetrating an enemy harbour at night, getting clear was important since the percussive effects of underwater blast meant that the crew were greatly at risk while close to the target.

The main bases for the Italian fleet were at Taranto (in Italy's 'instep'), Genoa in the north-west, and La Spezia, slightly further south, as well as Trieste at the northern end of the Adriatic, close to the border with Yugoslavia. Of these, only Taranto was well placed as a forward base as the war developed. It was near to Malta, and also provided the shortest mainland shipping route to North Africa, where Italian ground and air forces needed to be kept supplied. Being close to Greece, ships based on Taranto could also effectively cut the entrance to the Adriatic. Indeed, as the leg of Italy virtually bisected the Mediterranean, an active fleet based on Taranto could cut the Mediterranean in half.

Taranto offered everything a naval base could be expected to provide. It was a sheltered anchorage, with both an outer harbour, the Mar Grande, and an inner harbour, the Mar Piccolo. The outer harbour provided moorings for the battleships, while the cruisers and destroyers could use both harbours. A large breakwater shielded the outer harbour from the full force of the elements, for even the Mediterranean can be unkind in winter. In the inner harbour, ships used what was known as 'Mediterranean mooring', i.e. instead of berthing alongside, they were berthed stern to the quayside, packed close together 'like sardines in a tin' as one British airman put it. This had the incidental advantage of making a torpedo attack on any one ship very difficult.

A seaplane station was also provided at Taranto, largely for the aircraft that would be used by the battleships and cruisers once they were at sea, literally the 'eyes of the fleet', and in the absence of radar the only eyes for Italian warships other than their own lookouts. The ship-repair facilities were enhanced for wartime by the use of floating docks, while there was also a large oil storage depot.

Italy's geographical position, aided by air bases in Sicily, Sardinia and the Dodecanese, meant that the absence of an aircraft carrier in the Italian fleet was not as serious a drawback as it might seem. Italian aircraft could cover the entire Adriatic as well as a substantial proportion of the Mediterranean from shore bases, especially after Greek islands began to be occupied, and, of course, after the fall of Greece and then of Crete. Not having an aircraft carrier was certainly not as serious as it was to prove to the Germans in wartime, or for that matter, the Dutch forces in the East Indies.

COMPARISONS

Could the French fleet have been used to reinforce the strength of either the German or the Italian navies? Certainly, in some respects the French fleet was at the stage that the Germans wanted their fleet to be before going to war. In fact, it looks as if the more modern French battleships and the cruisers would have fitted more comfortably into the Italian navy, and so indeed would the two French battlecruisers with the same calibre armament as the Italian *Caio Duilio* and her sister the *Andrea Doria*.

The paradox was that the Italian navy between the wars had been modelled for a war with France, seen as the most likely enemy, and new construction had been driven by the need to commission ships that countered new French construction. The new Italian battleships were intended to balance the new French battlecruisers. There was also the problem that the Italian study of naval strategy for the war ahead was based on the theory that all future naval warfare would be based on engagements similar to the Battle of Jutland.

Membership of the North Atlantic Treaty Organization, NATO, later led to growing standardization of armaments, easing supply and logistics problems, especially when warships of different nationalities were operating together. The French have always been an exception to this standardization, and in fact for much of NATO's existence were outside its formal command structure, although ostensibly an ally. The fact is that the French have not always fitted the same calibre weapons to their ships as the British, and it is worth considering the French and German fleets more closely to see to what extent they were compatible.

In 1939, the two newest French battleships, *Jean Bart* and *Richelieu*, whilst similar in appearance to the Dunkerque class, had a main armament that would have been compatible with the Royal Navy, having eight 15-in guns as a main armament, and a secondary armament of fifteen 6-in guns, although the 3.9-in anti-aircraft guns would have been a problem.

Dunkerque and her sister ship, *Strasbourg*, were more problematical, with a main armament of eight 13-in guns and a secondary armament of sixteen 5.1- in guns. As both *Bismarck* and her sister ship *Tirpitz* mounted 15-in guns as a main armament, the *Jean Bart* and *Richelieu* would have fitted easily into the Kriegsmarine. On the other hand, *Dunkerque* and her sister ship, *Strasbourg* would not have done so easily, especially if one also looks at the two battlecruisers, *Scharnhorst* and *Gneisenau*, with their main armament of nine 11-in guns and secondary armament of twelve 5.9-in guns. The German armoured ships or *Panzerschiffe*, known to the British as 'pocket battleships', also had the unusual 11-in main armament and 5.9-in secondary armament, as well as 4.1-in AA armament.

The remainder of the French battle fleet were also out of step with the Germans. *Lorraine*, *Bretagne* and *Provence* all had 13.4-in main armament, and 5.5-in secondary armament, while *Courbet*, *Ocean* and *Paris* had 12-in main armament, but 5.5-in secondary armament.

The more modern French cruisers were more in line with their British counterparts in that they had main armaments of either 8-in or 6-in guns. The problem lay with their secondary armament, of which there was little standardization in any case, with guns of 3.9-in, and AA weapons at 3.5-in and 3-in. The German cruisers also had 8-in main armaments on the newer ships, such as *Admiral Hipper* and *Prinz Eugen*, but the secondary and AA armaments were 5.9-in and 3.5-in respectively, with only the latter compatible with the French. The older light cruisers had a main armament of just 5.9-in.

Nevertheless, there was little compatibility in armament between the destroyers of the French and German navies, with main armaments of 5.5-in on the French ships and 5-in on the German. The Royal Navy at the time had 4-in on the older destroyers and 4.5-in on the more modern vessels.

Given the German use of U-boats to shell unescorted merchant ships rather than use a more expensive torpedo, of which any submarine could only carry a finite number, usually with each torpedo tube being armed with a torpedo and having another one ready as a reload, the Germans may well have found the French *corsair* submarine *Surcouf*, with her twin 8-in guns useful, especially since she could also carry a seaplane for reconnaissance. She would also have been useful in the supply and replenishment role, although the one drawback of such a large submarine in those pre-nuclear days was that she had a large complement of 150 men.

Certainly, navies have had a long tradition of taking other warships as prizes and adding them to their own fleets. One of the most famous and distinguished British warship names, that of *Illustrious*, originated as a French prize, *L'Illustre*. During the Second World War, the Royal Navy succeeded in capturing a U-boat, *U-570*, which eventually joined the British fleet as HM Submarine *Graph*.

Germany was not adverse to seizing the military assets of occupied nations. Following the fall of France, materiel seized by the Wehrmacht amounted to 154 billion French francs, equal to 7.7 billion Reichsmarks. Given the highly artificial value of the Reichsmark at the time, it is perhaps more useful to note that the Germans gained 314,878 rifles, 5,017 artillery pieces, 3.9 million shells and more than 2,000 vehicles. Even as late in the war as 1944, 47 per cent of the German army's guns were of foreign origin, mainly French. It was not just guns that were seized. Transport was an essential component in modern warfare, both for the armed forces and to maintain war industry, but the German railway system's needs had been neglected during the 1930s as industry and raw materials were all concentrated on re-armament, so the Germans helped themselves to 4,260 French railway locomotives and 140,000 wagons.

The problem of operating ships with different calibre weapons and different equipment is one of logistics. The Germans repeatedly attempted to standardize their equipment as the war proceeded, which was the only way in which they could counter the massive industrial power of the Allies. This was taken to extreme lengths, so that the Messerschmitt Bf 109 fighter remained in production long after it had been outclassed by the latest Allied fighters, while at sea, the number of U-boat types was also kept to the minimum, but again at some cost in providing the navy with the best technology.

It would be tempting to think that the Germans could have taken the ships and simply kept the French supply chain in place, but while French industry was converted to war work for the Germans, productivity was well below that pre-occupation. If the ships had operated from French ports, all well and good, but the priority accorded Germany's pre-war arms build up had meant that industrial production was neglected, so that the German railway system, the Reichsbahn, lacked sufficient quantities of up-to-date locomotives.

Notes

1 *Lagevortage des Oberbefehlhabers der Kriegsmarine vor Hitler 1939–1945,* G. Wagner (Ed), Munich, 1972.
2 *A Sailor's Odyssey,* Cunningham, Admiral of the Fleet Sir Andrew, Hutchinson, London, 1951

CHAPTER SIX

Germany Strikes North

It says much about attitudes that the first winter of war was widely known as the 'phoney war' by the British and French, and as the *sitzkrieg* or 'sitting war' by the Germans. These were the views of the civilian populations and the opposing armies, but the war had been pursued at sea with major losses on both sides. While the air forces spent much of their time dropping propaganda leaflets, here too there were raids, although at this stage both sides were anxious not to attack the civilian populations of their opponents, and both sides tended to send small forces of aircraft against each other.

Hitler had in fact wanted to strike west shortly after the Polish surrender, but the weather was against it and there was the perennial problem that the Germans were short of ammunition. In fact, with Poland occupied, many German reservists were released back into their old occupations so that the war economy could grow once again.

In one sense, this was rather like making war in the old way, with armies raised after the harvest was in and fighting ending with the onset of the winter weather. But in the mid twentieth century, fighting began once sufficient fuel and weapons were stockpiled.

It was at sea that warfare was at its most brutal from the start.

On the very first day of war, the liner *Athenia*, with many of its passengers children being evacuated to safety in North America, and others citizens of the neutral United States, was torpedoed near the Hebrides, off Scotland's west coast, with the loss of 128 lives, of whom 28 were Americans. Just a fortnight after the outbreak of war, on 17 September, the Royal Navy lost an aircraft carrier, HMS *Courageous*, in the Western Approaches to the English Channel when she was torpedoed during an anti-submarine sweep. By comparison, the shooting down of a Dornier Do 18 flying-boat by a Blackburn Skua flown off Britain's newest aircraft carrier, HMS *Ark Royal*, on 26 September, didn't seem an adequate retribution, although it was the first German aircraft to be shot down by the British.

While the Royal Navy knew better than to assume that the major forward fleet anchorage at Scapa Flow, on the southern coast of the mainland of Orkney, to the north of Scotland, was impregnable, nevertheless it came as a major blow to British morale when the elderly battleship, HMS *Royal Oak*, was tor-pedoed and sunk whilst at anchor at Scapa on 14 October. The news didn't get any better in November, when the armed merchant cruiser *Rawalpindi*, a Peninsular & Oriental Steam Navigation Co., P&O, liner taken up from trade, was sunk by the German battlecruisers *Scharnhorst* and *Gneisenau* in a valiant but doomed attempt to save a convoy off Iceland.

The French navy or Marine Nationale had some good news in November, when the Simoun class destroyer, *Sirocco*, 1,300 tons, managed to sink two German U-boats within three days.

For the Royal Navy, it was not until December that the run of bad news seemed as if it might be nearing an end. On 13 December, the Battle of the River Plate was a spectacular success for the Royal Navy, not least because the three ships involved were outgunned by their opponent. Two light cruisers, HMS *Achilles* and *Ajax*, and one heavy cruiser, HMS *Exeter*, surprised the German pocket battleship, *Graf Spee*, officially known to the Germans as a *Panzerschiffe* or 'armoured ship', in the estuary of the River Plate. The German warship received such a serious battering from its opponents, themselves also seriously damaged, that her commanding officer put into Montevideo in neutral Uruguay for repairs. Limited by the neutrality of his hosts as to the time he could spend in port for repairs, on 17 December, he put most of his crew ashore, and left port to scuttle his ship at sea.

Graf Spee had been a commerce raider, attacking merchant vessels. Her two triple 11-in gun turrets should have been able to destroy the British cruisers even before she came within their range, with *Exeter* having 8-in guns and the other two, light cruisers, having just 6-in guns. The cruisers were also lacking armour protection and so should have been easy prey. By dividing his forces, the Royal Navy's Commodore Harwood, made it difficult for the *Graf Spee* to defend herself.

When this news reached the Germans, they must have thought with relief that before the war they had had the presence of mind to re-name one of the *Graf Spee's* sister ships, originally named *Deutschland*, *Lützow*. The feeling was that the loss of a ship with the original name would have an adverse effect on German civilian morale. There had been a clear warning of this possibility as the ship had seen action during the Spanish Civil War, when, as *Deutschland*, she had been attacked by Republican aircraft in Ibiza Roads on 29 May 1937. More than thirty members of her crew were killed. Even the bombast of the Nazi leadership was not proof against the meaning of such a message.

More good news for the British was to follow in the New Year. On 14 February 1940, the destroyer HMS *Cossack* found the *Altmark*, the *Graf Spee's* supply ship, infringing Norwegian neutrality by using that country's territorial waters to make her return to base. In her turn, *Cossack* also infringed Norwegian neutrality when she sent a boarding party aboard the German ship and released 303 British merchant seamen, who had been taken prisoners of war when their ships had been sunk. Even though the *Altmark* was allowed to continue afterwards, Norwegian diplomatic protests followed, but the British attitude was that Norway itself had failed to keep its waters free of belligerent shipping.

The problem for Norway was that it found itself in a vital strategic position from the start of the war. The Germans had few sources of iron ore of their own and depended on imports from Sweden, another neutral country. The direct sea route from Sweden to Germany was through the Gulf of Bothnia, an arm of the Baltic Sea, but this froze in winter and was impassable to shipping. The only all-year route was by rail from Sweden to Norway, where the iron ore was transhipped for passage through Norwegian territorial waters to Germany. So important was the supply of iron ore for German war industry that eventually, on 8 April, the Royal Navy began to mine Norwegian coastal waters, in defiance of the Geneva Convention. During the operation, it became clear that Germany was planning offensive operations in and around Norway. The following day, Germany forces occupied Denmark and began the invasion of Norway.

Having a land border with Germany, Denmark had no chance to oppose German forces that were numerically vastly superior and far better equipped. The situation in Norway was different. Recognising that the country was increasingly under threat, the Norwegians had already started to mobilise. Even though the Germans had recognised the fact that country was larger, and had a long coastline, while ashore the mountainous terrain, with most of the country still covered in snow, made movement difficult, they landed troops more or less simultaneously at Oslo, Kristiansand, Bergen, Trondheim and Narvik; backed these with air-landed troops at Oslo and Stavanger, but all did not go to plan. The troop transport *Blücher*, carrying the main headquarters staff, was sunk at Oslo, giving the Norwegian government and the King time to flee and mobilize resistance.

DEFENDING NORWAY

The Norwegian government asked the United Kingdom and France for help, and both countries were sympathetic to Norway's plight. While it was estimated that at least 50,000 troops would be needed to liberate the country, an initial expeditionary force of 13,000 British and 12,500 French troops was despatched, supported by air and naval forces. Unfortunately, most of the area was out of reach of aircraft based in the UK, and even more so those based in France. The aircraft carriers had to operate as transports, although finding suitable bases for land-based aircraft proved difficult, with few prepared airfields and improvised landing grounds often too soft for operations. The Royal Navy's Fleet Air Arm lacked high performance fighters at the time, otherwise this could have been the ideal campaign for carrier-borne aircraft.

At first, all went well. At sea, the Royal Navy soon established control. On 10 April, shore-based aircraft from the Royal Naval Air Station at Hatston, on the mainland of Orkney, sank the light cruiser *Königsberg*, the first loss of a substantial operational warship to aircraft. That same day, the first Battle of Narvik saw two German destroyers and several merchantmen sunk, although at the cost of two British destroyers later, but on 13 April, nine destroyers accompanied by the battleship *Warspite* sank the remaining eight destroyers. This was a serious blow to the Germans, who had few of these useful warships.

British and Free Polish forces were landed near Narvik on 12 April. The port was seen as being easier to take and hold than Trondheim, but it was the recapture of the latter that was seen by the allies as being essential for the reconquest of Norway. Unfortunately, the commander of the Narvik force failed to capture Narvik. First, he wanted to wait for the snow to melt, then he wanted his force to delay while a half brigade of French Chasseurs Alpins was sent to support him, although these troops had been assigned to other operations. Finally, he claimed not to want to cause civilian casualties through taking advantage of heavy naval gunfire! While this delay continued, the Germans were left to reinforce their defences at Narvik.

British troops had also been landed north and south of Trondheim. To the north of the town, they had landed at Namsos, between Narvik and Trondheim, while to the south, they had landed at Andalsnes. The northern force was expected to move south to Trondheim, a hundred miles away. The northern force had to contend with four foot of snow, and had no protection from German aerial attack, while those at Andalsnes were expected to cut vital railway lines, before moving north to Trondheim, while fighting off repeated German attacks from the south.

In London, the First Lord of the Admiralty, Winston Churchill, favoured an amphibious assault on Trondheim, but this was stalled by the chiefs of staff. They maintained that this would risk too many troops and place units of the Royal Navy at considerable risk. A revised plan, taking Trondheim by a pincer movement, was then considered but found to pose as many risks as the direct amphibious assault. Meanwhile, Churchill pointed out the dangers of the Germans persuading Sweden to allow troops to use the railway line between Sweden and northern Norway once the ice in the Gulf of Bothnia had thawed.

British and French troops then attempted to fight their way to Trondheim, despite the difficult conditions. One British brigade moving south managed to get within fifty miles of its objective by 19 April, before being forced back to its starting point at Namsos, from which it had to be evacuated during the night of 3/4 May.

To the south of Trondheim, the allies had managed to join up with Norwegian forces at Andalsnes, and together they advanced on Lillehammer, before being forced to retreat once more.

Apart from the reluctance to take Narvik, the entire operation was dogged by complacency, with one senior officer maintaining that if British and French troops found withdrawal difficult, the Germans would find advancing just as difficult. They didn't!

Inevitably, in any military operation luck plays a part, and the Norwegian campaign was no exception. A new commander for the southernmost British forces was appointed, but fell seriously ill later that same day. His successor was flown in by the RAF, but when the aircraft landed en route to Norway at Kirkwall in

Orkney, the plane crashed, killing two crew members and seriously injuring the rest of the occupants.

The Luftwaffe had quickly gained control of the air. Namsos and Andalsnes were both subjected to heavy bombing. Air cover was provided by aircraft operating from the two British carriers in the area, but, as already mentioned, at this early stage of the war the Fleet Air Arm lacked high performance fighters. The RAF was no better, with its main air component being obsolescent Gloster Gladiator biplane fighters operating off a frozen lake at Lesjeshogen, forty miles from Andalsnes. In short, the British fighter defences were no match for the Messerschmitt Bf 109s of the Luftwaffe. Towards the end of a campaign, a squadron of Hawker Hurricane fighters was based at an airfield ashore, though only after their first airfield was found to be unsuitable, but the Hurricane, manoeuvrable as it was, was still outclassed in fighter-to-fighter combat with the Luftwaffe, and in any case, there were far too few of them.

On 24 April, Narvik was shelled continuously for three hours by HMS *Warspite* and three cruisers, but the British troops surrounding the town, by this time 20,000, failed to attack even though the German garrison consisted of just 6,000 troops.

The French Marine Nationale did not enjoy the spectacular successes experienced by the British, but Admiral Derrien commanded the French naval contribution from the modern light cruiser *Montcalm*, 7,600 tons, while the light cruiser *Emile Bertin*, 5,900 tons, and the auxiliary cruisers *El Djezair*, *El Mansour* and *El Kantara*, which were converted merchantmen, escorted convoys with men and supplies and suffered constant Luftwaffe attack. In fact the two navies were working well together, prompting the two leading historians of the French navy, Auphan and Mordal, to write:

Never in history had there been more cordial relations than those established in the battle area off Norway. Not merely was this collaboration in the technical field, but the far more important field of human relations – the spirit of *camaraderie* between the French officers and their brethren of the Royal

Navy. Whether they sailed with the Home Fleet or on escort duty off the fjords of Norway, French and British ships, side by side, learned to sustain and to parry the fierce attacks of Germany's formidable air force.[1]

The French also suffered losses, losing the super destroyer, *Bison*, 2,400 tons, while in one of those accidents that add to the losses inflicted by combat, another super destroyer, the Aigle-class *Maillé-Brézé*, also 2,400 tons, was lost when one of her own torpedoes blew up while she was alongside at Greenock, on the Clyde.

Ashore, the Norwegian campaign was being dogged by poor leadership on land and a complete absence of effective air cover. It was likely to develop into a war of attrition, with the allied forces being gradually worn down, as by this time any chance of securing their objectives seemed hopeless. The whole situation changed with an even greater crisis much further south when, on 10 May 1940, German forces smashed their way into the Netherlands and Belgium, and headed towards France, completely by-passing the Maginot Line in which French hopes had rested. As the situation in France went from bad to worse, on 24 May, the decision was taken to pull the allied forces out of Norway and use them to reinforce France. This itself was typical of allied conduct of the early stages of the war, taking a decision too late for it to have the intended effect.

The paradox was that the allies finally had to occupy Narvik to provide a port through which their forces could be withdrawn. This was on 27 and 28 May using two battalions of the French Foreign Legion and a battalion of Norwegian troops, all under French command. More than 24,000 British, French, Norwegian and Polish troops were taken off by 8 June, but the following day German troops were on the Seine and Paris was cut off from the sea.

No doubt, the outcome could have been different, had the allies landed at Trondheim in the first place rather than leaving the forces intended to attack the town 100 miles north and 150 south of it in a country notorious for its rugged terrain and heavily indented coastline. The failure to save Norway was to have appalling consequences in the years that followed once the Soviet Union entered the war as an ally and expected to be supported by supplies carried on convoys that had to run the gauntlet of German air and naval attack on the long voyages past the North Cape.

Even the withdrawal was not without heavy cost. On 8 June, the aircraft carrier HMS *Glorious*, sister ship of *Courageous*, lost the previous autumn, was steaming from Norway towards Scapa Flow. Aboard, she not only had her own aircraft, but the surviving aircraft of the squadron of RAF Hawker Hurricane fighters, whose pilots had decided not to destroy their aircraft as originally intended, but instead, without arrestor hooks or deck landing training, had successfully flown them aboard the carrier so that they could be returned to the UK. Despite being in a war zone, no reconnaissance flights were being flown and there was not even a lookout in the crow's nest aboard the radar-less carrier. That afternoon, the ship was spotted by the German battlecruiser sisters, *Scharnhorst* and *Gneisenau*, shelled and sunk. While many of those aboard are believed to have survived the sinking, most drowned or died from exposure, and out of the 1,500 men aboard, just thirty-nine survived to be rescued.

Glorious was not the only casualty, as her two escorting destroyers, *Ardent* and *Acasta*, were lost making a valiant torpedo attack on the Germans.

Notes
1 *The French Navy in World War II*, Auphin, Amiral and Mordal, Jacques , US Naval Institute.

CHAPTER SEVEN

The Battle of France

I n anticipation of a another major war with Germany, British and French planning had simply assumed that the Second World War would be a re-run of the First, with German forces entering Belgium and being held along a front that would run from Belgium to the Swiss border. The Maginot Line was intended to protect France, but it ran only from the border with Switzerland to the border with Belgium close to the Ardennes. The heavy cost of this white elephant, that ignored the threat of a German invasion through Belgium, meant that it could not be extended to the Channel coast, while such an extension would have seriously harmed relations between France and her northern neighbour. The impact on Belgian morale of such a heavy and sophisticated fortification between the two countries is not hard to imagine.

Yet, already the Second World War was showing signs of being very different from the First World War. It was obvious that neither Italy nor Japan would be allies this time round, which made a big difference even if both countries were to remain neutral, which was increasingly unlikely. Another 'lost' ally from the First World War was Russia. Indeed, at the outset, it seemed that the Soviet Union, if not actually an ally of the Germans, was nevertheless hostile to the allies and that there would be no eastern front to distract the Germans. If there were any doubts that this was indeed a very different war, and not a repeat of the earlier conflict, it came when Germany ignored Danish and Norwegian neutrality and invaded both countries. This might have been foreseen, given German dependence on imported iron ore and also memories of just how successful the British blockade of Germany had been during the First World War, with many Germans starving to death in the final months of the conflict. Given this, it was strange that no one foresaw the Germans also invading the Netherlands, once again a neutral state, as it had been during the First World War.

The British and French assumed that there would be an invasion by way of Belgium, and for their part the Belgians calculated that they could only defend their territory with British and French help. Yet, knowing this, there were no combined exercises between any of the armed forces of these three countries, and indeed, Belgium once again placed her faith in neutrality until the Germans invaded on 10 May 1940, more than eight months after the declaration of war.

It was not as if the British and French had dithered at the outset of war. A British Expeditionary Force, BEF, had been planned and this was despatched to France on the day after war was declared, with an initial 152,000 men supported by an air component of twelve RAF squadrons and 9,393 personnel. In addition, the BEF was supported by the RAF's Advanced Air Striking Force, AASF, drawn from No.1 Group, Bomber Command, with ten squadrons of Fairey Battles, to which were added two squadrons of Bristol Blenheims and, later, two squadrons of Gloster Gladiator fighters. Eventually, the BEF's own Air Component, which was in addition to the AASF, was to rise to four squadrons of Hurricanes, four squadrons of Blenheims and five Lysander army co-operation squadrons. When the German advance started on 10 May 1940, an additional ten Hawker Hurricane fighter squadrons were moved to France within hours, ready for *Fall Gelb*, the German invasion of France.

To put the numbers into perspective, the number of troops

deployed with the BEF was around half as much again as the entire strength of the British Army today. It is often maintained that the British were consistently inferior to the German Wehrmacht in equipment, but the truth was that the British Army's equipment was uneven, neither uniformly good or uniformly bad. The 25-pounder field gun was very good, and the Matilda tank was difficult to knock out, although it lacked a gun capable of engaging the German panzers at a worthwhile range. Between the two world wars, the British Army had mechanised, in contrast to the Germans who depended heavily on horses for transport and for towing their field artillery. The Germans were also desperately short of medium and heavy tanks, but to make good this deficiency, they grouped their armour into compact fighting divisions able to bring maximum force on a point of the allied front lines. Just as they had eschewed attacking across the Maginot Line, along which much of France's manpower and armour was spread, they also waited for the British and French armies to dash north to help defend the Low Countries before attacking through the Ardennes, and striking at the Allies unexpectedly, with the sudden danger that the spearhead of the Anglo-French force could be cut off.

The problem was, as mentioned earlier in a quote from Admiral Sir Andrew Cunningham, that the French consistently refused to cooperate in an Inter-Allied War Council that could have kept strategy under review and evolved to meet the changing threat. Bad enough that there were no exercises with the Belgians and Dutch, worse that the collaboration between British and French was not as good as it could have been. At sea, liaison officers had been exchanged and the Anglo-French war codes brought up to date, and cooperation in Norway and off Norway had been good, but while facing the third threat to their country in less than eighty years, there was a certain inability amongst the French high command and politicians to cooperate. Did they see this as a sign of weakness, of lost independence?

There were other problems, inevitably. In modern warfare, control of the air over the battlefield, and along the supply routes, is essential, and the Second World War was a modern war. Air power cannot win a war on its own, but without it the 'boots on the ground' are vulnerable, and in this sense the air power deployed was hopeless; not only was it numerically inferior to the forces at the disposal of the Luftwaffe, but the aircraft were all hopelessly outclassed. Although highly manoeuvrable, the Hurricane lacked the speed of the Messerschmitt Bf109, while the biplane Gladiator was almost a museum piece. The Fairey Battle stemmed from a belief that a single-engined bomber could have the manoeuvrability of a fighter and much of its speed, but it didn't. Worse still, it had still to be recognised that bombing raids were best conducted by a concentration of as many aircraft as possible to force the defences to divide their fire, so attacks were often made by small numbers of aircraft, not even in squadron strength. Surprise was also often lacking.

Meanwhile, the British and French forces just sat and waited. It is impossible to judge, even with hindsight, whether the forces deployed would have had a greater impact if they had exercised together before the start of the German invasion, and especially if they had exercised with the Belgians. Given the attitudes that emerged once the German assault started, it is highly likely that exercises would have been regarded as provocative by both the French and the Belgians. As it was, all that happened were some limited discussions between the Belgians and their future allies during the winter of 1939–1940.

As in Norway, the odds were once again to be stacked against the defenders. The Luftwaffe had 3,834 aircraft, including 1,482 bombers and dive bombers, 42 ground attack aircraft, 248 fighter destroyers or *Zerstörer* (fighter-bombers), and 1,016 fighters. By contrast, the RAF had deployed 456 aircraft, of which 261 were fighters, 135 bombers and 60 reconnaissance aircraft. The main force of the French Armée de l' Air was in France and had 1,604 aircraft, many of them also obsolete or obsolescent, of which 260 were bombers, 764 fighters, 180 reconnaissance aircraft and another 400 or so aircraft in army support duties. Belgium had just 250 aircraft, of which 90 were fighters, just 12 bombers and an astonishing 120 reconnaissance aircraft, but only around 50 were modern. The Netherlands had 132 aircraft, of which 35 were fighters and 23 fighter-destroyers.

Against these forces, the Germans scored in both quality and quantity, and through having combat-hardened aircrew. The situation was not helped by the French insisting that neither of the two Allied air forces should press heavy bombing raids against German industry for fear of German reprisals against French targets.

The conflict was, after the Norwegian campaign, primarily a ground war with air support. The full impact of the U-boat menace had still to be realised, and so the Battle of France saw the two navies sidelined to a great extent. Even so, liaison officers were exchanged, those from the French Marine Nationale with the Royal Navy including:

> Alexandria – Capitaine de Vaisseau P.M. Auboyneau
> Dover – Dyevre and Eldin (ranks not given)
> Gibraltar – Capitaine de Frégate de Bryas
> Malta – Gayral
> Plymouth – Capitaine de Frégate Bos
> Portsmouth – Gelix (rank not given)

A comparative list of British and French officers' ranks is given in Appendix II on Page 232 but essentially, *capitaine de vasseau* was equal to a captain in the Royal Navy and *capitaine de frégate* to a commander.

DIFFERENCES BETWEEN THE ALLIES

It is worth noting that the British and French forces differed considerably. Unlike European armies, the British Army at the time was relatively small and based on professional soldiers, many of whom had long service and would have seen colonial peacekeeping and garrison duties abroad, mainly in Africa, India and the Middle East. It was supported by a reserve, the Territorial

Army, whose members were often known to the 'old sweats' amongst the regulars as 'Saturday night soldiers', just as to the Royal Navy, members of the Royal Naval Volunteer Reserve were known as 'weekend sailors'. The Royal Naval Reserve was mainly comprised of members of the British Merchant Marine, many of whom were highly experienced ship handlers, navigators and engineers.

While the 'Terriers' also went on an annual camp, the British Army as a whole was regarded as being unable to expand quickly in a crisis, lacking sufficiently strong and well trained reserve forces. In anticipation of war, conscription had been introduced while the Territorial Army had been expanded with considerable urgency.

At once a strength and also a weakness, the British Army devolved considerable decision-making to the generals in the field. This was all well and good given a general who was at least competent and, hopefully, talented, and who had the necessary resources and a good flow of reliable intelligence. As at Narvik, however, it was a major drawback if generalship was poor or indifferent.

The French Army, by contrast, was based on the continental pattern, with the majority of troops being conscripts, who afterwards spent a number of years in the reserves. Most of the regular troops were despatched to serve in the colonial forces, where their strength was augmented by locally recruited troops. Mobilization of the reserve forces was an important part of bringing the French Army up to its wartime strength. Nevertheless, having a large army mattered little if its equipment was out of date. The French Army had not mechanised between the wars, and still made considerable use of horses. Unlike the British, who by this time mainly confined horses to ceremonial duties, the French still had horses in two out of their three cavalry divisions. Much of the artillery dated from the First World War, while more modern pieces, such as the 47mm anti-tank gun, were in short supply. Even keeping the French Army operational was a logistics nightmare, with no less than eight different types of tank. Command was centralized, with a lengthy and cumbersome structure and only limited authority delegated to the generals in the field.

Both the French and British armies in wartime could depend on substantial numbers of colonial troops being posted to wherever they were needed. In the case of the British, troops from the dominions, that was Australia, Canada, New Zealand and South Africa, could only be moved with the consent of their own governments. The French made extensive use of troops from their African colonies.

The Belgian Army had started to mobilize on 25 August. During that first winter of war, it continued to expand, so that by May 1940, it had 600,000 men, a considerable proportion of its 8.2 million population, which amounted to a field army of 18 infantry divisions, 2 divisions of *Chasseurs Ardennais*, who were partly mechanized, and two mechanized cavalry divisions, although of armour itself there were just ten tanks. The Belgian Army was completely lacking in anti-aircraft guns, despite the fear of the bomber that had become almost paranoid in the democracies between the wars, and despite the well-publicised lessons of the Spanish Civil War, and indeed, of Abyssinia. It was slightly better off for anti-tank guns: it had four!

In one sense, like the French the Belgians had also decided that safety lay behind fixed fortifications, with modern forts covering the bridges at Eben-Emael, overlooking the junction of the Albert Canal and the River Meuse. Had the Maginot Line been extended northwards along the border between Belgium and Germany, it might have made more sense, although once again it could have been bypassed by German forces invading through the Netherlands. The Dutch, having maintained their neutrality successfully during the First World War, would have been unlikely to have accepted participation in an extended Maginot Line. In a different sense, the Dutch also believed in fixed defensive positions, but of a dramatically different kind – the use of flooding to check the enemy's advance. Nevertheless, the Dutch in their complacency had overlooked not only the rapid advances achieved by the German *blitzkrieg* tactics, but also the use of airborne warfare with paratroops and air-landed troops. Perhaps the lack of awareness of the potential for airborne forces of one kind or another was understandable, as these were first used in warfare in the German advances. On the other hand, air transport had played a part in Britain's colonial policing, especially in Mesopotamia, present day Iraq, while the Soviet Union had experimented with paratroops between the wars.

The Dutch had their most up-to-date aircraft, warships and other equipment in the Netherlands East Indies, present day Indonesia, could field an army of up to 400,000 men in wartime, organized as four army corps each with two divisions. This was singularly ill-equipped for modern warfare, having not one tank and just twenty-six armoured cars, which would have been unable to withstand a *panzer* force. The artillery consisted of 656 guns, all of them obsolescent or simply obsolete. Procurement policy and recruitment had been constrained by a strong pacifist movement in the Netherlands between the wars.

While the Dutch were indeed a nautical race with a strong maritime tradition, most of the modern warships were in the East Indies, while in home waters, there was just one cruiser and a single destroyer, some small craft and fifty or so elderly naval aircraft. The air force was little better, and resources had in any case pre-war been shared between the air force and the separate naval and army air arms in the East Indies. The Dutch could only muster 175 aircraft on 10 May, against 1,100 put into the air by the Germans, while the operational strength was even lower as only 132 Dutch aircraft were serviceable, and only slightly more than half of those could be considered modern.

These forces faced a German Army that was also based on the continental pattern, but within the conscript force had a strong central core of regular officers and non-commissioned officers. No less important, it was a mobilized and sizeable force, waiting, ready for the outbreak of war. In 1939, it had 2 million men in 106 divisions, but following the invasion of Poland, it expanded by 50 per cent, with another million men in 44 new divisions. In addition, the Nazi Party had its own armed force, the Waffen SS, which had another three divisions, while, unusually, paratroops were part of the Luftwaffe, which had a division of these key assault troops, while later a second division was added. The other element in the assault formations were the highly mobile Panzer divisions, of which there were ten, and another four motorised divisions. On the other hand, as already mentioned, transport was still largely horse-drawn, while the Panzer divisions had to be concentrated into strategically important groups to make the best use of the limited number available to the Germans for such a massive offensive.

THE GERMANS ATTACK

The belief exists that the Germans were so successful during the first eighteen months of the Second World War because they concentrated on just one front at a time, and that dividing their forces between the west, or more accurately, North Africa, and the east by invading the Soviet Union was the fatal move. This was not quite true, because the massive thrust westwards into the Netherlands and Belgium on 10 May 1940, started while fighting continued in Norway.

The German actions should not have come as a surprise. On 7 January 1940, a German aircraft force-landed inside Belgium, and a plan for the invasion of the country fell into Belgian hands. Naturally, the Germans revised their plans as a result of this, but the warning was ignored. One can only imagine that the Belgians felt that the plans were fake, intended to provoke a reaction, or that a sense of hopelessness had already taken hold.

What could not have been foreseen was that the Germans would exercise considerable imagination and ingenuity in their attack. On the other hand, it should have come as no surprise that the Germans did not intend to waste manpower and equipment on a costly assault through the Maginot Line. Going round it through Belgium was likely to be the only course, and, naturally, this was the route chosen during the First World War, before the Maginot Line had been built.

The Germans also treated the Belgian forts with considerable respect. At 0430 hrs on 10 May, a force of ten DFS 230 gliders was towed into the air by Junkers Ju52/3m transports, with the gliders carrying seventy-eight specially trained engineers from the Seventh Airborne Division. Despite the leader being left behind when his glider's tow broke, forcing it to land prematurely inside Germany, the remaining gliders landed on the roof of Fort Eben-Emael and in the area immediately surrounding it. Scrambling out of the gliders, the engineers used specially shaped charges to blow holes in the fort, and kept the 1,200 troops inside entombed for twenty-four hours while the Fourth Panzer Division swept across the river and canals into Belgium. The engineers had completed their mission by the time their leader caught up with them in his glider at 08.30. Fort Eben-Emael, that huge obstacle to an invasion, was neutralized at a cost of six German dead and another twenty wounded.

Another twenty-one gliders were used to seize other important crossings into Belgium, including the bridges at Veldwezelt and Vroenhoven. These bridges were taken completely intact after a desperate plea by the officer commanding the defence at Veldwezelt to destroy the bridge was refused by an incredulous officer at headquarters. The bridge at Kanne was blown, nevertheless, partly because German gliders had not been able to land close enough to maintain an element of surprise, but no doubt also because the permission came from the officer in command at Eben-Emael, who was in no doubt whatsoever that an invasion was in full swing.

As glider-landed troops seized the Belgian crossings, paratroops were overwhelming the Dutch defences, landing from 05.00 hrs in a long carpet to take the bridges at Dordrecht and Moerdijk, over the Nieuw Maas at Rotterdam, and the airfield at Waalhaven, where, despite continued heavy fighting, no fewer than 250 troop-carrying aircraft landed during the day. In this way, a 30 mile stretch of Dutch territory was secured in advance of the Panzer armies. Other paratroops took the airfields at Delft and The Hague, in an attempt to seize members of the Dutch Royal family and the leaders of the main political parties – presumably also including a few pacifists. The Dutch put up a stiff resistance, but decided not to destroy the bridges in the vain hope that these could be retaken, but this was impossible. Even when lightly-armed paratroops seized the bridge at Moerdijk, they were able to fight off strong Dutch counter-attacks for two days, until they were finally relieved by a Panzer division. Had the Dutch maintained effective armoured forces of their own, recapture might have been possible.

The Germans did not have it all their own way. Out of thirteen Junkers Ju52/3m transports assigned to take troops to seize Ypenburg, several were shot down. The infantry division assigned to take The Hague suffered heavy losses after only 2,000 out of the 7,000 troops had been landed or dropped, so that the attempt to seize the capital had to be cancelled and the division re-assigned to the battle for Rotterdam. Despite Rotterdam being declared an 'open city' after furious fighting, it was heavily bombed by the Luftwaffe. The Dutch air force lost half of its aircraft on the first day of fighting, and was virtually wiped out by the time the Netherlands surrendered on 14 May.

The invasion of the Netherlands diverted British and French attention, with French troops hurriedly sent north to help, while other British and French troops moved into Belgium to assist the defences. The allies in effect spread their forces too thinly and were distracted as the Battle of France began to develop. It also meant that preparations were not made to stop German forces advancing through the Ardennes, where the panzer forces in particular could have been vulnerable to a well coordinated anti-tank defence as they negotiated the narrow roads of the forests. As it was, the French and Belgians regarded the Ardennes as virtually impassable, especially for a substantial army with heavy equipment and tanks, and left them poorly defended. The result was that the Germans raced through the Ardennes, onwards to the plains of northern France, and came close to cutting the British and French armies in two.

Meanwhile, with British and French help, the Belgians continued fighting until King Leopold negotiated a surrender on 28 May, much to the anger of his ministers who had wanted him to join a government in exile in France. Just as there were to be divisions amongst the French after surrender, there were similar divisions within Belgium, with the sovereign blaming the politicians for having failed to provide strong leadership and prepare for an invasion, while they resented his attempts to establish a relationship with the Germans in the hope that his country might regain some autonomy.

Autonomy was not on the German agenda. Tiny Luxembourg, for example, with no standing army, was overwhelmed on 10 May, and later its territory was incorporated into that of the Third Reich, despite some 97 per cent of citizens opposing the occupation in a referendum in 1941. The Germans even endeavoured to conscript the Luxemburgers into their armed forces, despite a general strike being called which resulted in more than twenty of the strikers being shot.

When these nations surrendered, the general pattern was that they did not concede an end to the war, and it was clear that they would continue to fight to regain their territory. Many personnel from the Scandinavian countries, Belgium and the Netherlands, followed the Poles to the United Kingdom, although many Poles had first gone by way of France and saw action there. The Norwegians also called upon their substantial merchant fleet to sail to British ports and place themselves at the service of the authorities – which was a substantial bonus at a time when the British Merchant Navy was under considerable strain with many of its ships taken up for the needs of the armed services, including, of course, many passenger liners which because of their size and speed became armed merchant cruisers until it was realised that these were completely inadequate in any battle with major German fleet units.

FALL GELB – THE INVASION OF FRANCE

Numerically, the German and Allied armies in France were roughly equal. Apart from the Germans having drawn the British and French northwards by invading the Low Countries and leaving the exposed northern border between France and Belgium undefended, the French also wasted thirty divisions who were left sitting behind the Maginot Line ready for a German assault that never came. Whether or not the Maginot Line was the biggest white elephant in the history of warfare, it was the longest. The mobile reserve formation designated to support the French commander, General Gamelin, the French Seventh Army under General Geraud, had been sent racing northwards in a belated and vain attempt to help the Dutch.

The French frontline had advanced into Belgium, but the front between Namur in Belgium and Sedan on the French border was held by the French Second and Ninth Armies, often described as consisting of poor quality troops with poor morale which had suffered during the eight months of phoney war.

While the British had ten divisions in France, it was in the air that the country displayed its weakness. The best of the RAF's fighters, the new Supermarine Spitfires, were held back for the defence of the United Kingdom. The RAF's idea of a heavy bomber at this stage of the war was the Vickers Wellington, later re-designated as a medium bomber, and even this effective aircraft was kept at home, along with the Handley Page Hampden, a peculiar thin aeroplane known as the 'flying pan handle' to its crews, which was another useful aircraft by the undemanding standards of the day. Already, it seems that the British were looking ahead to the day when France might be occupied and building up their forces for a last ditch defence of the mother country. Yet, the French themselves were far from taking the offensive against the Germans.

In both cases, the aircraft, if moved forward to France, could have attacked German industrial centres and troop concentrations, as well as communications targets – but the French didn't want this in case it brought retribution upon French cities.

Indeed, the French could have shelled the industrial area of the Saar with their heavy artillery had they been determined to do so. The French were not alone in this. Many in the British government objected to attacks on ammunition factories because these were 'private property'. RAF crews were allowed to strafe German airfields with their machine guns (British fighters were yet to receive the more effective heavier calibre cannon), but not to bomb them. Machine gun fire from a strafing aircraft could kill and maim, but for the most part it had nuisance value rather than inflicting serious damage.

While Hitler wanted to strike west as soon as possible, even before the end of 1939, he was held back by his generals, who wanted to consolidate their Polish gains, especially as they were now facing their declared enemy, the Soviet Union. What some at the time described as the 'worst winter on record' was another factor, and traditionally, armies had not moved during the winter. There were also those who thought that a prolonged period of inactivity in the west would encourage the United Kingdom and France to accept that helping Poland was out of the question and that once again the two allies would back down, as at Munich. While some members of the British government might have considered a negotiated settlement during that first winter, by spring attitudes had hardened and in May 1940, the British cabinet decided that it would reject any German peace proposals.

British and French armoured units were poorly deployed, often in small numbers ready to plug gaps in the line, and the same could be said about their air power. Poorly deployed, slow to react, and when they did so, they flew offensive sorties with such small formations that the defences quickly disposed of them.

It was not a case of targets being in short supply. The main obstacle for the German forces advancing through the Ardennes was not British and neither was it French, it was the poor highway network, which resulted in traffic jams some fifty miles in length which, had they known about them, would have presented ideal targets for the Royal Air Force and the Armée de l'Air.

The First World War mindset exhibited by both British and French senior officers, and by their intelligence officers as well, also failed to recognize the urgency of the situation. When, just three whole days after the attack had started, at nightfall on 12 May, Whit Sunday in 1940, seven panzer divisions were poised on the east bank of the River Meuse, it was the consensus amongst both allied armies and those in their capital cities, that it would be another five or six days before the Germans would try to force a crossing. Within twenty-four hours, the first units were across.

The Germans had preceded their attack with an aerial blitz by around a thousand aircraft. Casualties amongst the French Second Army, on the receiving end of the attack, were not substantial, but the real impact was that the poorly trained troops were unnerved by the Junkers Ju87 Stuka dive-bombers with their 'trumpets of Jericho' sirens that screamed as the aircraft dived towards the target. Anti-aircraft gunners stopped firing and 'went to ground', recalled one French general, while the infantry cowered in the trenches. By the time darkness fell, the Germans had a bridgehead across the Meuse some three miles wide and up to six miles deep.

It took just two days for the RAF's bomber strength in France to be cut from 135 aircraft to 72, and of these another 40 were shot down by the third day. Bomber squadrons based in southern England also attacked the advancing German forces, but to little effect and at great cost. Typical of the actions that took place was on 12 May, when six AASF Battles, with an escort of two Hurricane fighters, were sent against the Vroenhoven and Veldwezelt bridges, across which the German forces were streaming. Four of the aircraft were shot down as they approached the targets, which were left undamaged. One of the Battles was burning 'like a torch' as it dropped its bombs, but its pilot, Flying Officer McIntosh, managed to land it safely behind enemy lines, and the crew spent the rest of the war as prisoners. One German officer pointed out to McIntosh that they had taken the bridges early on the Friday morning, but the Germans had been left with the whole of Friday and Saturday to build up anti-aircraft defences before the RAF had arrived on the Sunday.

By 21 May, the air component of the BEF was down to its last few Lysanders, while the few surviving Battles were limited to night operations to keep losses to an acceptable level. As the Germans swept through Belgium and the Netherlands, forcing British units which had ventured into Belgium back into France, the British soon started to husband scarce resources and trained aircrew for the defence of the British Isles. Two more Hurricane squadrons had been despatched to France in response to desperate pleas from the army, but Air Chief Marshal Sir Hugh Dowding, AOC-in-C, Fighter Command, successfully opposed sending more, arguing that to do so would 'bleed white' the air defences of the United Kingdom. During the withdrawal and then the evacuation from Dunkirk, the RAF used units based in the south of England to provide air cover. Hitler had been persuaded to let the Luftwaffe finish off the British troops with their backs to the sea at Dunkirk, but in desperation Fighter Command expended valuable resources in an attempt to ward off the Luftwaffe, even obtaining local air superiority at times, but at a heavy cost. This was despite the difficulty of providing constant fighter cover given the short range of fighter aircraft at this stage of the war. While Fighter Command could not always stop ships being bombed as they loaded troops, Coastal Command and the Fleet Air Arm helped by ensuring that enemy U-boats as well as E-boats (fast motor gunboats and torpedo boats) were prevented from attacking the evacuation fleet. Once Italy entered the war on 10 June, Wellingtons and Whitleys based in the south of France mounted some limited attacks against Genoa and Turin, and there was also an attack by instructors in a Fleet Air Arm Swordfish training squadron that had been using the elderly aircraft carrier, HMS *Argus*, and a base in the South of France for training.

A flying visit to Paris by the First Lord of the Admiralty, Winston Churchill, found the French government undecided over whether the Germans were heading for Paris or the Channel.

Meanwhile, the Germans were beginning to grow wary of their constant successes, and expected a counter-attack. At least twice, the advanced was halted so that forces could be consolidated in anticipation of a repulse, but none came. Having moved forward on 10 May, by 19 May, the Second Panzer Division was on the English Channel close to Abbeville, having covered 200 miles in just ten days. A large part of the British and French armies were trapped with their backs to the sea in a pocket stretching towards Dunkirk. A successful British armoured counter-attack southwards from Arras on 21 May was not backed up by French forces, and so the British withdrew towards the Channel ports.

The British could only do one thing, evacuate as many of their own troops from Dunkirk as they could manage. During a period of just over a week from 26 May to 3 June, more than 338,000 British, French and Free Polish troops were evacuated from Dunkirk, mainly by the Royal Navy and by merchant vessels taken up from trade, although many small vessels, including motor yachts and fishing boats were also used, especially in ferrying men from the shore to larger ships that were unable to get closer in. The Marine Nationale also deployed a number of its ships for the evacuation.

The evacuation saw great sacrifice by units ordered to fight rearguard actions, and by the French and Belgian troops, many of whom remained fighting until the evacuation was over and they too had their backs to the sea. The French resisted a renewed German onslaught on their final line of defence on 5 June, but the Germans broke through leaving Paris defenceless when it was occupied on 14 June. The troops manning the Maginot Line and those based behind it were simply mopped up by the Germans, while in the south the Italians finally entered the war, invading the South of France and earning themselves the title of the 'harvest hands' from their cynical German allies.

The aircraft of the AASF remained in France after the evacuation of Dunkirk ended, with its few remaining Blenheims and Battles continuing to make offensive sorties as the remnants of the BEF and French forces were squeezed into the Cherbourg peninsula. Only as these too were evacuated did the aircraft return to the UK, with the fighter squadrons acting as a rear guard and being last to return.

In all, during the Battle of France, RAF losses totalled 931 aircraft with 1,526 casualties. Of these aircraft, 229 were from the AASF and a further 279 were from the BEF's air component, with around 200 from Fighter Command and more than 150 from Bomber Command, while around 60 were from Coastal Command. A number of Fleet Air Arm Fairey Swordfish units were placed under Coastal Command control and helped to patrol the waters north of the evacuation area.

The Germans had estimated that the occupation of Luxembourg, Belgium and the Netherlands, and France, would cost them 90,000 dead and 200,000 wounded, with perhaps 1.9 million prisoners; it had instead it had taken just six weeks and cost 29,640 dead, and 133,573 wounded. On 22 June, French leaders signed an armistice in the very same railway carriage where Marshal Foch had accepted the German surrender in 1918.

The impact on the Germans was immense. They had not anticipated such an easy or complete victory, and had few plans to follow up the collapse of France. The light casualty figures ensured that the mass of German public opinion viewed the victory as having little cost, and enthusiasm for the war grew. While the United Kingdom was forced onto the back foot and had saved most of its army, but without most of its equipment, Germany hesitated, leaving the British time to rebuild their forces and, without knowing what was to come, prepare for the Battle of Britain.

CHAPTER EIGHT

Surrender and the French Forces

Although an agreement signed on 28 March 1940 committed the two allies not to conclude a ceasefire or peace with the German separately, the surrender of French forces had been foreseen some time before the event. Churchill's demands for ever greater numbers of aircraft to be sent to France had been resisted by the Royal Air Force, realizing that these scarce assets and their even scarcer aircrew would simply be thrown away, with no tactical or strategic benefit, and leave the United Kingdom critically unprepared for whatever might follow. The British already had plans for the evacuation of their troops well before the actual order was given on 24 May. These plans were comprehensive, and involved not only the military but the railways, shipping companies, although many of the ships used were in railway ownership, and many voluntary organisations, as an unknown number of troops would have to be fed and watered during what could be a lengthy journey from the Channel ports to their barracks. The big unknown was just how many troops could be taken off the beaches, and the eventual total of 338,000 was far beyond even the most optimistic expectations of the British government.

Even before Dunkirk, a number of French warships had begun to arrive in British ports, where they were less vulnerable to air attack. The Dutch had already moved a cruiser, two destroyers, nine submarines and a minelayer to Falmouth in Cornwall.

During the Dunkirk evacuation, Admiral Abrial commanded the French warships providing assistance and also the ground defence of the port. This was known to Admiral Darlan, but the start of the evacuation caught the French army's high command by surprise. There was considerable confusion, as Darlan's orders to Abrial were that the forces protecting the evacuation were, once they were sure that any forces outside the defensive line would be unable to make their way to it and join the evacuation, to join the evacuation leaving as small a rearguard force as possible. This meant that French troops were expected to ensure that as many as possible of the British and Free Polish forces got away, before they could follow them.

In Paris, Churchill assured the French government that British and French troops would be evacuated on equal terms, and that the rearguard would be provided by British troops. This was a classic case of politicians agreeing one thing while the situation on the ground was completely different.

As the Germans reached the Channel coast of France, the French 2nd Destroyer Flotilla, commanded by Capt Yves Urvoy de Pozamparc in the small Simoun class destroyer *Cyclone*, 1,300 tons, dashed to Boulogne, and began firing at the German forces attacking the port. The Luftwaffe counter-attacked, setting her sister ship, the destroyer *Orage* on fire so that she had to be abandoned. The flotilla's ships were small destroyers of the Simoun class, just 1,400 tons, and sometimes classed as *torpilleurs*, or 'torpedo-boats'. The surviving French destroyers then withdrew to Cherbourg to take on more ammunition, while their place was taken by a flotilla of British destroyers which managed to snatch 4,000 British troops from the port. Some idea of the speed of the German advance can be taken from the situation at Walcheren, where a French torpedo-boat, the *Bouclier*, just 600 tons, attempted to come alongside, and it was not until he had a bullet pass through both cheeks that her commanding officer, Capitaine de Frégate (Commander) Fourniere, realised that the men on the wharf who he thought were waiting to take his lines were Germans.

On 28 May, the French navy started to take an active involvement in the Dunkirk evacuation. Under the command of Rear Admiral Marcel Landriau in the sloop *Savorgnan de Brazza*, 2,000 tons and larger than many of the destroyers, a hastily improvised force of 250 assorted vessels formed what became known as the 'Pas-de-Calais Flotilla'. The force included two *contre-torpilleur* super destroyers and seven other destroyers as well as smaller naval and civilian vessels. Landriau placed himself and his force under the command of Admiral Sir Bertram Ramsay at Dover.

Further south, the elderly battleships *Courbet* and *Paris* arrived at Cherbourg from Brest to provide anti-aircraft cover for the evacuation from there. They then joined the evacuation fleet of warships and merchant vessels. One ship, the destroyer *Bourrasque*, 1,300 tons, every inch of her decks filled with men, was sunk with the loss of all 1,200 men aboard. A sister-ship, the *Sirocco* delivered 500 men at Dover, and then the next day was unfortunate enough to become one of the few ships in the evacuation to be attacked by German E-boats, whose torpedoes were followed by bombs from Junkers Ju87 Stuka dive-bombers. Another destroyer, the *Mistral*, had her bridge completely wrecked, but managed to limp into Dover.

Sirocco, as mentioned earlier, had had a distinguished war career, having sunk two U-boats.

Back at Dunkirk, the elderly *Oriole*, a minesweeping paddle steamer, did not have boats to ferry men from the shore, but her commanding officer drove her onto the beach so that men could scramble aboard, and use her as a jetty to board other ships that took them off over her stern. Before beaching, two anchors had been dropped off the stern so that the ship could be kedged off after her service as a jetty. It worked, and the ship was later spotted by the Luftwaffe steaming to England.

Another minesweeper, the *Emile Deschamps*, was less fortunate. She struck a mine off the Kent coast and went down with
400 men. The loss of life when such a small ship struck a mine or
was hit by a torpedo was almost always complete.

Other ships, both British and French, took troops off at other
ports, including Cherbourg and St Nazaire.

Often overlooked, the French participation in the evacuation
helped towards the total of 338,226 men rescued, of whom
around 123,000 were French. Dunkirk, as Churchill was quick to
remind the British people, was not a victory as 'wars are not won
by evacuations', but it saved a force more than three times the
size of the British army today, and these experienced and battle-
hardened troops provided the basis for the expansion of the
British army in the years that were to follow.

FRENCH SURRENDER

The big difference between France and the other nations
invaded by the Germans up to June 1940 was that it was not
entirely overrun. This was never the German intention. Another
difference was that, in common with Luxembourg, the Germans
had high hopes that at least some of the population would join
them, as Alsace and Lorraine had long been disputed territories
with both France and Germany regarding these provinces as
theirs. They had come under German control during the Franco-
Prussian War of 1871, having become French territory during
the late 17th and early 18th centuries, and returned to France
after German defeat in the First World War. Now, in May 1940,
they were back in German hands. In both provinces, known to
the Germans as Elsass-Lothringen, the majority of the local
population was German-speaking.

Strangely, the territories were not covered by the Armistice
Agreement of 1940, but they were nevertheless re-annexed by
the Germans. To drive the point home, some 200,000 French-
speaking members of the population were forced to abandon
their homes and flee westwards into metropolitan France.

Gauleiters were appointed and the territories were subjected to German law. French prisoners-of-war found to have been born in Alsace Lorraine were released into the German Army, and some of the pro-German element in the population even managed to join the Waffen SS. Nevertheless, the population remained effectively second class citizens within the Reich, probably because even though they were German speakers, their sentiments, if not anti-German, were for the most part anti-Nazi, having lived in the freer atmosphere of inter-war France. Alsace and Lorraine brought additional natural resources to the German war effort, mainly in the form of coking coal, while the inhabitants were subjected to the direction of labour, as indeed was, increasingly, the population of Germany itself.

While fighting continued between French and German forces, arranging an armistice was difficult. It was also a difficult political question as earlier that year the British and French had concluded a treaty that didn't simply commit themselves to an alliance, but forbade either to conclude a separate negotiation with Germany or Italy. French warships in the Mediterranean had shelled Italian ports and coastal installations after Italy entered the war belatedly on 10 June.

Nevertheless, as the Battle of France started its final phase, it was a senior French army officer, General Weygand, who began to urge his political superiors to negotiate a cease fire. In lobbying for this, Weygand went far beyond what was acceptable for a member of his country's armed forces. His concern was that since defeat was inevitable, it would be much better if it came while the French armed forces retained the order and discipline to avoid complete anarchy after surrender. When Paul Reynaud, the prime minister, offered Weygand the written authority for the army to surrender to the Germans, the general became very angry and indignant, maintaining that the army did want to have the shame of surrender, but that it should be the state that should do so. This created an impasse. If France had to capitulate, Reynaud wanted to do so along the lines of the Dutch surrender, under which all Dutch soldiers engaged with the enemy had to lay down their arms, but the state retained the right to continue the war. In this case of France, this would be possible from its North African and Middle Eastern territories.

There was a third view, emanating from Pierre Laval, another member of the government who had surrounded himself with a power base of senators and deputies. Laval wanted not simply surrender, but for France to change sides. His argument for the policy was that by allying herself with the victor and continuing the war against the United Kingdom, France would not only retain her sovereignty, but also all of her overseas possessions.

A former lawyer, Laval had entered French politics as the Socialist Party's youngest deputy, but later became an independent socialist, and his policies and attitudes changed while he had three terms of office as prime minister. When Hitler rose to power, he was initially opposed to his policies and the threat of a resurgent Germany. In December 1935, he was one of the proponents of the unsuccessful Hoare-Laval plan which would have given Mussolini a substantial part of Abyssinia, with Laval's long-term strategy being for France and Italy to form an alliance to counter the growing military might of Germany. When the United Kingdom rejected the plan, Laval resigned. He was brought back into office by Pétain on 25 June 1940 as vice-premier.

The irony was that the man who was ultimately responsible for the armistice was Marshal Henri Philippe Pétain, a regular army officer brought out of retirement as minister of state and vice-premier to act as a rallying point for the French Army and the people. Pétain had been due to retire in 1914, holding the rank of colonel, but the First World War intervened and he rapidly rose to high command. The victor of Verdun, he became a popular hero and was made a Marshal of France.

In 1940, Pétain was eighty-four years old, feeble and without any of the fire necessary to drive a country to victory even in conditions more favourable than those that existed. From the start, Pétain advised an armistice, and having been appointed vice-premier by Paul Reynaud, on 18 May 1940, he replaced him as premier late on 16 June. The following morning, his first act was to ask the Spanish government to act as an intermediary with the Germans.

THE ARMISTICE

As it happened, despite the constant successes on the battlefield, Hitler was responsive to the idea of an armistice. He did not want to stretch his armies by occupying the whole of France, since his original plan was to occupy only the northern part of the country, with its coal and industry. More importantly, he knew that the French could continue the war from their North African territories, and if they managed to get their substantial fleet (the fourth largest in the world at the time) away to North Africa, they could, with British help, dominate the Mediterranean. While French forces in North Africa would be cut off from their usual supply of war materiel, the United Kingdom, and perhaps the United States, could be sure to make up much of any shortfall. At the time, the French had colonial possessions in Algeria, part of Morocco, Tunisia, the Lebanon and Syria, while they also had strong forces in Egypt.

On the other hand, surrender, with a substantial part of France unoccupied and with its own government, would make it much more difficult for France to continue the war. In fact, Hitler's appreciation of the threat posed if the French chose to continue the war from North Africa, and perhaps the Lebanon and Syria as well, was astute. Paul Reynaud had understood all too well that the Battle of France was lost. He intended to continue the war from Africa and the French Empire using the French fleet. This was not implausible. None of the other countries overrun by the Germans had actually stopped fighting, but had continued to do so using those of their citizens who had managed to escape, first to France and then to the United Kingdom. The French had the advantage of strategically placed territories around the world that gave them the room and the manpower to continue fighting, as well as, in some cases, the natural resources to help pay for it. Their fine naval bases in North Africa would undoubtedly have been an asset for the two allies, although the British were also well off in this respect, and overall, the French forces in the Mediterranean theatre had been stronger than those of the British. The only weakness in the French continuing the war from their colonies was the lack of a manufacturing base, for which the British and the Americans, and perhaps the Canadians who were rapidly industrializing, would have to provide a substitute.

In the terms of the armistice, Hitler allowed France to continue to be regarded as a sovereign power, and allowed her to retain her colonies to avoid these siding with the British. While the French Army would be demobilized in occupied France, the unoccupied area could retain armed forces, although limited in size. The French Navy would be neutralized in either German or Italian ports, but it would not be taken over by either country, and a promise was made to France that once the war was over, the ships would be returned to it. There would be no formal demands for French territory, despite the annexation of Alsace and Lorraine, until a peace settlement was negotiated.

On 21 June, the terms of the armistice were presented to the French delegation in the Forest of Compiègne, and as mentioned earlier, the meeting used the same railway carriage as was used in the German surrender of 1918. There were no negotiations. This was partly because Hitler wanted to see British reactions, but it was also meant to emphasize that the French had been defeated in the field. As a result, the leader of the French delegation, General Huntziger, was simply handed the armistice agreement with its twenty-four articles, and told that they were non-negotiable. While the Armistice with Germany was signed the following day, one condition was that it would only come into effect once a separate armistice was signed with Italy. Italy had declared war on the United Kingdom and France on 10 June, and had invaded the south of France on 21 June. Nevertheless, Mussolini's venture in France was far from successful, and a further armistice was signed between France and Italy in Rome on 24 June.

With the Anglo-French alliance effectively in tatters, the British were not privy to the conditions of the armistice, which consisted of a twenty-four article document. British suspicions of French intentions were also aroused at this stage. It took Sir Ronald Campbell, British ambassador to France, some time to persuade Paul Baudouin, the Minister for Foreign Affairs, to release details of the armistice agreement. Baudouin eventually released the details, adding that Admiral Darlan had proposed that the fleet should be allowed to proceed to North African ports. This was unacceptable to the British as they feared that the ships could then be seized by the Italians, and they demanded that the fleet should be removed from the Mediterranean. Baudoiun replied that if there was any danger of the ships being seized, they would be scuttled.

When they did get to see it, the condition of most interest to the British was Article 8, which read:

The French fleet (with the exception of that part which is left at the disposition of the French government for the protection of French interests in the colonial empire) will be concentrated in ports to be determined and will be de-mobilized and disarmed under the supervision of Germany or, respectively, Italy. The peace-time bases of these vessels will be used to designate these ports.

The German government solemnly declares to the French government that it has no intention of using during the war for its own purposes the French fleet stationed in ports under German supervision, other than the units necessary for coastal patrol and minesweeping. It further declares solemnly and formally that it has no intention of making claims in respect of the French fleet after the conclusion of peace.

With the exception of that element of the French fleet to be determined which will be allocated to the defence of French interest in the colonial empire, all warships at present outside French territorial waters should be recalled to France.

If one could trust the Germans, this article would seem to provide all of the reassurance that the United Kingdom could want, but at this stage no one trusted the Germans. After all, had not the pledges upon which the Munich Agreement of 1938 had been founded been broken?

Nevertheless, this was not the only one of the terms that was to be of concern. Article 10 in particular made grim reading. In essence, the French government was not allowed to transfer any assets or personnel to the United Kingdom. Any individual who left to join the United Kingdom, or any other state, to continue the war against Germany would be designated a *franc-tireur*, essentially an outlaw and outside the Geneva Convention. As the Germans had shown themselves to be merciless during the First World War, there could be no question that the position of a *franc-tireur* would be unenviable. During the First World War, the master of a British merchant vessel who attempted to ram a U-boat was executed when he eventually was taken prisoner by the German Navy. This condition also implied that those French forces resident in the colonies would also be classed as *franc-tireurs* if they attempted to continue the war with Germany.

Early on 23 June, Campbell telegraphed London:

Diabolically clever German terms have evidently destroyed the last remnants of French courage. If, as I presume to be certain, Germans reject French counterproposal as regards the fleet, I do not believe for a moment that the French, in their present state of collapse, would hold out against original German condition to recall the fleet to French ports, and might even reverse scuttling order. They could still square their conscience by saying ships could not be used against us. We are thus thrown back on Darlan's pathetic assurances to First Lord of the Admiralty.

To the British, the French Admiralty maintained that they were prepared to send ships as far away as Madagascar if possible, but that the ships could not be handed over the Royal Navy without specific orders from the government. Such orders were, of course, unlikely, given that the French were doing their best to convince the Germans of their good intentions in an attempt to obtain as favourable armistice terms as possible. Admiral Darlan, at Bordeaux, by this time the seat of government, maintained that the French fleet would never be surrendered to the Germans or the Italians, but had also refused to send the fleet to the UK while French troops were still fighting and declared that the fleet had to remain in French waters while the fighting continued. This had implied that the situation would be different once France surrendered.

Writing later, a one-time head of the French Naval Historical Section, Contre-Admiral (Rear Admiral) Jean Kessler, explained:

> France was anxious to limit the consequences of its defeat in the Battle of France, while the United Kingdom sought to assert its unwavering determination to continue fighting and to obtain the assistance of the United States to win the world war.[1]

Just as the use of the railway carriage had been symbolic of the changed order, the army allowed Vichy under the terms of the armistice was just 100,000 strong; the same size as that allowed Germany under the Treaty of Versailles.

The armistice between Germany and France did not encourage the British to discuss an end to the war, and indeed, by this time, British attitudes had hardened. It would be tempting to suggest that the British were being remarkably prescient, and this may well have been the case, with a general distrust of the Nazi regime. This distrust was to prove to be right, for in November 1942, in a complete breach of the armistice agreements, Germany and Italy moved to occupy the entire area of France. Vichy, which had held sway over its own part of France, but had been subjected to German overlordship in the occupied zone, now became a complete puppet of the Germans.

To drive the point home, Paul Reynaud, the former prime minister, was first interned by Pétain in September 1940, and then in November 1942, taken by the Germans who imprisoned him in the concentration camp at Oranienburg, before finally moving him to Itter Castle in Austria. The leading advocate of continuing the war, Reynaud had also welcomed Churchill's offer of an indissoluble union between the United Kingdom and France, although most Frenchmen had little enthusiasm for the idea.

As we will see later, the occupation of Vichy France was prompted by a volte-face by none other than Admiral Darlan just two days after the Allies invaded North Africa. Yet, Darlan's involvement with the Vichy regime was one reason for British distrust. Admiral Jean Francois Darlan had been instrumental in building up the French Navy between the two world wars, and was appointed admiral in 1939. He supported Pétain in pressing for an armistice with Germany, and later became first minister of marine, then foreign minister and finally vice-premier in Pétain's administration.

At the time of the armistice, Darlan went to great lengths to assure the United Kingdom that the French fleet, the Marine Nationale, would not fall into German hands. He ordered commanding officers to scuttle their ships should the Germans attempt to take them. Unfortunately, the British didn't trust Darlan, and seized or sank whatever ships they could, except at Alexandria, as we will see in the chapters that follow.

British distrust of Darlan was not without foundation. He was one of those Frenchmen who harboured strong Anglophobe tendencies and attitudes. He also wanted a more equal relationship between France and Germany. In May 1941, Darlan offered Hitler the use of French bases in Syria, and after a visit to Berchtesgaden he returned to France with plans for joint Franco-German operations in the Middle East. Pétain refused to agree to these proposals, which were undoubtedly of great appeal to the Germans who had been unable to encourage their First World War ally, Turkey, to join them.

Distrust was further justified in the British view by Laval's presence in the Vichy administration. He had changed from trying to counter German expansionism to embracing it.

THE FATE OF THE FRENCH FORCES

The fall of France in 1940 put the United Kingdom in a difficult position in every way. An ally had been lost, and in the Mediterranean and in North Africa, the forces belonging to France had been far stronger than those available to the United Kingdom. All at once, the British Empire was fighting Germany alone, without an ally.

The full extent of the German occupation was not known at first, and indeed from the British perspective, matters could have been very much worse than they were. The entire French Atlantic and Mediterranean coastline could have been in German hands, but it was bad enough. While the French naval base at Toulon was in Vichy territory, all of the Atlantic and Channel bases from Brest northwards were in German hands. In practical terms, this meant that the German U-boats no longer had to make the long and difficult voyage from bases in Germany, around the north of Scotland and into the Atlantic, but could more easily be based in French Biscay ports with a clear run into the Atlantic. At first, this advantage was also shared by the surface raiders until they were recalled home.

Britain had lost bases in France from which to strike at Germany, while the Germans had acquired bases in France close enough to the south coast of England for bombers to cover all of the United Kingdom. The hit and run raids on the east coast of Scotland that had occurred during the first winter of war could now be replaced by massed concentrations of aircraft over Britain's major cities as far west as Belfast. In the Mediterranean, almost the entire coastline from Morocco to the border between Libya and Egypt was in hostile hands, as was the Levant, or the Lebanon and Syria.

Many French soldiers and airmen had managed to escape to the United Kingdom following the fall of France to continue the war against Germany. The real problem was that of the French fleet, most of which was not at its home bases but instead at bases in its colonies, including Mers el-Kebir, near Oran, and Dakar, in North and West Africa respectively, at Alexandria in Egypt and at Portsmouth in the south of England. This fleet was a valuable asset.

In 1939, France was not a leading maritime power and it could be fairly said that, where the Royal Navy had fleets, the French had squadrons, as in the Atlantic and Mediterranean. Like the Royal Navy, however, the French had the problem of a wide colonial empire across which the armed forces were spread.

The French had belatedly realized that their sole aircraft carrier *Béarn*, 22,000 tons, would be inadequate for the coming conflict, and had ordered two new ships, the *Painlevé* and the *Joffre*, of unusual design, with the flight deck and upper hangar offset to port to balance the starboard superstructure island. Both ships were scrapped on the slipways after the invasion, no doubt with German agreement, so that the German Kriegsmarine denied itself one of the greatest prizes of the Second World War given the delays in completing its own first carrier.

Few of the ships in the French 1936 programme had been completed by the time of the German invasion, with the exception of three submarines.

This fleet was a prize worth having. Although it was not known at the time, the German Navy had not been expecting war to break out in 1939, and had expected to have until 1944 to build itself up to its wartime strength. A succession of naval plans had been approved, starting with Plan X, which was followed by Plan Y, which itself was superseded by Plan Z, which foresaw an initial four, later rising to six or eight aircraft carriers, and a dramatic expansion of the submarine fleet, which in 1939 consisted of just 59 U-boats. The pride of the fleet, the two modern battleships *Bismarck* and *Tirpitz* were still under construction in 1939. The two battlecruisers, *Scharnhorst* and *Gneisenau*, had been sent to sea with just 11-in guns, although it was planned that these would be replaced by higher calibre weapons later, while the so-called 'pocket battleships'or

Panzerschiffe, were not designed for fleet actions but as commerce-raiders.

The appeal of the French fleet to the Germans was clear.

ALLIES AT SEA

While the opening of the Second World War offered few early opportunities for the French Navy to see action, although a destroyer sank two U-boats in November 1939, it cooperated with the Royal Navy in running convoys, and many of the ships were present during the Norwegian campaign, while others helped in the Dunkirk evacuation. Overlooked in most accounts of the fall of France was the evacuation of British forces from Cherbourg and from Brittany, in which the French Navy played an important role, rescuing thousands from the latter peninsula.

The surface fleet remained virtually intact during the first winter of war, but the submarine fleet suffered badly, with twenty-four boats sunk.

The Battle of France, nevertheless, had seen the French Navy effectively sidelined. This was inevitable given the continental nature of the war. Unlike the largely conscript army, the navy consisted mainly of long-serving professionals. The Navy continued to operate and was unaffected by the collapse in morale amongst the French ground and air forces. It was undertaking acceptance trials of one new battleship, *Richelieu*, 35,000 tons, and as surrender grew closer, all seaworthy units of the fleet were moved from their French ports, while the other new battleship, *Jean Bart*, completing at St Nazaire, was moved, even though uncompleted, to Casablanca.

What amounted to almost a diaspora of the French Navy was taking place.

Two old battleships, together with eight destroyers and three submarines, accompanied by a number of smaller vessels, made their way to the major British naval bases at Portsmouth and Plymouth. The two battlecruisers, *Dunkerque* and *Strasbourg*, 26,500 tons, both fine modern ships, with two older battleships, six destroyers and a seaplane carrier, sailed to the naval base in Algeria at Mers-el-Kebir, near Oran. Six cruisers went to Algiers itself. Many of the remaining submarines went to Bizerte, also in Algeria. The French squadron in the Mediterranean, under Vice-Admiral Godfroy*, which had been working closely with the British Mediterranean Fleet under Admiral Sir Andrew Cunningham, remained at Alexandria. This force had a battle-ship, four cruisers and three destroyers, which was a somewhat unbalanced formation as a far larger destroyer force would have been expected. Many smaller warships moved to Toulon, while there were also smaller vessels in the Caribbean and in French Indo-China, as well as a number of ships at Dakar.

The aircraft carrier *Béarn*, 22,000 tons, unable to find a role at this stage, was being used as an aircraft transport, moving aircraft ordered by the Armée de l'Air from the United States to France. The Armée de l'Air, like the Royal Air Force, had been late in ordering aircraft from the United States because, until the German invasion of Poland, many American politicians had objected to compromising American neutrality by selling arms to belligerent powers.

The British found themselves with a dilemma. What were the chances that the French fleet would defect to Vichy, or even worse, be taken over by the Germans?

German naval weakness and the lack of time in which even to start fulfilling the targets set by Plan Z meant that the Kriegs-marine was short of ships. Despite some incompatibility between the two fleets, many French warship types were avail-able in far larger numbers than their German counterparts. Indeed, at this still early stage of the war, the French had more submarines than the Germans. Manpower was one reason for the Germans not taking over the French ships, as German industry still needed skilled men and the army and air force had absorbed large numbers of men. Because a far higher proportion of German women already worked before the war, in wartime

* Some accounts spell the name Godefroy, but this is the spelling used in Cunningham's autobiography.

that gave the Germans less scope in mobilizing additional women for war work than the British, who effectively mobilized every fit adult other than mothers with young children, with direction of labour.

Part of the problem was that the Germans would have needed to seize Vichy France to be sure of seizing all of the ships actually in French home waters, with many of the large surface units at Toulon. The Germans were, nevertheless, concerned that the ships in ports outside of France might have been handed over to the Royal Navy.

Yet another problem was simply what use the Germans could make of the French surface fleet. Even with it, they did not have enough large ships for a major set-piece battle with the Royal Navy, and in any case they would have needed to find a way to bring the former French ships and their own together, which would have been very difficult, the Channel Dash* notwithstanding.

While there would have been problems with different calibre guns, these would not have been insurmountable, even with German war production under considerable strain, and the emphasis on standardization mentioned earlier.

Yet, the main reasons for failing to make full use of the French

---

* The Channel Dash – On 12 February 1942, three German warships succeeded in a dash through the English Channel. The two battlecruisers *Scharnhorst* and *Gneisenau*, and the heavy cruiser *Prinz Eugen*, had been based at Brest, where they were repeatedly bombed by the RAF, and although the chances of sinking or seriously damaging any of the three ships with the bombs then available were remote, the ships did suffer minor damage. The British anticipated the ships being recalled to Germany, and had laid plans accordingly. To their surprise, Hitler, instead of having the ships take the route west of Ireland, out of the range of British aircraft, decided that the shorter and direct route through the English Channel would catch the British unawares and have the greatest chance of success.

A heavy fighter escort was provided by the Luftwaffe as well as a strong destroyer escort. Nevertheless, German success was mainly due to a series of equipment failures, poor inter-service collaboration between the Royal Air Force and the Royal Navy, bad weather which, for example, meant that the coastal artillery at Dover could not see the ships, and, worst of all, excessive secrecy that meant that too few people knew of the plans.

maritime booty were threefold. The first was that the Germans saw a blockade of the British Isles using submarines as a way to force the United Kingdom into starvation and capitulation, and did not see a strategic plan in which naval forces would play a major role. This was due to the continental, land-centred, mentality. The second was that Hitler quickly became dis-illusioned with the German surface fleet's performance, whose one great success of the war was the sinking of the British battle-cruiser *Hood*. When the Germans lost the *Bismarck*, the pride of the Kriegsmarine, shortly afterwards, it was the second in a growing list of major German warship losses, following on from the *Graf Spee*. There seems to have been a sense of pessimism amongst the German naval high command, as the *Panzerschiffe Lützow* had been renamed in November 1939 having originally been commissioned as *Deutschland* – someone had thought about the impact on the national morale of *Deutschland* being reported sunk! As it happened, she was not lost until near the end of the war, by which time she, with the rest of the major surface units, had been confined to port.

There was a third reason for not making use of the French fleet, again unknown to the British at the time, and that was the German fuel situation. It was simply not possible to maintain the panzer units and the Luftwaffe and also have a thirsty

---

The operation was famous not just for the British humiliation in not being able to prevent the ships' passage through the English Channel, but for the desperate attack by just six Fairey Swordfish torpedo-bomber biplanes of No.825 Naval Air Squadron. In the gloom of a winter afternoon, Lt Cdr Eugene Esmonde led his aircraft into the air, expecting an escort of sixty Supermarine Spitfire fighters, but just ten appeared over the target area. The slow Swordfish pressed home their attack, but were caught in heavy fire from the German fighters above and intense AA fire from the ships below. With his own aircraft badly damaged, Esmonde kept in the air long enough to launch its torpedo, after which he crashed into the sea. He had aimed at the *Prinz Eugen*, but the heavy cruiser managed to take evasive action. All six Swordfish were shot down, and out of the eighteen naval airmen aboard, just five survived. Esmonde was not one of them and he was awarded one of only two Victoria Crosses gazetted to members of the Fleet Air Arm during the Second World War.

surface fleet. The situation was so bad that many minor warships, including minesweepers, were converted to coal-firing, as this was the one natural resource that Germany had in abundance. The manpower needs of burning coal in warships and the reduced range, as well as the time taken to re-coal, was a major drawback and indicative of the extent of the fuel crisis.

Yet, while for whatever reason, the Germans did not take advantage of the French fleet, these reservations were unknown to the British, who had every reason to fear the worst. Darlan's anti-British attitudes were well known in British naval circles while there had been considerable reluctance to share the details of the armistice with the British. It was also the case that in August 1940, Reichsmarschal Hermann Goering, the second highest member of the Nazi regime, demanded the complete exploitation of the occupied territories. This was to be taken to its most extreme in the east, where starvation was the fate of many and the German occupying forces were supposed to live off the land.

While the British resented an ally negotiating a separate armistice with the Germans, the French resented being abandoned, as they saw it, by the British. The scene was set for a confrontation. The British wanted the French warships out of harm's way, away from the Germans and the Italians, while the French wanted them to stay in their colonial bases. The Germans wanted the ships returned to France, which made their promise not to use the ships all the more doubtful.

THE GERMANS TAKE OVER

The collapse of a strong defence brings with it chaos. Two French admirals, Abrial and Le Bigot, were taken prisoner after Abrial had attempted to repeat his defence of Dunkirk at Cherbourg.

At Brest, France's main naval port on the Atlantic, Admiral de Laborde was attempting to load a thousand tons of gold into his auxiliary cruisers to be taken to Dakar, when the port's defences collapsed. As it happened, German troops were not close, leaving him ten hours in which to get 159 ships, of which 83 were warships, out of the port. In the end, he succeeded in getting 74 warships away and destroyed the remaining nine. Of the 76 merchant vessels, one was scuttled and another sunk by German bombs, but the remainder escaped.

At St Nazaire, the uncompleted 35,000-ton battleship *Jean Bart* sat amidst yet another evacuation, with 40,000 British and 2,500 Polish troops leaving this port. The *Jean Bart* had been launched, but ships are far from ready at the time they first enter the water, as work on the superstructure, armament and much of the interior fitting out and the installation of equipment remains. The battleship only had two of her four screws, or propellers, fitted. In the case of the *Jean Bart*, the ship was sitting in an open basin with a massive dyke of earth separating her from the harbour itself. She barely looked like a ship, with much of her deck covered in scaffolding, which also surrounded her superstructure.

Before the ship could be moved, the dyke had to be opened up, and a channel dredged through that would be wide enough not just for the battleship to squeeze through, but to enable tugs to handle the ship. At the time, those working on the ship had not planned for her to be ready until October, allowing plenty of time to complete their work, open the dyke and dredge the channel.

As the situation began to look increasingly grim, the battleship's commanding officer, Capitaine de Vaisseau Pierre Ronarc'h, gave orders that the dyke was to be breached and then dredged on 25 May. This may seem to have been an excess of pessimism on his part, but there was clear logic on his side. Not only was the Dunkirk evacuation about to start, but he knew that the work would take some time and if he was to have any chance to get his ship to sea, it would need the benefit of the high tides between 18 and 22 June, or have to wait another lunar month for the next spring tides. The night of 18 June was selected, but within the time available, dredging could only be to

a depth of 26 ½ ft, 8 metres. This meant that the ship would have
to be almost completely de-provisioned and have her fuel
pumped out, to lighten her – no water, no provisions, and only
a minimal quantity of fuel oil – but fortunately she had only one
of her heavy twin 15-in turrets in place. If this limitation wasn't
difficult enough, the ship had a beam of more than 114 ft, 35
metres, and the dredged channel would be just 164 ft, 50 metres,
wide. In fact, the target date was missed, with dredging not
completed until 02.00 on 19 June. It takes around eight hours for
a large ship to raise steam from cold, and since this would be the
first time that any of her boilers had been fired, this work had
started several days early, on 11 June. Even so, until water was
in the basin, the turbines had not been turned.

Since weight had to be kept to a minimum, the ship was
without fire control systems and none of the weapons fitted so
far was in a condition to be used, as aerial attack was a real
possibility. As the time to leave drew closer, the dockyard was
scoured for weapons, and in the end a few anti-aircraft machine-
guns, including two 90mm twin mounts and a few 37mm guns,
were hurriedly swung aboard and bolted down.

Time was short, as the Germans had already reached Rennes
and it was likely that they would break through to St Nazaire the
next day. It was a case of leave or have the ship blown up to
prevent her falling into German hands.

There was no time to delay any further, it was time for the
battleship to leave, and within ninety minutes of the channel
through the dyke being completed, she started to move, as
Auphan and Mordal recounted:

At 0330, the time of high tide, the operation began. There
was no power on the main engines, or on the rudder, or the
windlass, or the aft winches. Everything had to be done by
hand – with capstan bars aboard and pushing tugs
outboard. The ship managed to get clear of the basin
without too much difficulty, but in the darkness she missed
a buoy in the too narrow channel and ran aground. It took
six tugs to pull her off again. Then at 0440, just as the *Jean*

Bart was clearing the entrance to the Loire, the Luftwaffe appeared. The ship sustained but one hit, and that caused only minor damage. Then after the German attack was over, the French fighter planes, which had been scheduled to give air cover, belatedly arrived – and were warmly greeted by the *Jean Bart*'s gunners. Luckily only one Morane fighter was hit, and no lives were lost.

Then, little by little everything straightened out. Luck was with the ship. The main engines began to turn over; there was steam for the auxiliaries, and electric power for the steering; the oil tankers were on time at the refuelling rendezvous; and two German submarines, which had been lying in wait, never made contact.

The *Jean Bart* was saved. Even though she had no steering compass, she could follow the destroyer *Hardi* on which Admiral de la Borde had hoisted his flag. At 1700 on June 22, the *Jean Bart* steamed into Casablanca harbour, in French Morocco, having made the whole trip at an average speed of 21 knots.[2]

Captain Pierre Ronarc'h had saved his ship from the Germans, and from the British. Had she not escaped from St Nazaire, the British destroyer *Vanquisher* had been waiting outside with orders to enter the port and sink the battleship to save her from falling to the hands of the Germans. The British must have known about the channel being dredged, otherwise the chance of the destroyer being able to hit the ship through the earth dykes would have been absolutely nil, and even with her in the water with the dyke breached, it would have been difficult for a torpedo attack to overcome her anti-torpedo armour belt and cause serious damage. To be successful, the torpedoes would have had to hit the ship below the armour belt, or ahead or aft of it.

Meanwhile, under article 14 of the armistice, all French radios were sealed and the armed forces were reduced to sending messages by courier. The last broadcast by Darlan to the French fleet was that, if their ships were in danger of being seized by the

Germans or the Italians, they were either to scuttle their ships or sail them to the United States. While bribery had been attempted to encourage the masters of merchant vessels to sail to a British port, many did not do so for lack of fuel or because of resistance by their crews, who were simply anxious to return to their families.

Despite Darlan, a number of French naval vessels had arrived in British ports, usually on operations, such as assistance with the evacuation of troops, rather than as a concerted attempt to continue the fighting.

Portsmouth had the veteran First World War battleship *Courbet*, 22,200, later joined by her sister ship, the *Paris*, as well as a destroyer and three submarines, three torpedo boats, a patrol vessel and two submarine chasers. Plymouth had a destroyer, two submarine chasers and six tugs and trawlers. French merchant vessels in British ports were delayed, but a few were eventually allowed to depart for ports in the French colonies. The French authorities had sent the light cruiser, *Emile Bertin*, 5,900 tons, to Halifax, Nova Scotia, with $300 million in gold, to be transferred from the Bank of France to the Bank of Ottawa, but the gold was never unloaded and she left for Martinique, in the French West Indies, with the cruiser *Devonshire* shadowing her.

After the British heard that Admiral Darlan had ordered the commanding officers of the warships in British ports, including Admiral Odend'hal at Portsmouth, to take their ships to Dakar, initially the Admiralty decided not to oppose this move. The Admiralty had ordered the port admirals at Portsmouth and Plymouth to 'grant all facilities to French warships for their departure to North Africa', but the orders were almost immediately countermanded. It was then decided to contact Darlan to seek control of the ships.

From the time of their arrival at Portsmouth and Plymouth, the French warships had been stuck in port, with their crews denied shore leave by the British, and essential supplies such as food grudgingly given.

'We behaved very stupidly,' recalled Sub-Lieutenantt Peter

The French destroyer *Bourrasque* sinking off Dunkirk – none of those aboard survived. (*IWM No HU228*)

Not everyone could get away at Dunkirk, and those left behind included many who had held on to defensive positions to allow others to be evacuated. Here are British and French prisoners of war. (*IWM No MH2396*)

Dunkirk was not the only evacuation point. Here members of the British Expeditionary Force prepare to leave St Nazaire. (*IWM No HU47951*)

A substantial part of the French Mediterranean Squadron was at Alexandria when news of the French surrender came. The destroyer in the foreground is the *Forbin* and she is alongside the cruiser *Tourville*, while in the background the destroyer *Le Fortune* is alongside the cruiser *Duquesne*. (IWM No A9937)

Efforts were made to negotiate a transfer of the French fleet, but at Merse-el-Kebir, force had to be used. This is Captain Holland returning to HMS *Ark Royal* in a Fairey Swordfish floatplane. Note the arrester wires have been removed. (*via S.H. Wragg*)

The Swordfish touches down on *Ark Royal*'s notoriously flimsy flight deck (*S.H.Wragg*)

Incredibly, the landing was made without damage to aircraft or ship – here a handling party races out with wheels. (*S.H.Wragg*)

One of the more dramatic seizures of French warships by the British was that of the *corsair* submarine *Surcouf* at Portsmouth, where British naval officers were killed. Here a Briish naval commander walks ashore after showing army officers over the submarine – the twin 8-in guns can be seen. (*IWM No A410*)

General Charles de Gaulle leaves a Free French sloop at Portsmouth, 1940. Behind him is a Royal Navy captain standing beside a French Lieutenant de Vaisseau. (*IWM No A2170*)

The British occupation of Madagascar in 1942 prevented the Axis powers using the island, which had become strategically important as it sat astride the convoy route from Cape Town to the Suez Canal, essential for supplies to British forces in Egypt. This shows the merchantman *Warenfels* in the dry dock at Diego Suarez. (*IWM No K2574*)

Although initially only one or two positions on Madagascar were to be occupied, under South African pressure the whole of the island was eventually taken. Here British troops storm ashore at Tamative. (*IWM No K3517*)

A French Foreign Legion band playing in Syria – where members of this elite force were fighting on both the Vichy and Free French sides. (*IWM No E5139*)

The Second World War saw aircraft used as VIP transports for the first time – here General Claude Auchinleck arrives in Syria to inspect Indian troops. The aircraft is a de Havilland Dominie, the RAF version of the Dragon Rapide. (*IWM No E5199*)

Despite British fears, when the Germans tried to seize the French warships at Toulon, they were scuttled and explosive charges were set off to ensure that even if refloated, they would require considerable attention before returning to service. This is the condition of the battlecruiser *Strasbourg* afterwards, with a scuttled cruiser lying alongside. (IWM No A25666)

But happier days for the battleship *Richelieu*, as she returns to Mers-el-Kebir after refitting in New York. (IWM No A20299)

Simpson-Jones, RNVR, who was a high angle gunnery control officer who spoke fluent French. 'We let them sit in port without leave or enough decent food.'[3]

SEIZURE!

On 30 June, the Admiralty received a copy of a message telegraphed from the French Admiralty to Admiral Odend'hal at Portsmouth, advising him that the Italians had permitted the stationing of the French fleet at Toulon and in North Africa, with half crews aboard. The telegram continued to say that the Vichy authorities were optimistic about obtaining a similar agreement from the Germans, and ordered Odend'hal to insist on the British government releasing both merchant and naval vessels in British ports. In fact, while the Germans did agree, there was no time to let Odend'hal know. What did happen was that the following day, both the Germans and the British demanded that they should have control over the French warships, with the Germans insisting that all French warships should be returned to France, or the armistice conditions would be changed.

What then followed was that the British implemented plans to seize all French ships in British ports, with those anchored outside being called into port on a number of false, but plausible, pretexts.

At Portsmouth and Plymouth, Operation Catapult, the seizure of French warships, was implemented during the early hours of 3 July. British sailors and marines swarmed aboard the French ships, with armed men stationed at every hatch and in every passage, while British naval officers, armed with pistols, confronted the French commanding officers, demanding that the ships be handed over to the Royal Navy, while their crews would be detained. Aboard the large corsair submarine *Surcouf*, 2,900 tons surfaced, with her twin 8-in guns and seaplane hangar, the commanding officer insisted on first changing from his pyjamas and into uniform before meeting the British naval officers, Lieutenant-Commanders Griffiths and Sprague. It was explained to Capitaine de Frégate Paul Martin that he and his fellow officers were under arrest, and that they, with their crews, would shortly be taken ashore, after which they could either be repatriated to French territory, meaning North Africa, or could remain in the UK to continue to fight against the Germans. Reasonably enough, Martin asked if he could visit the battleship *Paris* to discuss the matter with his admiral, and permission was given him, along with the assurance that none of the submarine's crew would be taken away until he returned.

As Martin was leaving, a pistol shot was heard, and when Sprague ran into the submarine's wardroom, pistol in hand, he was shot in the head by Bouillaut, the submarine's gunnery officer. Griffiths shot Bouillaut in the shoulder, before tripping over Sprague's body, and as he fell, he in turn was shot in the chest by the *Surcouf*'s surgeon, who then turned his gun on a marine sergeant, who was lunging at him with his rifle bayonet, but not before he first bayoneted another French officer.

The turmoil aboard the *Surcouf* was the only such event in the whole exercise, and possibly was caused by a misunderstanding in an emotionally charged atmosphere. Nevertheless, an attempt was made to scuttle the destroyer *Mistral*, 1,300 tons, at Plymouth. As the officers were being assembled in the ward-room, sea valves were opened and the ship started to flood. The British officer leading the boarding party simply threatened to leave the ship's crew, who had been locked in their messes, to go down with the ship, and the sea valves were closed.

Around 8,000 French seamen were assembled ashore and moved to an internment camp at Aintree, near Liverpool, where they were to wait until they could be taken aboard British ships to Casablanca. When the French admirals requested that they be allowed to return to their ships with their crews as the camp was insanitary, permission was refused for fear of further scuttling attempts. According to some accounts, the merchant seamen were not always herded into the camps, and some seem to have remained aboard their ships.

The French naval personnel in the internment camp were

offered the chance of joining the British in the war against Germany, but, disillusioned with their former ally, most of them wanted to be repatriated. This started during July. Rather than using a British ship or taking them to North Africa, 1,100 men were loaded aboard the French liner *Meknes* at Southampton and she departed for Vichy France. After nightfall, the ship steamed with all lights showing, hoping to indicate that she was a neutral vessel, but at 22.00 she was hailed by a German E-boat, which, when she refused to reply, machine-gunned her before sinking her with a torpedo. Many Frenchmen blamed the British for the loss of 400 lives when she went down. As a result, future repatriations took place using clearly marked hospital ships, whose movements were announced in advance. By the end of 1940, around 30,000 French seamen, soldiers and civilians returned to France in this way.

'About 90 per cent of the French seamen opted to return to France,' commented Peter Simpson-Jones. 'There was much ill-feeling. Later, I became one of the first British naval liaison officers aboard a French warship, *Le Triomphant*, and it was very tricky at first as I went aboard just three weeks after the problems at Oran.'[4]

Le Triomphant, which Simpson-Jones liked, was one of the Fantasque-class *contre-torpilleur* 'super destroyers', a ship of 2,600 tons and capable of more than 40 knots.

This was, one feels, an almost impossible situation. The British could not have allowed the ships to leave for fear that they might fall into German or Italian hands, and the French would not surrender them without orders from Vichy France for fear of being regarded as traitors. Just how long the ships could have been contained at Portsmouth and Plymouth without a decision being taken one way or the other by either the French or the British is something we can never expect to know. In the fearful and uncertain atmosphere of summer 1940, when Germany seemed unstoppable, and the British were on their own, possibly no other decision could have been reached. For the French, however, this was drastic action by a former ally and one with whom they had cooperated well during the Norwegian campaign and then assisted in the evacuation from France. For the British, Vichy France was in danger of becoming a German ally rather than a neutral.

Notes
1 and 2 *The French Navy in World War II*, Auphin, Amiral and Mordal, Jacques , US Naval Institute.
3 and 4 Imperial War Museum Accession No 15320

CHAPTER NINE

Vichy France

As France drew close to surrender, the government was in Bordeaux, but this did not become the new capital. Vichy France took its name from the spa town of the same name, to which Marshal Pétain's administration moved temporarily following the armistice agreements. Pétain did not regard the town as a permanent capital. His plan was to follow the armistice with Germany, which he regarded as being the one that mattered, with peace negotiations followed by a return of government to Paris, in the occupied zone of France. In fact, such peace negotiations never took place since the armistice was non-negotiable, although Pétain was allowed to rule as the dictator of Vichy.

The desire amongst those in the Vichy regime to cooperate with the Germans seemed to know no bounds. Not only did the Vichy regime expedite the transfer of Belgium's gold reserves to Germany, the Germans were also offered the French-owned shares in Yugoslavia's Bohr copper mines. Behind all of this was the French deputy-premier, Pierre Laval, and as a result of his efforts he gained an audience with Hitler on 22 October 1940, which proved to be the preliminary to the disappointing meeting that followed between Pétain and Hitler.

COLLABORATION

Encouraged by his vice-premier, Pierre Laval, Pétain had met Hitler in October 1940, and offered the Fuhrer collaboration. In effect, collaboration did take place, but on Germany's terms. Hitler took it as something that he expected, nothing less than what was due to the victor from a defeated enemy, and Pétain, it seems unwittingly, had no option. In fact, Hitler was not concerned about creating a Fascist satellite in France, and had no strategic vision for a united Europe. The one aim of official German policy was to establish itself as the dominant power in Europe and acquire the resources for the successful prosecution of the war. The manpower, natural resources and industry of the occupied territories were therefore harnessed to this end. The one advantage of Vichy rule was that its citizens had the possibility of volunteering to work in the Reich, whereas in the eastern occupied territories, forced labour was used.

At the outset, friction between Pétain and Laval was a feature of Vichy rule, with the vice-premier despising his superior and eventually being dismissed in October 1940. It seems that Pétain entertained naïve and completely unrealistic hopes of a rapprochement with Germany, and was blind to the predicament of France. Reality probably did not dawn on the man until he met Reichsmarschal Hermann Goering in late 1941. When Pétain mentioned that his view of collaboration was that it involved dealings between equals, Goering lost his temper and demanded to know whether Germany or France had been the victor!

Meanwhile, Pétain had sacked Laval, but his successor, Pierre Flandin, did not meet with German approval, and neither did the next vice-premier, Admiral Darlan, so in April 1942, Pétain was forced to reinstate Laval. Pierre Laval soon settled back into his post, and despite the snubs provided by the Germans, by June he was broadcasting to call upon Frenchmen to volunteer to work in German industry. He concluded his broadcast with a fervent wish for a German victory in the war to prevent Communism establishing itself throughout Europe.

Despite his strong pro-German stance, Laval could not prevent the Germans from occupying Vichy France in November 1942. Despite being given considerable authority by Pétain, including the right to issue decrees, Laval could not extract concessions from the Germans, even when he offered to have France declare war on the Allies, and raise a strong French force to re-conquer North Africa. Not only had the Germans lost interest in France and the French, other than as a source of manpower and raw materials, the attitude was close to one of contempt which was if anything only worsened by the efforts of Laval to ingratiate himself with the Nazi regime. Overall, the authorities in each country had come to distrust the other.

In late 1943, with the whole of France occupied by the Germans, Pétain tried to resurrect the French National Assembly and make that body his successor, to German anger. Pétain's reaction was to sulk and refuse to cooperate with the Germans, but he was forced to yield under intense German pressure, including warnings of dire consequences for both France and Pétain from Hitler himself. The Germans then effectively took over the Vichy administration, dictating its policies and its membership, forcing Pétain to accept Marcel Deat as a member, after which Pétain refused to attend any further meetings, although he did not actually resign until August 1944. Eventually Pétain moved first to Germany and then to Switzerland, where he was when the war ended, later returning to France of his own accord to face a war crimes tribunal, which found him guilty and sentenced him to death, although this was commuted and he spent the rest of his life on the Ile d' Yeu.

Deat had been a French socialist and after the French surrender, had edited a pacifist newspaper, L'Oeuvre, in Paris, although he later adopted Nazi ideology, becoming a staunch supporter of Pétain's prime minister, Laval. He was appointed minister for labour, which effectively meant running the German scheme of conscripting French workers for their factories in Germany. He was detested by Pétain and had to work from Paris rather than Vichy.

Meanwhile, from summer 1940 through to November 1942, the surviving units of the French Navy had been used to protect Vichy convoys between France and her North African colonies, an ever present reminder to the British that here was a great naval asset that could be used against them. While the United States was still neutral, Darlan used the US embassy in Paris to warn the British not to interfere with French convoys, while also assuring the United States that the French colonies and the French navy would not be offered to the Germans. Indeed, once the United States started to become more overt in its support of the United Kingdom, Darlan secretly offered the United States Navy free passage through the waters of France's Caribbean terroritories.

Darlan was in French North Africa, in Algiers, when the Allies invaded on 8 November 1942. Initially, he assumed command of Vichy forces and resisted the British and American invasion forces, but after negotiations with Vichy and with the Americans, he surrendered his forces on 10 November, and agreed to work for the Allies, becoming high commissioner for French North Africa. Undoubtedly his earlier courting of the United States had not been in vain, and indeed many senior US officers as well as the government favoured Darlan over de Gaulle. Nevertheless, Darlan's appointment was short-lived, as he was assassinated on 24 December by a young Frenchman.

THE VICHY REGIME

While Pétain chose to believe that he was in control of France, his room for manoeuvre was limited. True, he had more power in the so-called *zone libre* than in the *zone occupée*, but the conditions of the armistice limited his powers even in the former, while in the occupied area Vichy simply provided an administrative function for the German authorities.

In many ways, Vichy was something of a throwback. Possibly because it was denied real influence, it chose to turn its back on the world and sought to promote the values and traditions of rural France rather than the delights of the cities. Pétain was a dictator and the Vichy regime was authoritarian. It took as its creed the puritanical message, *Travail, Famille, Patrie*, or 'work, family and fatherland'. These policies emphasized the return to the rural ideal and the sanctity of the family, with the place of women being firmly in the home. Economic policies were in tune with national socialism in that corporatism, the bringing together of government and industry, was encouraged, while anti-Semitic policies were adopted which were to see the internment of the Jewish population and their despatch to the death camps. As in Nazi Germany, youth organisations were encouraged and the idea of sport and the healthy outdoor life promoted. Not all of this went down well with the Germans, who were sensitive to the dangers of any movement that appealed to patriotic sentiment, and so many Vichy initiatives were banned from the occupied zone.

Direction of labour soon followed, but first enticement was used, with workers being encouraged to seek jobs in German war industry for their sake, that of their families and that of their country. While vice-premier, Laval established a scheme under which one French prisoner-of-war held in Germany would be returned home for every three Frenchmen who volunteered to work in Germany. A French legion was formed for the veterans of both world wars, the *Legion Française des Combattants*, and youth work camps, the *Chantiers de la Jeunesse*. At first, Vichy was not a puppet regime, but a reflection of anti-democratic elements in France that had decided that democracy had failed the country, and consisted of disillusioned politicians, senior members of the armed forces and financiers and industrialists who believed that the corporatist state could rebuild the country.

Many observers have stated that the public admiration for Pétain, and their initial willingness to accept his leadership in the wake of defeat, was mistaken by Pétain and those around for approval of Vichy policies. If such approval existed, it didn't outlast the winter of 1940–1941. The Vichy regime moved quickly to disband town councils and replace the mayors with

their own nominees. Both trade unions and employers' fed-
erations were banned, as was Freemasonry. Initially, Jews
became second-class citizens, while those who had fled to France
to escape persecution elsewhere were moved to internment
camps originally established for refugees from the Spanish Civil
War. A commissioner was appointed to supervise the Jewish
population and their businesses acquired or liquidated, before
the appointment in May 1942 of Louis Darquier de Pellepoix, a
racist and supporter of deportation. The Popular Front that had
governed France since 1936 was purged.

In August 1942, the Jewish immigrants in the camps were
deported to Germany.

Part of the problem for Vichy was that France was effectively
isolated, surrounded by Germany and her allies, amongst which
could be counted non-combatant but Fascist Spain, with the
exception of strictly neutral Switzerland. Vichy politicians
believed that the country stood alone having been abandoned by
the United Kingdom, which in its turn would be unable to stand
up to German attack. After all, the Third Reich had won every
battle and conquered every opponent. The optimists believed
that France had everything to gain by throwing in its lot with
Germany, which would head a new European power bloc, but
as mentioned earlier, Hitler had no such vision other than
Deutschland über Alles. Pétain and others had a vision that
entailed cooperation and sharing, but Hitler had no intention of
sharing and cooperation was the only option open to the
defeated French.

When General Charles de Gaulle appealed for support on 18
June, he was treated as a deserter and sentenced to death in his
absence, making him the leading *franc-tireur*.

Any illusion that France and Germany were moving closer
together was later finally dispelled when German and Italian
forces occupied the *zone libre* on 11 November 1942. The small
army of 100,000 men allowed under the terms of the armistice
was disbanded and finally the Germans seemed that they would
have the remnants of the French Navy, a still substantial fleet at
Toulon, under their control. In fact, as it turned out, Darlan's

assurances to the Allies were to be kept, and as we will see later, the French fleet was scuttled, disabled or, in the case of a few ships, escaped. The official reason for the German occupation of the remainder of France was the Allied invasion of North Africa, but even more important than this was the realisation that if such a senior member of the Vichy regime as Darlan could, within two days, transfer his allegiance to the Allies, the entire regime could not be trusted.

Although Vichy lost its army after the occupation, a new force was formed in January 1943, the Milice. Effectively, the Milice was an internal security force and acted in conjunction with the Gestapo throughout France, and its priority was the elimination of resistance against the regime. Dismay at the turn of events had led many, including Vichy-appointed mayors and officials, to adopt a policy of non-cooperation and passive resistance. The Anglo-American landings in North Africa had highlighted the fact that, not only was the war far from over, German victory was no longer assured and was beginning to look distinctly uncertain. Units of the Milice fought against resistance groups as the latter grew stronger and more daring.

The liberation of France following the Allied landings in Normandy, and then in the South of France, saw members of the Vichy administration escape to Germany, but while some went into exile, many more returned to France to face trial.

The inevitable question arises, just how big a risk was it that the French Navy might come fully under German control? Despite the assurances given by Darlan to the British in 1940, the risk must have been considerable. Darlan himself courted Hitler with the offer of French bases and the French fleet, while Laval broadcast across France calling for a Germany victory to prevent the spread of Bolshevism throughout Europe. It might be possible to excuse Pétain for his sense of grandeur and his inability to accept a changed order, but Laval and Darlan actively cultivated the German connection, and it does seem that much more was due to German reluctance to enter a true partnership than to Vichy scruples.

THE END OF VICHY

The Allied invasion of France in June 1944 did not mark the end of the Vichy regime. Indeed, for a period it seemed as if the Allies would be stuck with a bridgehead in Normandy and not much else, as it took some time to fight their way out of the landing zone. In any event, the main thrust of the Allied advance was first to Paris, then into Belgium and then towards Germany. Even the northern areas of the Netherlands were by-passed in the desire to invade Germany, and the south of France had to await the landings, Operation Dragoon, in August. In the south, the Germans had had neither the time, the manpower or the resources to build a Mediterranean version of the famous Atlantic Wall, which in itself had failed to keep the Allies out. Indeed, the landings went so well compared to those in the Italian campaign, that Allied aircraft were soon operating from bases in the South of France. Germany no longer had the army or sufficient aircraft in its air force to fight in Italy, northern France and Belgium, in Eastern Europe and then in the South of France as well.

Strangely, the Germans didn't abandon the Vichy government as the Allies began to press in around them. Vichy itself was facing not just the Allies but also an increasingly powerful and confident resistance movement, and the regime consisted of firm collaborationists and those who wanted to perpetuate their rule in France.

In August 1944, the Vichy government was ordered by the Germans to move to Belfort, on the border between France and Germany. Later, it was moved to Sigmaringen in southern Germany, with the irony of Vichy itself now becoming a government in exile. By this time, there was little for the members of the regime to actually do, except wait for the end.

Oddly, the Germans, despite having precious little fuel, or indeed anything else, left, flew Laval to Barcelona in Spain in May 1945. No doubt he saw the Franco regime as one that would be benevolent to a supporter of Fascism, but on arrival he was told in no uncertain terms that Spain didn't want war criminals.

He is reputed to have claimed that he was a 'peace criminal'. In July, Laval flew to Austria, an unwise move if he wanted to evade capture as the country was occupied by the Allies, and inevitably he was arrested and handed over to the French authorities. He was tried, found guilty and sentenced to death. He tried to escape the firing squad by swallowing cyanide just before he was executed, but he was still alive when the firing squad took aim.

Pétain fared rather better. Unlike Laval, he was popular with many in France and was even warmly received on his last visit to Paris in April 1944. On 19 August 1944, when asked to move to Belfort, he resigned, but like Laval, he too ended up in Sigmaringen in southern Germany, and in April 1945 managed to persuade the Germans to let him move to Switzerland. It is claimed that de Gaulle even secretly requested the Swiss government not to accede to any extradition requests that France might make, but it mattered not, as Pétain, supremely confident of the justice of his case and the rightness of his actions to the end, chose to return to France of his own accord. In July 1945, he was put on trial. He mounted a vigorous defence, maintaining that he had resisted German demands, 'Every day, with a knife at my throat . . .' He too was condemned to death, but the sentence was commuted and he spent the final years of his life as a prisoner on the Ile d'Yeu, where he died in 1951 at the age of ninety-five years.

Marcel Deat also found his way to Sigmaringen, for after all, he had no choice. When the war ended, he sought sanctuary in an Italian monastery, and managed to remain there until his death in 1955 at the age of sixty-one years.

CHAPTER TEN

Stand Off at Alexandria

For the British, the big fear was that in the fall of France, they had not simply lost an ally, there was the danger that French forces might change sides, given the long history of enmity between the two nations or, more probably, the Germans would be able to seize the French fleet. This was a prize worth having. In 1940, not only was it the fourth largest in the world, it bridged the gap between the projected strength of the German Kriegsmarine in 1944 and its 1940 strength. In fact, the 1944 strength of the Kriegsmarine's Plan Z was an increasingly remote target as the Germans were soon forced to cancel all projects other than the U-boats and those surface vessels such as the two battleships, *Bismarck* and *Tirpitz*, that were nearing completion. Expansion of the Marine Nationale had been helped by a naval race between France and Italy between the wars, with both countries seeing themselves as the rightful masters of the Mediterranean. France, after all, had her colonial possessions in North Africa to consider.

Unknown to the British at the time, the Germans had other problems, most notably that of fuel and of maintaining ammunition production at a satisfactory level. The fuel crisis was such that maintaining a large surface fleet would have been impossible, forcing Hitler to decide whether he wanted a navy or an air force – he couldn't have both. In desperation, many minor surface vessels, such as minesweepers, were converted to coal burning. Since dropping aerial mines had been a major activity for the Royal Air Force, helped on occasions by the Fleet Air Arm, minesweepers were one of the few types of surface vessel that had to continue operations. Coal firing was a measure of last resort, as re-coaling needed to take place more frequently than refuelling with oil, and it took much longer and was a messy and unpopular labour-intensive activity. Coal may seem to have been a safer fuel than oil, but large quantities of coal or coal dust could produce latent heat and catch fire.

This was the crux of the problem. The British were scared that the French fleet would be taken and used against them by the Germans, but the Germans probably couldn't have made use of them.

The major fleet units of the Marine Nationale were scattered around the Mediterranean, much to the dismay of both the British and the Germans. The British wanted them out of harm's way, fearing either a German or, more likely, an Italian take-over of the fleet, and a French suggestion, soon withdrawn, of Madagascar had sounded attractive, at least at the time. Later, Madagascar itself would be seen as a dangerous spot for naval forces that could be used against the Allies, once British forces in Egypt had to be supplied not across the Mediterranean, but through the Suez Canal after convoys had made the long detour via the Cape of Good Hope. The Germans wanted them safely in a French port, ostensibly so that the British could not seize the ships, but the fear was that they had them in mind for their own operations. After all, the German navy had come a poor third in the pre-war reconstruction and expansion of Germany's armed forces. In addition, its reconstruction during the 1930s had tended to be reactive rather than innovative, with the battlecruisers *Scharnhorst* and *Gneisenau* built to rival the French *Strasbourg* and *Dunkerque*.

ALEXANDRIA

The British Mediterranean Fleet had moved to Alexandria before Italy entered the Second World War, and in anticipation that Italy would ally herself with Germany. In peacetime, Malta was the Royal Navy's main base in the Mediterranean, and indeed had been the main base during the First World War when Italy had been an ally. With Malta just some eighty miles from Sicily, the Royal Air Force and the British Army had both declared the islands to be impossible to defend in any war in which Italy was an opponent, but the Admiralty insisted that the islands could be defended and would provide a forward base for offensive operations, mainly by submarines and light forces. The Admiralty won the argument, but for safety's sake moved most of its ships to Alexandria, where they were joined by several units of the French Mediterranean Squadron, itself a powerful force.

The decision to move the British Mediterranean Fleet to Alexandria was not taken lightly. Gibraltar and Malta offered the Royal Navy the full depth of repair facilities with dry docks and a skilled workforce experienced in dealing with warships and working under the overall direction of naval engineers. Alexandria had little of this, although a floating dock was moved from the UK to provide some form of repair facility, even if unsuitable for anything heavier than a cruiser, and major work still had to be done elsewhere. Incidentally, it is worth noting that the floating dock at Malta, which would have been the obvious one to move to Alexandria, was rejected as unsuitable because of its poor condition.

Moving to Alexandria was not simply a defensive measure for the fleet itself, it was also to allow the fleet to continue to maintain one of the United Kingdom's rights enshrined within Anglo-Egyptian Treaty of August 1936, the right to defend the Suez Canal. The canal was the short cut to Britain's colonies east of Suez, including India, Ceylon (now Sri Lanka), Burma, Malaya and Singapore, as well as the link with the dominions of Australia and New Zealand.

In fact, the British were so well established in Egypt that the country was run almost as a colony and had indeed been a British protectorate between 1914 and 1922. During the Second World War, the Royal Egyptian Navy was headed by a British admiral.

The 1936 treaty had also given the British very extensive rights in the event of war to make full use of Egyptian 'ports, aerodromes and means of communication', and established that the monarch, King Farouk, would give 'all the facilities and assistance in his power.'

While the French did not share the rights held by the British in Egypt itself, they were shareholders in the Suez Canal, and basing ships at Alexandria made sense as long as the UK and France were fighting on the same side.

Even so, the Italians had also a strong hold on the country. Both the young king, (Farouk was just twenty when Italy entered the war) and his prime minister were basically pro-Axis in their sympathies. During the 1930s, they had been allowed to maintain this position and with the League of Nations being impotent in the face of Italian aggression in Abyssinia, nothing had been done to discourage it. Indeed, the British and French had portrayed nothing but weakness. This was bad enough, but the prime minister, Ali Mahir, headed a coalition government which included many anti-British elements.

In Egypt, as in other parts of the Middle East, the British position was threatened by increasingly strident Arab nationalism, something which the Germans exploited through supporting an uprising in Mesopotamia, present day Iraq. There was also some concern early in the war that Turkey, which had been a German ally during the First World War, might also enter the war on the Axis side.

On the outbreak of war in September 1939, Mahir became military governor of Egypt, imposing martial law, censorship and strict economic measures. Reluctantly, the Egyptian authorities ensured that German nationals were arrested and diplomatic relations with Germany were cut off, but the country did not declare war on Germany. Later, when Italy entered the war in June 1940, diplomatic relations were severed, but the country did not declare war on Italy and Mahir once again acted against Italian residents within Egypt with considerable reluctance. The Egyptian army was told that its frontier troops were not to fire on Italian troops in the desert. It was not until the British forced Farouk to dismiss Mahir that the Italian legation finally left Cairo on 23 June 1940, almost two weeks after Italy entered the war.

With Italian troops over the border in Libya, the threat of Italy seizing the French warships at Alexandria became very real indeed. Another concern was that at this stage, Egypt continued to maintain diplomatic relations with Vichy France, which had forces and bases in the Lebanon and Syria, not that far distant from Egypt, with only British-mandated Palestine in between as a buffer zone.

THE FRENCH CONNECTION

The fall of France had created an unexpected problem for the Royal Navy. The ships of their erstwhile ally were scattered at a number of ports, in the Atlantic from Portsmouth and Plymouth in the UK to Dakar in West Africa, and in the Mediterranean from Casablanca in French Morocco, Mers-el-Kebir and Oran in Algeria, to Alexandria in Egypt. While the Royal Navy was reluctant to take action against the French, the attitude of the new Vichy French government was an unknown quantity, although it was known to include pro-Axis elements. It was important that the ships should not fall into German hands. At Portsmouth and Plymouth, the ships were seized by boarding, while action was taken against those at Dakar and Mers-el-Kebir by major surface units, including aircraft carriers. The ships at Alexandria posed yet another problem for Admiral Sir Andrew 'ABC' Cunningham, commander-in-chief of the British Mediterranean Fleet.

Cunningham had every sympathy with his French counterpart, Vice-Admiral Godfroy, who knew that he was under orders from his Admiralty to sail, but was trying to confirm that the order was authentic. While de Gaulle was already in the United Kingdom intent on establishing the Free French forces, this move was not universally accepted by all French émigrés and at this early stage of the war, with so few personnel available to de Gaulle and the future policies of the Vichy regime not known, few were inclined to commit themselves. Aftre all, the Germans had not occupied the whole of France, and they did not wish to be classed as traitors. They were also still being paid.

Naturally, most of the personnel involved wished to return home to their families. Although Darlan had issued orders that ships were to be scuttled if there was a risk of them being seized by the Germans, it was also clear that they were not to be handed to the British either. Cunningham recalled:

Though I had no doubts of the good faith of Vice-Admiral Godfroy, it was impossible for the British fleet in Alexandria to go to sea for operations against the enemy leaving behind in harbour fully efficient units of the French Navy. Immediately we were out of sight they might sail for Beyrout (Beirut), or even go back to France, where there was no assurance that they would not fall into German or Italian hands and be used against us.

During the last days of June we became aware that an operation was being planned against the French ships at Oran. An ultimatum was to be given to the French admiral in command, giving him four alternatives. He might sail his ships to British ports and continue the fight with us, or sail his ships with reduced crews to a British port from which the crews could be repatriated whenever desired; or sail his ships to a French port in the West Indies where they would be demilitarized to our satisfaction, or, if preferred, entrusted to United States jurisdiction for the duration of the war, the crews being repatriated in either case; or, finally, to sink his ships.[1]

In fact, there was a fifth option, demilitarizing the ships at Oran in their berths, provided that this could be done inside six hours. By 'demilitarizing', the British meant putting the ships into such a condition that they could not be returned to service for at least a year, even with the assistance of a fully equipped dockyard.

The Admiralty pressure on Cunningham to act decisively and quickly was considerable – with their lordships brooking no argument. It says much for Cunningham's character that he refused to be hurried into taking action that could further affect Anglo-French naval relations.

Realising that Godfroy would be aware of the action taken against the rest of the French warships elsewhere, Cunningham knew that his only alternatives were to intern the ships or risk unnecessary bloodshed on both sides by sinking them. After initially appearing to accept internment with the repatriation of most of his ships' companies, while the vessels would be relieved of their fuel and the warheads taken off their torpedoes, the Vichy government's orders to sail forced Godfroy to change his mind. He instructed his ships to raise steam – a process that would take up to eight hours. Cunningham was alerted and, going on deck, saw not only that the ships were raising steam, but that their guns had been uncovered and they were ready for action, with the real possibility of a close-range gun battle in Alexandria harbour. The British warships immediately did the same, removing the tompions (muzzle covers, usually made from steel or brass and often decorated with the ship's crest) from their guns.

Each French warship had been given a British opposite number and it was the job of her commanding officer to maintain liaison with his French counterpart. Cunningham immediately ordered his COs to visit the French, while the flagship signalled each French warship in turn advising them of the British government's offer of repatriation if the warships were put out of use. The visitors to the French warships were not unwelcome. The captain of a cruiser welcoming Captain Rory O'Connor of the battlecruiser *Neptune*, admitted: 'When I saw the tompions being removed from your guns, I immediately ordered the tompions to be placed in mine.'[2]

In many cases, the decision was taken out of the hands of commanding officers as French ratings held meetings on deck, while the French commanding officers visited Godfroy on his flagship, *Dusquesne*. An hour later, Godfroy asked to see Cunningham. They agreed that all fuel oil was to be discharged from the French ships, their guns were to be disabled, and some 70 per cent of their crews were to be landed and eventually repatriated.

No attempt was made to press the French ships into the Royal Navy. As mentioned earlier, apart from any question of honour, another consideration was that the French often used different gun calibres – 5.1-in instead of 6-in, and 3.5-in instead of 4-in or the increasingly common 4.5-in – from the British, and this would have compounded the problem of inadequate ammunition supplies already being experienced. It was unlikely that sufficient spare personnel would have been available to man them in any case. Leaving small crews behind meant that the ships were maintained ready for the day of liberation.

The French fleet no longer presented a threat by 7 July, allowing the British to leave Alexandria without any concern over possible French action to seize the port or the Suez Canal. Cunningham had shown considerable skill and diplomacy in a difficult situation – in modern terminology he had defused the situation.

Notes
1 and 2 *A Sailor's Odyssey*, Admiral (later Admiral of the Fleet) Sir Andrew Cunningham, RN, Hutchinson, London, 1951

CHAPTER ELEVEN

Conflict in North Africa

Algeria was one of France's most prized colonial possessions, and had been settled by the French who lived
alongside the indigenous Arab population. It was the
most extensively colonized part of the French empire, with more
than a million French settled in the country.

The country had a long and not always distinguished history.
Having been ruled first by Carthage and then by Rome, it
became part of the Ottoman empire in the sixteenth century,
having earlier managed to avoid being ruled by Spain. Under
the Ottomans, it became a centre for the slave trade with the
sultan's writ observed more often by neglect. In the eighteenth
century, the country became a pirate state with the effect of the
Barbary pirates being felt throughout the Mediterranean and
even as far north as Cornwall. The age of piracy was brought to
an end in 1816, when an Anglo-Dutch-American naval squadron
intervened, and at one stage bombarded Algiers itself. In 1830,
Algiers was seized by French troops, and by 1847, the French
had occupied the entire northern area of the country and established the *départements* of Algiers, Oran and Constantine, and in
1881, these regions came to be counted as part of Metropolitan
France – a distinctive feature of French rule in many of her
colonies – by which time the mountainous regions were also

occupied, although the Sahara did not come completely under French control until 1909. Substantial migration from France ensured that the country was effectively colonized during the second half of the nineteenth century.

Algeria had in fact originally been a colony of neighbouring Tunisia, to the east of Algeria, which was settled as Carthage by the Phoenicians, who themselves had come from what is present day Lebanon, and then fell under Arab rule until it became part of the Ottoman empire in 1574. Like Algeria, it was a base for the Barbary pirates. Tunisia became a French protectorate in 1881.

Further west, with a coastline that included both the Atlantic and the Mediterranean, Morocco had also had a history of being subjected to successive waves of colonists, including the Portuguese, who for a while occupied the port of Ceuta, today still one of two Spanish enclaves in Morocco. Both Spain and France became involved in the country during the nineteenth century, but it was not until 1912 that the country was formally divided into French and Spanish protectorates. The main French naval base in Morocco was at Casablanca, but this was far less important than Oran and Mers-el-Kebir.

THE FRENCH NAVY IN NORTH AFRICA

As with the British, who had a major naval base on the island of Malta and had others around the world in their colonies, the French had established an important naval base in Algeria at Mers-el-Kebir, just outside Oran, although a number of ships were also based on the latter port. The importance of the bases can be understood by the fact that they even included training facilities for the Marine Nationale.

Overseas bases for the colonial powers not only relieved pressure on the home ports in days when navies were far larger than today, but they also helped to maintain the dignity and power of the colonial power, as well as providing opportunities for overseas service for the personnel of all three services. In some cases, and especially the further flung parts of empire, the bases were necessary for refuelling warships, something that had been needed much more frequently in earlier days when using coal rather than oil and, of course, such bases provided opportunities to re-victual ships and take on fresh water.

In 1940, after the fall of France, Mers-el-Kebir had two elderly French battleships plus the modern battlecruisers *Dunkerque* and *Strasbourg*, as well as six large destroyers of the *contre-torpilleur* type, sometimes described as 'super destroyers' and intended to oppose Italy's light cruisers, with seven smaller destroyers and four submarines at Oran. Since the declaration of war, the French Navy had been busy escorting convoys between metropolitan France and Algieria, seen as vulnerable to Italian attack. *Dunkerque* had only recently returned to Mers-el-Kebir, having visited Gibraltar,

The German Navy was known to be short of major fleet units, and the two battlecruisers as well as the *contre-torpilleur* type of destroyer would certainly have accelerated the development of the Kriegsmarine. Alternatively, the ships could have been of use to the Italian navy, the Regia Navale, which had six battleships, two modern and four elderly, but rebuilt, and had neglected the battlecruiser. It also seems that the Italians were short of destroyers, sometimes using cruisers to escort Mediterranean convoys, even though these were of little use in anti-submarine warfare.

Not fully appreciated by the British was that the Italians themselves were soon to be short of fuel, and later in the war, when the Eastern Front began to collapse and Germany experienced growing shortages of oil, their Italian allies had their supplies drastically reduced. The Germans were to become very cynical about the use of the Italian navy, which they had expected to venture out and bombard Malta, before occupying the islands, on entering the war.

ULTIMATUM

Concerned at the loss of French naval support in the Mediterranean, the British reacted quickly to fill the gap in capability. On 28 June 1940, Force H was formed. Officially, Force H was seen as a powerful naval squadron, although in the balance of its ships, with an aircraft carrier and capital ships, and numbers, it was really a small fleet. Based on Gibraltar, it was able to range out into the Atlantic or across the Mediterranean, operating as far east as Malta and actually attacking Italian naval installations and warships as far north as Genoa. Once the Germans became active in the Mediterranean at the beginning of 1941, effectively cutting the 'Middle Sea' in half, with the British Mediterranean Fleet moved from Malta to Alexandria even before Italy entered the war, Force H almost became a 'Western Mediterranean' fleet.

Given the difficulty of operating in the Mediterranean under Axis control of the air, it often took Force H to escort convoys attempting to reach Malta. The situation in the Mediterranean was such that large fleet carriers often escorted convoys, whereas on the Arctic convoys, escort carriers were judged sufficient, although often with fleet carriers in the distant escort, while on the North Atlantic, the MAC-ships, merchant aircraft carriers with a primitive flight deck above the cargo holds, and cargo, of oil tankers and grain carriers, were effective.

On its formation, Force H was commanded by Vice-Admiral Sir James Somerville, who had been brought out of retirement and had taken a considerable demotion from his original career rank of Admiral of the Fleet: in other words, Somerville had gone from five star rank to three stars to serve his country.

Despite his age, Somerville was one of the most daring and competent British naval commanders of the war, and ideally suited to a flexible and independent command such as Force H was to become. His record comes across as almost being swashbuckling. Earlier in the war, he had assisted Ramsay at Dover in organising the Dunkirk evacuation.

Force H was a balanced fleet, with battleships and an aircraft carrier, the still new HMS *Ark Royal*.

The British government was not aware that Darlan had ordered his commanding officers to scuttle their ships rather than allow them to fall into German or Italian hands. As subsequent events were to show, the Germans were eventually to want to seize as many French warships as they could, after the occupation of Vichy France in November 1942, although most probably to stop them falling into Allied hands. Even if they had been aware of Darlan's order, the French admiral himself was not trusted by the British, who were well aware of his anti-British feelings, while the British also felt a sense of betrayal that the French had negotiated a separate armistice with the Germans. In any event, a scuttling order depended on the crew of a ship having the time to put it into effect, and a ship scuttled in harbour could often be re-floated and re-commissioned.

After those French warships that had fled to British ports had been seized on 3 July, Force H was despatched to Mers-el-Kebir and Somerville attempted to open negotiations with the local French naval commander, Admiral Marcel Gensoul. This was easier said than done. In the confusion following the collapse of France, Gensoul was in a difficult position, not knowing the policies of his government and whether or not his country would expect him to continue the war or accept surrender and, perhaps, neutrality. He had a substantial part of his country's naval forces entrusted to his care and some excellent bases. Somerville's emissary was refused a meeting with Gensoul and so the negotiations had to begin in writing.

This was a crucial difference between the situation in Alexandria being handled by Cunningham and that in Algeria. Contact was well established at Alexandria with the flag officers knowing each other and liaison even reaching down to commanding officer level, but no such possibilities existed at Mers-el-Kebir and Oran.

Somerville wrote offering Gensoul four options, of which the first was that he should take his fleet to sea and join forces with the Royal Navy, even though this would mean that he would be branded as a traitor by the Vichy regime. As a variation on this proposal, the second option was that the ships could be sailed with a reduced crew to a British port, possibly Gibraltar, which was close, but probably not Malta because of its proximity to Italy. Once in the British port, the crews would be repatriated. The third option was that the ships could be taken, again with a reduced crew, to a port in the French West Indies, and the ships would be immobilized. The fourth and final option was that the ships should be scuttled at Mers-el-Kebir and Oran within six hours.

A fifth option given to Somerville by the Admiralty in London was that the ships could be immobilized at Mers-el-Kebir and Oran. This was unrealistic, given the dockyard facilities at Mers-el-Kebir, which meant that the ships could be returned to service reasonably quickly, and Somerville, wisely, did not offer this option to Gensoul. By 'immobilize', the Admiralty meant that the ships should be so disabled that they could not be used again without a substantial time, perhaps a year, receiving attention in a well-equipped dockyard. This was unrealistic, and had it occurred, could later have counted against the Allies and the Free French.

Finally, Gensoul was told that if he did not accept one of the four options, his ships would be sunk by the Royal Navy. What might have happened had Gensoul forwarded the full list of options to his political superiors will never be known, as he simply told the French Admiralty that he had been given six hours to scuttle his ships or they would be attacked by the Royal Navy. Given this stark choice, Vichy naturally enough ordered him to resist with all of the force available to him.

Somerville, in common with most British sailors, was very unhappy about having to use force against a navy that had, just weeks before, been an ally, and which had taken part in the Norwegian campaign and later assisted in the evacuation of British troops from not just Dunkirk, but also from the Cherbourg peninsula and Brittany. As a final gesture, Somerville sent one of his most senior officers, Captain Holland, commanding officer of the aircraft carrier, *Ark Royal*, to see

Gensoul with an ultimatum. Holland was flown in a Fairey Swordfish seaplane from Holland's flagship. While Holland was aboard Gensoul's flagship, the battlecruiser *Dunkerque*, the French Admiralty signalled *en clair* for all French naval forces in the Mediterranean to converge on Oran and put themselves under Gensoul's command. Not surprisingly, this message was immediately picked up by the Admiralty in London, which lost no time in ordering Somerville into action while he still had only the forces already at Mers-el-Kebir and Oran to contend with, rather than face the overwhelming might of all French warships in the Mediterranean.

Captain Holland left the *Dunkerque* at 17.25 on 3 July, having already informed Somerville that Gensoul was refusing to accept any of the four options presented to him. It was important that Holland resumed command of his warship, Somerville's only carrier, immediately. Aboard *Ark Royal*, the arrester wires were removed from her flight deck, and the Swordfish float-plane flew safely onto her paper-thin flight deck, without damage to the aircraft or the ship, something which could only have been done with an aircraft with such low speeds as the venerable 'Stringbag'.

At 17.54, Somerville opened fire, soon joined by aircraft from the *Ark Royal*. The old battleship *Bretagne* blew up and several other ships were badly damaged, including *Dunkerque*, which although only slightly damaged in the initial salvoes of gunfire, was then crippled in an attack by Swordfish torpedo-bombers from the British carrier on 6 July. Total French losses were 1,297 men. The warships were not the only targets, with a single broadside from a British battleship blowing a French army barracks off the crest of a hill.

The French warships fired back, and Joseph Rockley, a leading seaman aboard the battlecruiser, HMS *Hood*, remembers the shells passing over the ship.

'It was my first experience of naval gunfire,' he recalls. 'Some shells passed overhead like an express train, but others wobbled, and I learned later that this was due to the rifling in their barrels being worn. They sounded like someone blowing hard into a glass in short, sharp breaths.

'It was impossible to tell at the time how much damage we had caused, but we later learnt that it had been considerable.'[1]

'Mers-el-Kebir was Churchill's biggest mistake,' maintained Matelot (Able Seaman) Jean-Pierre Gauthier, a gunner aboard the destroyer *Casque*, which was in the port at the time. '*Casque* was not hit while she was in the port, but after she left port she was hit and began to sink. Men dived into the water, but the *Strasbourg* raced through them like a knife through butter. It was all over in five minutes.'[2]

Despite the gunfire and the air strikes, the battlecruiser *Strasbourg* and six smaller ships managed to slip out of Mers-el-Kebir and make their escape to Toulon, where they were soon joined by a small force of cruisers that had been at Algiers. Several British ships gave chase, including the *Hood*, but they failed to catch the French ships.

One French matelot who had been actively campaigning to continue the war alongside the British was Arsene Le Poittevin, but Mers-el-Kebir made his objective so much more difficult to attain.

'It was terrible for us,' Le Poittevin recalls. 'Lots of sailors dead, and ships sunk or damaged. It was impossible to say anything nice about the British for a long time. Later, people began to say that perhaps they had no choice.

'At the same time, rather than simply rejecting the British ultimatum, had the commanding officers had the courage of their convictions, they should have gone to sea and fought, rather than just staying in harbour.'[3]

Needless to say, the British attitude was different, even though they had every sympathy for the French.

'It was a sobering thought, as we had been allies fighting the Germans just a short time before,' recalls Joseph Rockley. 'Amongst my own circle, we knew that we had been operating alongside the French, and we were upset for a time.

'No one doubted that the government had no choice as there

was this big fleet that the Germans could have taken and used against us.'[4]

The Germans were seen by many British sailors as being the big threat, especially if they managed to seize the French ships, rather than the Italians, who seemed to be reluctant to fight.

The Battle of Mers-el-Kebir was sufficient to help Cunningham, Commander-in-Chief of the British Mediterranean Fleet, enjoy greater success at Alexandria, but the consequences of the fighting were to be felt for many years to come.

Not surprisingly, the Vichy government immediately broke off all diplomatic relations with the United Kingdom, although how long these could have been maintained on any worthwhile basis must be open to question. Torpedo-bombers of the Aeronavale, the French naval air arm, also mounted a retaliatory raid on the home base for Force H, Gibraltar, although little damage was caused.

In the short term, however, the threat of major French fleet units being transferred to Germany or Italy was eased, although it was not completely out of the question with so many ships still at Toulon in the South of France. The signal was also sent to the Axis powers and to the United States, that despite being isolated and having lost much of her army's equipment in France, the United Kingdom was determined to fight on, whatever the odds.

DAKAR

Dakar, the capital and chief port of Senegal, was a major naval base. The history of the country differed considerably from Algeria and the North African protectorates, and indeed, Senegal had been a French colony for far longer than any of the others, with Dakar itself becoming a French possession in 1659, although it was not until 1865 that the interior of the country was fully occupied by the French. In 1895, the country became part of French West Africa.

The most significant part of the French fleet which was far

from France and the Mediterranean was based at Dakar. Once again, there was little contact between the two navies, but in any case, events elsewhere would have hardened the resolve of commanders on both sides.

On 8 July 1940, French warships stationed at Dakar were attacked by aircraft from the diminutive British aircraft carrier, *Hermes*, and two British cruisers, damaging the battleship *Richelieu*, but not putting her out of action.

Dakar had posed a different problem for the British. It was not just a case of ensuring that any French warships based in Dakar did not pass to the Germans, it was also important that the base itself be kept out of Axis hands. Port and aerodrome facilities at Dakar would be ideally placed to attack British shipping on the convoys between the UK and South Africa, and indeed could also be used as a base to attack those heading for South America, the source of fresh meat. The West African port also had the only dockyard facilities between Gibraltar and Cape Town, an invaluable resource, even in peacetime but more so in wartime, to whichever power held the port. These considerations were to lie behind a Vichy attempt to take the port.

Even so, in July 1940, few probably appreciated just how important the Cape route was to become, as the war in the Mediterranean, North Africa and the Balkans went against the British, the Mediterranean became impassable to British shipping. Malta began to starve. Instead of being the direct route to British possessions in Asia and the Antipodes, the Suez Canal, and the Cape route, became the very roundabout way of keeping British forces in Egypt supplied.

FURTHER FAILURE AT DAKAR

After the failure of the attack on the French warships at Dakar, it was decided to send an Anglo-French expeditionary force to seize the territory. By this time, sufficient French troops, most of them lifted off the beaches at Dunkirk, and from Cherbourg and Brittany, were in the United Kingdom to form a sizeable Free

French force. On 31 August 1940, 2,700 Free French troops and 4,200 British troops left Liverpool under the command of Majoor General N. Irwin, with Vice-Admiral John Cunningham (not to be confused with 'ABC', the commander-in-chief of the Mediterranean Fleet) in command of the naval force. The force was accompanied by General Charles de Gaulle, despite it being known that he would not be welcomed by the Vichy forces holding Dakar. After all, he was the *franc-tireur* personified.

Dakar, in the French colony of Senegal, was an important prize. It wasn't simply a port, it had the only dockyard between Gibraltar and Cape Town. Whoever held Dakar could command the mid-Atlantic.

There were some grounds for optimism. Another French colony, the French Cameroons (originally part of the German colony of Cameroon, but which had been mandated to France at Versailles), had tried to repudiate the armistice between Vichy and Germany, but Vichy forces had intervened. A bloodless *coup d'état* had followed in August, and the French Cameroons were by this time aligned with the Free French.

The person behind these moves in the French colonies was a Major (later Lieutenant-General) Philippe Leclerc, the *nom de guerre* of Captain Viscount Philippe de Hauteclocque, who had joined de Gaulle in London after the fall of France. De Gaulle had promoted Leclerc to major and sent him to the French colonies in West Africa and Equatorial Africa to rally support for the Free French cause. It was Leclerc who had organized the coup in the French Cameroons, and another coup in the Congo.

British intelligence regarding Vichy was generally very poor at this stage of the war, and it was even worse regarding the French African territories. While the Anglo-French force was on passage from Liverpool to Dakar, a Vichy French cruiser squadron managed to leave its home port of Toulon and slip out of the Mediterranean. The squadron's mission was to return the French Cameroons to Vichy control and to support the regime's forces in Gabon, but it also put in to Dakar. This became known to the British, and, realizing the danger, Churchill wanted to recall the expeditionary force.

The French squadron had managed to leave unmolested because of confusion between the naval commander in Gibraltar, Admiral Sir Dudley North, the Admiralty in London and Somerville's Force H. North had earned a sharp reprimand from the Admiralty after he had protested over the action at Mers-el-Kebir. North was ordered to avoid incidents with the Vichy French Navy and so he allowed the French cruiser squadron through the Straits of Gibraltar believing that if the Admiralty had wanted them stopped, it would have ordered Force H to do so. In fact, the Admiralty was unaware that the French ships were at sea.

Aboard the *Audacioux*, 2,600 tons, a Fantasque-class *contre-torpilleur* or 'super destroyer', often regarded as being close to a light cruiser in armament, was Matelot Jean-Pierre Gauthier, formerly of the *Casque*. He had changed ships at Toulon because he had volunteered to serve in Madagascar, largely because he thought that it sounded a better posting. Led by the cruiser *Georges-Leygues*, they had steamed past Gibraltar at 35 knots and called at Casablanca for two days before continuing to Dakar.

What Churchill did not know was that the Free French in London had been lax in their security, and the departure of the expeditionary force soon became known to the Vichy regime, although it could only speculate on the destination.

On 19 September, before the Anglo-French force arrived at Dakar, the six Vichy cruisers attempted to leave, but were intercepted by British warships. Two of the French cruisers returned to Dakar, but the other two were forced to surrender and were escorted to Casablanca, while another two escaped.

Churchill had planned that the Anglo-French force would arrive and so overawe the resident forces in Dakar that they would quickly agree to joining the Free French. All prospect of surprise was also lost when de Gaulle broadcast just before the arrival, alerting the governor and military commanders to the presence of the force. When it did arrive, on 23 September, instead of tropical sunshine the area was shrouded in fog. Free French officers were sent ashore to negotiate an agreement, but they were not welcome, and a hostile response awaited the advance landing party. The battleship *Richelieu* opened fire, as did the port batteries, badly damaging both an elderly British battleship and a cruiser. In the event, both sides exchanged fire over two days, while the fog persisted and was strengthened by smoke screens, before the operation was called off.

Gauthier was still aboard the *Audacioux* when she was hit, and ended up in the water, which, fortunately, was warm, as he remained there for some ten hours before he was rescued, by which time he had swallowed some sea water and also some fuel oil.

'They pulled me out of the water, grabbing me around the stomach, which was badly swollen,' he recalled. 'Once aboard they gave me coffee mixed with salt to make me sick. In the water, I never thought that there might be sharks, but perhaps the noise kept them away.'[5]

The hospital accommodation at Dakar was overwhelmed with casualties, so any not requiring surgery were billeted aboard merchant ships in the port.

This was not the end of Free French involvement in France's African colonies. Using the French Cameroons as a base, the Free French invaded Gabon on 12 October 1940, with additional forces moving in from the French Congo. Fierce resistance was encountered from French Senegalese troops, and it was not until 7 November, that an attack could be launched against the capital, Libreville, which took four days to capture. In this case, no British forces were deployed ashore, such was the lack of enthusiasm in London following the Dakar fiasco, although a British sloop managed to capture a Vichy submarine.

Meanwhile, when the Redoubtable class submarine *Sidi Ferruch*, 1,400 tons displacement on the surface, 2,100 tons submerged, arrived at Dakar from Martinique in the French West Indies, Gauthier joined her and went first to Casablanca, and later to Toulon. He saw no action for some time, until he transferred to an oil tanker and was in Casablanca when the

Americans invaded, after which he joined the Free French along with the ship and the rest of the crew, and they went to New York for a refit.

Notes
1 IWM Accession No 12422
2 IWM Accession No 19773
3 IWM Accession No 19773
4 IWM Accession No 19864
5 IWM Accession No 19773

CHAPTER TWELVE

The Cross of Lorraine

Britain's wartime leader, Winston Churchill, faced what for many men would have been an impossible task following the French surrender, and there can be little doubt that there were few times during the years that followed when the situation was easy. Nevertheless, one of his most famous remarks of the war years was that: 'The hardest cross I have had to bear was the Cross of Lorraine.'

The 'Cross of Lorraine' was a none too oblique reference to the leader of the Free French, the then Brigadier-General Charles de Gaulle, although the symbol had been chosen by the Free French in 1940.

A career army officer, de Gaulle was one of those, along with the British strategist Basil Liddell-Hart and indeed the Führer himself, who believed in mechanised warfare and the close collaboration of air power and ground forces. He had written extensively on the subject between the wars, but his views proved controversial and were not acceptable to the military establishment. He had first hand experience of life in the trenches during the First World War as a young officer, and was wounded three times before being taken prisoner by the Germans in March 1916, at the age of twenty-six years, something to which many ascribe his survival given the high mortality rates amongst infantry officers in the conflict. His progress through the ranks between the wars was slow, no doubt due to a combination of his radical (in terms of strategy) views and to the low priority accorded defence and the maintenance of adequate armed forces by the democratic governments.

De Gaulle's two most significant works were two books, *The Edge of the Sword* published in 1932, which was followed in 1934 by *Towards a Professional Army*. The main thrust of his arguments was the creation of a professional army centred around highly mobile forces, including armour, rather than the European system of largely conscript armies. In Europe, conscript armies tended to be ill-equipped, partly because of the high cost of equipping such large forces and also because of the considerable time needed for technical training. The full extent of the differences between de Gaulle and the French military establishment can simply be judged by the fact that while he advocated mobile warfare, France built the fixed Maginot Line. Many of the older generation of senior officers must have wished that de Gaulle would go away, but he was persistent, and was active in promoting his ideas in the press. He also found a political patron, Paul Reynaud.

Reynaud had been a prominent member of the Democratic Alliance from 1930, and on 21 March 1940 succeeded Daladier as president of the council of ministers, which was in effect the French cabinet with Reynaud effectively equivalent to prime minister. He also took on the role of foreign minister. A week later, Reynaud made an agreement with the United Kingdom that neither country would sign a separate peace with Germany. More aggressive than his predecessor Daladier, Reynaud was fully in favour of Anglo-French intervention in Norway. Famously, after the German offensive against France started, Reynaud told the French National Assembly that only a miracle could save France, before adding: 'I believe in miracles.'

Daladier was appointed foreign minister on 20 May, the same day that Reynaud added the post of minister of national defence to his role as prime minister. This was not especially radical or dramatic, as in wartime the British prime minister exercised a similar combination of powers. He immediately made changes to the leadership of the Allied forces fighting in France, and appointed Marshal Pétain as deputy prime minister. Despite these changes and the later appointment of his protégé de Gaulle as under-secretary for war on 5 June, what had by this time become a coalition government took a markedly defeatist turn. To avoid the German encirclement of Paris, the French government had evacuated the capital and by 15 June had based itself in the south-west of France at Bordeaux. That day, the French cabinet asked the British government to release France from the commitment not to sign a separate peace with Germany made on 28 March, to the dismay of Reynaud who had to be dissuaded from resigning.

The British acceptance of the French request the following day was conditional on the French fleet leaving France and the French colonies and sailing to British ports. Reynaud's next move was to propose that while the army fighting in France should surrender, the French government should continue the war against Germany from North Africa. His colleagues refused to accept this proposal, and his deputy, Pétain, resigned. In the UK, Winston Churchill proposed an indissoluble union between the two countries, but this somewhat eccentric idea (post-war, Churchill favoured European union, but emphatically without the UK being a part of it) was also rejected by the French cabinet. With no options left, Reynaud then resigned and was immediately replaced by Pétain, who began negotiations for an armistice almost immediately.

Realising that Reynaud's connections with de Gaulle, by this time leader of the Free French, could pose a threat to the Vichy regime, Pétain interned Reynaud in September 1940, and two months later, he was imprisoned by the Germans in Oranienburg concentration camp, before eventually being taken to the Itter Castle in Austria. Reynaud survived the war to be released by the advancing American forces, and was later a witness at Pétain's trial.

De Gaulle, meanwhile, had been simply the commander of a tank regiment when war broke out in September 1939, a post which he had held since 1937. He was put in command of the armoured units of the French Ffth Army, and after Reynaud became prime minister, he was promoted to command the 4th Armoured Division. He was soon in the thick of the battle, fighting successfully at Laon on 17–20 May, and then at Abbeville on 28–30 May. Given his responsibilities, it seems strange that promotion to the rank brigadier-general (equivalent to the British rank of brigadier, the British Army having dropped the suffix of general after the First World War) did not come until 1 June.

DE GAULLE AND POLITICS

Despite his pre-war lobbying over the shape of the French army, de Gaulle's first active involvement in the political arena did not come until 6 June 1940, when Reynaud appointed him under-secretary for national defence. This meant that as France moved to collapse, de Gaulle was the French army's most junior general and a minor minister in a governing coalition that was itself on the verge of collapse. Nevertheless, de Gaulle's term of office took him to London where he first met Churchill on 9 June, and he was present at Churchill and Reynaud's last two meetings in France on 11/12 and 13 June. These three meetings were his only chance to make an impression on the British prime minister – he did not fail to do so.

De Gaulle's period as a government minister was indeed brief, lasting just ten days, as he lost his position when Reynaud resigned to be replaced by Pétain on 16 June. While Pétain sought an armistice, de Gaulle was flown out of France by the Royal Air Force. While Pétain was seeking an armistice from Germany on the night of 16/17 June, on 18 June de Gaulle went on the air, broadcasting on the British Broadcasting Corporation, to his fellow countrymen to continue the fight against Germany, an action only possible with the authority of Churchill.

The British hesitated to take the next step, but on 28 June, they formally recognized Charles de Gaulle as the 'leader of all free

Frenchmen, wherever they may be.' De Gaulle took Churchill at his word, and it seems that the British premier was often to have cause to rue his description of the French general as 'leader of all free Frenchmen.' It was not until 7 August that the decision was taken to create the Free French forces, fully paid for by the British taxpayer.

In fact, the British were investing considerable political and strategic capital in de Gaulle, as well as money. They believed that he would bring with him a considerable number of French men and women, and that a large proportion of the French colonies would also rally to his cause. Despite broadcasting six times in late June and again a further six times throughout July, de Gaulle's radio calls for the continued fight against Germany met with little response. No other significant political or military figure followed him, and, apart briefly from support from the governor-general of Madagascar, the colonies all quickly switched their allegiance from the now defeated Reynaud government to that of Vichy and Pétain.

THE FREE FRENCH

De Gaulle's Free French forces faced a difficult and uncertain start. Anyone with less confidence, and less arrogance, would have failed within weeks of taking up the challenge. The French colonies had all declared their allegiance to Vichy and Pétain. While around 123,000 French soldiers had been taken off the beaches at Dunkirk and Cherbourg, and from Brittany, in mid-August 1940, the Free French Army in the United Kingdom consisted of just 140 officers and 2,100 other ranks; a token force. Those units of the French fleet that had been in harbours controlled by the British had been seized or, as at Alexandria, had surrendered the ships, with more than 30,000 French seamen being repatriated to France. Repatriated personnel were of no use to de Gaulle or the Free French.

While he had held a relatively junior political post in the hectic period immediately prior to the French surrender, on arrival in

London de Gaulle seems to have quickly come to the conclusion that he was now the true head of the French state, and not just those elements resident in Britain. It was not enough to serve as a rallying point for Frenchmen opposed to the armistice and wishing to continue to fight the Germans, or even to go a step further and gather around him all those who opposed the Vichy regime. For many, to have led the Free French would have been enough – for de Gaulle, it was not.

Of course, this raises the question, if not de Gaulle, who else? After all, this still relatively young army officer was overnight projected into a position where he was dealing with a statesman like Churchill, and then later Stalin and Roosevelt. If Paul Reynaud had managed to leave France and move to London, then Reynaud would have been the obvious choice for French leader. As a democratic politician of considerable seniority and experience, Reynaud would also have been a credible leader.

One of the early members of the Free French was Marcel Ollivier, a French merchant seaman, one of the engineers aboard a motorship which had been diverted first to Milford Haven and then to Liverpool at the time of the armistice. His ship was carrying ammunition and aircraft, disassembled and in crates, from the United States. He recalled many of his fellow seamen being angry about the armistice.

On 3 July 1940, the British seized our ships, but the merchant seamen were not sent to camps like the naval personnel, then on 7 July, I decided to leave to join the Free French, but when I told the captain, he told me I could not go. Even the company's agent in Liverpool tried to stop me by impounding my papers.

So, I just left and went to London, where all the volunteers were assembled at Olympia. The accommodation was poor, as we had to sleep on the floor, but there was plenty of food as the supplies originally intended for a Foreign Legion unit had been held nearby.

One day, I was given two shillings and sixpence and told that I was to act as an emissary between the people at

Olympia and the Free French headquarters because I could speak English. I duly arrived at a building in the centre of London, and found it empty, no furniture, nothing. I hunted through the rooms until I found a room with about five people in it, sitting on chairs or on boxes. If there was a table, it was well hidden. This was the Free French headquarters.[1]

Ollivier found much anger against the British amongst the Free French, and while he didn't feel quite as angry as his comrades, he was convinced that if the British had taken their time, many more French naval personnel would have eventually agreed to support them. Of course, the question remains, would their ships have come too, and how long would the Royal Navy have had to keep watch on the French fleet, just in case it did try to escape.

Subsequently, Ollivier was put into the Free French army, where he was asked if he wanted to take Canadian citizenship or to change his name, the first to protect himself if captured and the second to protect his family from reprisals. He decided to do neither. Free French servicemen were all given numbers that ended with the year of their enlistment, so the lower the number, the earlier the man had joined. This was a concern for Ollivier later when he deserted from the army to join the navy, as he wanted to return to sea. The captain of a sloop made it easy for him as in the early days of the Free French, almost anything could happen, with very weak central control and considerable lack of discipline, but to avoid any complications, he changed his date of birth so that he was unlikely to be detected. Unfortunately, although he had joined the Free French in July 1940, he had switched to the navy in March 1941, so his new service number ended in 41!

SUPPORT FROM EQUATORIAL AFRICA

The first signs of light came from some of the darkest parts of the so-called 'dark continent', Africa. In an inspired move, in

August 1940, de Gaulle sent Major (later Lieutenant-General) Philippe Leclerc, to garner support in French Equatorial Africa and French West Africa. Clearly, de Gaulle had decided that North Africa was too committed to Vichy rule, and intended to see whether a power base could be established further south. This was important to de Gaulle, for having some territory of his own meant that he could place greater emphasis on what he perceived as his 'independence' from first the United Kingdom and then, once the United States and Soviet Union were in the war, from the Allies.

Leclerc could hardly have expected to be so successful. By the end of August, he had organized coups in the French Cameroons and the Middle Congo, in each case without loss of life, before leading a force of French colonial troops to seize Gabon, including the capital, Libreville. The governor of Chad, Félix Eboué, joined the Free French cause and Leclerc established his headquarters there, starting a series of campaigns that incredibly ended with his men seizing the Libyan oasis of Kufra before fighting their way north to join up with the British Eighth Army near Tripoli in January 1943.

Despite these successes, as mentioned earlier, there were also some failures, notably the disaster at Dakar, where Vichy forces retained the upper hand. Plunged into despair, de Gaulle continued, bypassing Senegal to make a tour of French Equatorial Africa where he did much to strengthen his links with the more far flung supporters of the Free French cause.

Marcel Ollivier had encountered de Gaulle after the fiasco at Dakar, and when Ollivier was still in the Free French army. Aboard a merchant ship carrying the equipment that they had expected to deploy to Dakar, he was on deck when he saw de Gaulle coming up from below.

'I was terrified at having to meet the great man,' he recalled. 'De Gaulle turned me and said "My boy, we are almost in France" as we approached Douala in French Cameroon. I saw a small tear in the corner of his eye and was never again afraid of de Gaulle.'[2]

The Dakar fiasco was the first of many blunders by de Gaulle, who had alerted the defences by making a premature radio broadcast, but he survived the debacle largely due to Churchill's expression of continued confidence in him. Churchill had little choice, as at that stage there was no other obvious leader for the Free French. Nevertheless, as mentioned earlier, the seizure of Libreville, Gabon's capital, by Free French forces was done with little help from the British. While their attitude was understandable, it also allowed de Gaulle to take a more independent line in the future.

Independence was also the keynote in his next move, the so-called Brazzaville declaration, made while he was visiting the French Congo on 27 October. This declared the Vichy government illegal and maintained that French government no longer existed as Vichy was subordinate to German policies and decisions, and was followed in November by a further declaration setting out the reasons for the Vichy regime being considered illegal. This was undoubtedly true, but it was questionable whether his next statement had any greater legality than that of Vichy. He maintained:

> It is therefore necessary that a new authority should assume the task of directing the French effort in the war. Events impose this sacred duty upon me. I shall not fail to carry it out.

A Council of Defence for the French Empire was then established, which de Gaulle would consult on important decisions, but, of course, only when he considered it appropriate. Nevertheless, this showed growing confidence on the part of the Free French, followed by the announcement of a new war decoration, the Order of Liberation, on 16 November.

This was the point at which de Gaulle started taking decisions without any reference to Churchill. Indeed, he had this much in common with the early Vichy leaders, in that he seemed to be able to overlook the experience of defeat. Possibly, this had been so traumatic that attempts to ignore it were inevitable. The Free French, and certainly those most closely associated with de

Gaulle, liked to maintain their independence, but they were heavily dependent upon the British, and even the progress made in the Lebanon and Syria, and Madagascar, as well as the early gains in French Equatorial Africa, were not enough for a substantial power base. It was not to be until after the Allied landings in North Africa that the situation began to change, but even then, the Free French had no industrial base of their own, and were dependent entirely on British and, later, American provision of equipment and other supplies.

FRENCH INDO-CHINA

Meanwhile, the first six months of Free French operations had been ones of slow and limited progress. The former governor-general of French Indo-China, General Georges Catroux, had been replaced in June 1940 by a Vichy nominee. He left French Indo-China to become the first senior army officer to align himself with the Free French. He was given command of the Free French element in the Syrian campaign, afterwards gained the somewhat long-winded appellation of 'Delegate-General and Plenipotentiary for the Levant', and later became one of the founding members of the French Committee for National Liberation, CFLN, when this was formed in June 1943, less than a year before the Normandy landings. In the meantime, in September 1941, de Gaulle had established the French National Committee, effectively a cabinet in waiting ready for the liberation of France, but at first only the USSR recognized this organization.

Catroux's position in French Indo-China, present day Vietnam, Laos and Cambodia, had been a difficult one, and in some ways similar to the British predicament in Malaya and Singapore. In contrast to the North African colonies, French Indo-China had just about 40,000 European inhabitants. The French ruled Vietnam directly, but in Cambodia and Laos the indigenous royal houses remained in place. The Japanese threat to French Indo-China became increasingly obvious during the late 1930s, and appeals to Paris for additional forces resulted in very little being supplied, although extra money was provided with which Catroux was able to raise his army, the main part of his forces, to around 100,000 men, including 20,000 French Foreign Legion troops.

In June 1940, making the most of French preoccupation with the Battle of France, the Japanese demanded that they be allowed to establish a military mission in French Indo-China and also provide troops to close the Haiphong-Yunnan railway along which travelled most of the supplies for Generalissimo Chiang Kai-shek's Nationalists. Even with 100,000 men at his disposal, Catroux was in no position to deny the Japanese demands. His masters in Vichy disagreed and promptly sacked him, replacing him with Vice-Admiral Jean Decoux, but despite this, when the Japanese returned with further demands, Vichy ordered him simply to negotiate and not to fight.

In fact, the Japanese soon had everything they wanted from French Indo-China without having to take the trouble to run the country or occupy it fully. They achieved this by careful negotiation and bullying. On one occasion, they feigned ignorance of a new agreement and attacked from bases in China, capturing two towns and killing more than 800 French troops, after which they withdrew and apologized for their 'mistake', which was of course simply a campaign to further remind the Vichy administration who was in control and of the consequences of failing to accede to their demands. When French naval forces in the area defeated a Thai attempt to take disputed territory in Cambodia and Laos, the Japanese forced the French to cede the territory to Thailand. In July 1941, the Japanese occupied Saigon and Cambodia with 35,000 troops, and proceeded to take possession of the annual rice and corn harvests, as well as the country's coal and rubber, all of which was either used by the Japanese garrison or shipped to Japan. This was done without concern for the local population, and matters worsened once the territory became cut off from Japan by the Allied advance towards the Japanese home islands, with rice being used as fuel and jute and cotton planted to provide the garrison with textiles. As a result, in 1945, as many as two million people died from starvation in French Indo-China.

It was not until early 1945 that de Gaulle extended his authority to French Indo-China with the formation of a Free French Council of Indo-China, which also decided to finally confront the Japanese in order to retain the territory for France. The United States, by contrast, had been favouring the Communist Viet Minh, who after the war were to fight the French for independence. When Decoux refused Japanese demands to place his forces at their disposal, he was arrested, his forces surrounded and those who resisted were killed, with the loss of almost 2,000 French troops.

The problem here was that the United States had decided not reinstate French colonial authority in Indo-China, despite Chiang Kai-shek refusing the offer of this territory at the Cairo conference in November 1943. Undoubtedly, the friction between Roosevelt and de Gaulle did not help, but the United States generally had little sympathy for the colonial powers, even though some Pacific territories, such as the Philippines, had been run almost as colonies by the United States.

DE GAULLE DIFFICULT

De Gaulle was to prove to be extremely difficult to deal with. When Syria and the Lebanon were occupied by British Empire and Free French forces, de Gaulle rejected the armistice terms, partly because the territories passed straight from Vichy France control to that of the British, and partly because the troops that had fought so well for Vichy were allowed to be repatriated without the Free French having a chance to recruit them. The fact that Catroux had agreed to the armistice terms didn't matter. De Gaulle was also blind to the fact that in the Middle East, the British were under opposing pressures from Arab nationalists who wanted both the Lebanon and Syria to become independent. Elsewhere, as an imperial power itself, the UK was generally happy to see territory move directly from Vichy to Free French control.

Based in Cairo at the outset of the campaign, de Gaulle moved to Brazzaville, which he used as his power base, and from whence he publicly denounced the armistice terms. On his return he insisted that the armistice be revised, and that if it was not, he would withdraw the Free French forces in the Middle East from British command. He was assured that France's historic interests in the Lebanon and Syria were recognized by the British, and given a chance to recruit the Vichy troops for the Free French, eventually gaining some 6,000 men, which increased his forces considerably.

Again, when British, East African and South African forces invaded Madagascar, de Gaulle was angered because he was not consulted, for which one can understand his frustration, and because the British entered into negotiations with the local Vichy administration, hoping not to have to occupy the whole island. Possibly the British did not inform de Gaulle in case he made another of his infamous broadcasts and jeopardized the operation, but his insistence that there should be no negotiations with Vichy representatives was wholly unrealistic, especially as the commanders of over-stretched British forces naturally wanted to end the fighting as quickly as possible. For his part, de Gaulle should have welcomed any attempt that reduced the risk of bloodshed amongst his fellow countrymen. As it happened, in the end, the British had to occupy the entire island, and it was handed over to the Free French in November 1942. Before this, de Gaulle put out feelers to Stalin to see whether he could operate from the Soviet Union if the relationship with the British continued to decline. Even had Stalin accepted, it is doubtful whether de Gaulle would have found a base in the USSR to be acceptable or effective, and certainly independence would not have been on the agenda.

In July 1942, the commander-in-chief of the United States Navy, Admiral (later Fleet Admiral) Ernest King, visited London. He recalled an audience with His Majesty King George VI, who met him in the uniform of an admiral of the fleet, and offered him whisky or tea; the two then had a comfortable chat about naval matters. King's biography recalls:

> None of this comfortable atmosphere prevailed when General de Gaulle called at Claridges to pay his respects to King and Marshall (General George Marshall, US Army C-in-C) . . . De Gaulle, feeling himself to be the head of a state, seemingly considered that *he* should be called upon, rather than call, but as it had been pointed out that he had two stars (major general), while Marshall and King had four, he presented himself at Claridges, although with rather ill grace. He appeared at the proper time with a single aide, but conducted himself very stiffly, and after delivering himself of a long speech in French, in which he asked for many things that we needed ourselves at that moment, took his departure. It was scarcely a call calcu-lated to make friends![3]

Nor were relationships within the Free French always entirely harmonious. De Gaulle had objected to the armistice agreed by General Georges Catroux in Syria, and he followed this by having problems with the commander of the Free French naval forces, Vice-Admiral Emile Musilier.

Musilier has generally been credited with proposing that the Cross of Lorraine be the symbol for the Free French. De Gaulle later tried to change the name of the organization to the 'Fighting French' in mid-1942, but the name never became widely or publicly accepted.

De Gaulle and Musilier had an unhappy relationship, but this did not prevent de Gaulle coming to his aid when, in January 1941, Musilier was arrested by the British on charges of conspiring with the Vichy regime. Musilier was released following de Gaulle's intervention. Despite this, in September of the same year, Musilier attempted to displace de Gaulle as leader of the Free French, a move that had the support of a number of British officials and which was almost certainly known to Churchill. De Gaulle managed to survive this attempt on his position, eventually regaining Churchill's support, despite the 'independence' of the Free French. The idea of independence seemed to be contagious, as in March 1942, Musilier struck once again, attempting to remove the Free French fleet from de Gaulle's overall command, and in this he had the support of the British Admiralty. De Gaulle protested furiously, refused to accept the loss of the fleet, and once again the British gave way. After this, there was no position for Musilier amongst the Free French, although he returned to favour after the Allied landings in North Africa, being given a senior command in the liberated territories.

Meanwhile, from November 1941, the United States extended the Lend-Lease programme to include the Free French forces. This not only opened up vast new possibilities in terms of equipment, it also eased the pressure on the United Kingdom of being the sole provider. The move was one of necessity, as de Gaulle distrusted the Americans for maintaining a good relationship with the Vichy regime, as well as suspecting them of wishing to use the French Caribbean territories, and President Roosevelt returned the compliment, taking a deep personal dislike to de Gaulle, and refusing to accept him as the sole representative of France.

The following month, Musilier, with de Gaulle's support, occupied the French colony of St Pierre et Miquelon, close to Newfoundland, on 24 December 1941, giving the Free French the Christmas present of another Vichy territory and France's oldest colony. This marked another major problem in the relationship with the United States as de Gaulle had promised not to invade the islands, and then had promptly ordered Musilier to lead a small naval task force to take them. The problem arose because the still neutral United States had entered into an agreement with the Vichy regime, which the US wished to discourage from allying itself with the Germans, which committed the Americans to maintaining the status quo for all French possessions in the Americas. Despite this, a radio station in the colony had been causing concern to the British and the Canadians, who were anxious to protect the Atlantic convoys from the growing menace posed by German U-boats. Ideally, the Canadian government should have intervened, as the islands dominated the sea lanes used by convoys coming from Halifax, Nova Scotia, but the Canadians had difficulty in acting for fear of antagonizing their French Canadian population, many of whom had links with Vichy. This single act so incensed the United States that initially the US government threatened to invade the islands and oust the Free French, but in the end settled for the islands being demilitarized and declared as neutral territory.

FREE FRENCH SUCCESSES

Ideally, de Gaulle wanted some form of power base in France itself. This was difficult to achieve at first, although a few agents were inserted. Resistance groups appeared spontaneously throughout France, and especially in the occupied zone, but at first there was little linking of the groups and no established link with de Gaulle's forces in the UK or Africa. It was not until 1942 that the resistance groups started to become a national movement and established links with British intelligence and with de Gaulle's Free French. To encourage the resistance and gain their support, de Gaulle committed himself to democracy once France was liberated and, in an attempt to appeal across the political spectrum, also affirmed his support for a welfare state in postwar France. This was a practical concession, not only because it gave de Gaulle a broad power base and enabled him to portray himself as a national leader and not simply the leader of a group of émigré Frenchmen, but also because it avoided the infighting between different factions that so plagued the resistance movements in some other countries, notably Yugoslavia.

The Free French also continued to enjoy military success and gain credibility as an effective fighting force. In late May and early June 1942, Major-General (later Lieutenant-General) Marie-Pierre Koenig's 1st Free French brigade of 3,600 men successfully defended Bir Hakeim, an oasis and fortress in the

Libyan desert, helping to hold the British Gazala Line against Rommel's *Afrika Korps* with the support of the Desert Air Force, until ordered to withdraw during the night of 10/11 June. Three-quarters of those involved survived the fighting and avoided becoming prisoners of war to make a successful withdrawal.

Nevertheless, such progress, while appreciated by the other Allies, was threatened time and again by de Gaulle's determination to be the supreme and sole arbiter of what was and was not acceptable in the French empire. In this, he ignored what might be described today as the *realpolitik* of fighting a war. He overlooked the fact that since Vichy had not actively sought to engage British and American forces, and that since there was considerable sympathy for the predicament of many in the Vichy territories, there was a tendency to seek an accommodation as the war advanced.

To British and American commanders, risking the lives of their personnel in fighting the troops of a former ally seemed to be a waste, especially if concessions could not only avoid bloodshed, but also switch former Vichy troops and equipment to the Allied cause. It was also the case that taking over a colony with its administration and policing intact meant that order was maintained without a further drain on Allied resources, a lesson that the Germans understood to some extent in their conquests but which was forgotten by the British and Americans in their invasion of Iraq in 2003. In this sense, de Gaulle was unforgiving and unyielding, taking the view that those who had not followed him were against him, and that he was against them for all time.

DE GAULLE VERSUS GIRAUD

These considerations meant that Operation Torch, the Allied invasion of North Africa, in November 1942, was the cause of yet more tension rather than the start of a major advance in Allied fortunes from the acquisition of strategically important territory and the conversion of Vichy forces to the Allied cause. The root cause was the decision by the British and the Americans to treat with Admiral Darlan, who happened to be in Algiers at the time. As commander-in-chief of the French armed forces and Pétain's Minister of Marine, Darlan was one the most senior members of the Vichy administration. He was known to have collaborated with the Germans, yet always insisted that he would scuttle the French fleet rather than allow it to fall into German or Italian hands. The Allies did not consult the Free French or even inform them of their plans in North Africa. This may have been high handed and thoughtless, but de Gaulle had shown a tendency to allow plans to slip out through his desire to broadcast; and on other matters, the Free French in London had shown themselves prone to unfortunate leaks or to penetration by Vichy agents – either way, it made no difference.

On the other hand, the deal to allow Darlan to become high commissioner in French North Africa held out the possibility of a rapprochement between the Allies and Vichy, one that could mean that after liberation it would be the Vichy regime rather than that of the Free French that would prevail. This was the fear that influenced Free French attitudes.

In the end, the Darlan issue was resolved by his assassination on Christmas Eve, 1942, something which so suited the Free French that many immediately suspected that they were implicated. If they were implicated, the outcome was still not to their satisfaction, as the Allies turned next to General Henri-Honore Giraud, a senior army officer who once again had strong links with the Vichy regime.

Giraud had commanded the Seventh French Army at the start of the war, and then the merged Seventh and Ninth French Armies during the Battle of France. He was captured and imprisoned by the Germans, but managed to escape from Germany, the most senior officer of any side in the war who managed to do so, and ended up in Vichy France, where he was treated as a hero, but is generally believed to have been viewed as an assassination target by the Gestapo. He next appeared in Gibraltar, and was flown to the UK, where he was welcomed by the Allies as a counterbalance to de Gaulle. They also saw him as a possible leader of the French troops in North Africa if, after the invasion, these could be turned from Vichy to the Free French.

Not content with simply having the Americans want him to command all French forces in North Africa, at first Giraud's agreement was conditional on not having any involvement with the British or the Free French, which was unrealistic. When his conditions were rejected, he initially refused to cooperate, and when he eventually decided to do so, he found that French senior officers refused to obey him. Completely unabashed by this setback, he raised a fresh volunteer army to fight alongside the Allies, and when Darlan was assassinated, Giraud replaced him as high commissioner in North Africa, whilst retaining his own position as commander-in-chief of French forces in North Africa.

As can be seen, Giraud and de Gaulle were rivals with an intense dislike of one another, but the other Allies needed them to work together. At the insistence of Churchill and Roosevelt during the Casablanca Conference of January 1943, the two eventually had to bury their differences and after prolonged negotiations, agree to becoming joint chairmen of the French Committee for National Liberation, CFLN, which was set up in Algiers the following 3 June. Cooperation between the two men had not been without some behind-the-scenes arm-twisting, as became clear in the American Admiral King's biography.

In the course of the Casablanca Conference, General de Gaulle, who was in London, had been invited by the (British) Prime Minister to come to North Africa. De Gaulle had been offended that he had not been invited further in advance, and in one way or another proved to be his usual difficult self. Mr Eden, the Foreign Secretary, had to exert great pressure to induce him to leave London for Casablanca. When he arrived there the firmest treatment by Mr Churchill was required to persuade him to call upon Giraud. Finally, in the interests of at least good public feeling a "shot-gun marriage" was arranged. At a press conference on 24 January, de Gaulle and Giraud were made to sit in a row of chairs alternating with Mr Roosevelt and Mr Churchill, and to be photographed shaking hands. As the newsreel cameras finished their work, each French general dropped the other's hand as though it were red hot.[4]

This was barely a show of cooperation. Indeed, with the media present, it risked rumours of discord amongst the Free French. Initially, the British and Americans had wanted de Gaulle to be subordinate to Giraud, but the former held his ground stubbornly, and in the end what seemed to be equal status was accorded both. Despite this, it was an unequal partnership as the politically aware de Gaulle was soon running circles around the politically inept Giraud, and it simply took from June to November 1943 for de Gaulle to gain complete control of the committee, with Giraud off it entirely. In April 1944, his position of commander-in-chief was scrapped, and while he was offered the role of inspector-general, he refused and instead resigned, fading into obscurity.

De Gaulle's dominance of the CFLN was all the more impressive since during the first few months of the committee's existence, Roosevelt had manoeuvred to have de Gaulle removed.

Most of 1943 and 1944 were concerned with transforming the Free French from a largely émigré organisation to the new government of France. The leadership of de Gaulle, who had moved his headquarters to Algiers, both because it was French territory and to emphasise his independence, was the first step in the process. The other stage that overlapped with this was the vexed question of merging the Free French forces with those of Vichy in North Africa, bearing in mind that the Free French were, after all, officially still *franc-tireurs*. In short, each group saw the other side as traitors. Even at this stage, with the Normandy landings the best part of a year away, there were disputes with the British and Americans over the way in which liberated France would be governed, and, finally, but obviously connected with this, the need for de Gaulle to be able to assert his authority over the resistance groups, and especially those run by the Communists. While France was not on Stalin's list of territories where the Soviet Union would be the dominant power, pre-war French governments had been well to the left of centre.

The issue of merging the two armies saw de Gaulle being uncharacteristically prepared to compromise. His own forces numbered around 50,000, while those of Vichy in North Africa, as opposed to the 100,000 men permitted in Vichy France's *zone libre*, totalled some 230,000. The Free French had fought alongside the British Eighth Army and had shared some of its battle honours, and were known as *hadjis*, or pilgrims, while the Vichy troops were known as *moustachis*, a reference to the moustaches of most French regular troops. The Free French had had an active war, while the Vichy troops had been largely idle on garrison duties, and because of this, some commentators have suggested that the Free French provided the spirit and the Vichy troops the numbers, but the latter also had an outstanding regular officer, General Alphonse Juin, although, it would seem almost inevitably, Juin's own position was viewed by many Frenchmen as compromised.

Juin's problem was that he had been loyal to the Vichy regime, and had even gone beyond simple loyalty by joining Jacques Benoist-Mechin's mission to meet Goering.

Juin and de Gaulle had been contemporaries at the French military academy at St Cyr, and were promoted through the officer ranks at about the same pace, so that in 1940, both were brigadier-generals. In command of the 15th Motorized Infantry Division, Juin commanded the desperate defence of Lille during the Battle of France, helping to make the evacuation of Dunkirk possible by delaying the German armies. Taken prisoner, the Germans nevertheless were persuaded to release him in June 1941, and he was sent to join General Weygand in North Africa, where he was promoted to major-general and put in command of the army in French Morocco. Further promotion to lieutenant-general followed as early as November 1941, when he was given command of all French army units in North Africa following Weygand's departure for France.

After the Allied landings in North Africa and the cease-fire that followed quickly, Juin's forces were handed over to the Allies, and fought a successful action in Tunisia against the Germans during late 1942, eventually becoming the 19th French Corps. The action against the Germans brought from de Gaulle an all too rare warm letter of congratulations. Juin was then promoted to full general (that is four star rank), and while continuing to have responsibilities for his troops in North Africa, his main priority became the formation of the French Expeditionary Corps, FEC, with which he moved to Italy in November 1943. Strangely, whilst in command of the FEC, he requested to be demoted to lieutenant-general, but was promoted again later after the Normandy landings to become chief of staff for the French National Defence, and in 1952, was given the honour of being promoted Marshal of France.

Meanwhile, another Vichy officer, Lieutenant-General Jean-Marie de Lattre de Tassigny, who had been imprisoned by the Vichy authorities for resisting the German occupation of the *zone libre*, had managed to escape from prison at his fourth attempt and make his way to the United Kingdom with help from the British Special Operations Executive, SOE, and joined de Gaulle. In December 1943, he was flown to North Africa and took command of what eventually became *Armée B*, and later his forces saw action first in Italy and then during the landings in the South of France.

The invasion of North Africa meant that the Free French forces were now substantial, with the army alone around a third of a million strong.

DE GAULLE'S PRIORITIES

Amidst the continuation of the war, de Gaulle had another priority, which was to secure the government of France following liberation. This led to the formation of a consultative assembly in November 1943, which effectively acted as a parliament in exile. The next step was to create *Commissaires de la Republique*, who would replace the prefects as areas were liberated. This was not a step towards parliamentary democracy, however, as de Gaulle was emphatic that their role was to 'represent the government to the people, and not the people to the government.' There would be no sharing of power with the resistance groups, which were to be disbanded. It was also made clear to the consultative assembly in a speech by de Gaulle on 27 March 1944, that the French Committee for National Liberation would act as the provisional government of the liberated areas of the country, which the CFLN itself authorized in an ordinance published on 3 June 1944, just three days before the Normandy landings.

Despite these moves by de Gaulle, who had failed to let the British and Americans know the full scope of his proposals, even though British, American and Canadian troops would bear the brunt of the Normandy landings, the question of how France would be run had not been resolved on 6 June. The British basically favoured the idea, but Roosevelt opposed it, possibly because it was undemocratic, but his distrust of de Gaulle may have been the main reason. There was also the question of the attitude of the resistance groups. Basically, the Allies wanted to use military government for the immediate administration of areas after they had been liberated, but in the end, practicalities prevailed and the CFLN was left to follow its plans. The first *Commissaire de la Republique* was formally installed in Normandy at Bayeux on 14 June by de Gaulle personally, who also enjoyed a warm welcome by the crowds.

The return to his own country did nothing to improve de Gaulle's attitude, as was again noted in Admiral King's biography.

Prior to the landings de Gaulle had made it clear that he wished to be definitely recognized as the ruler of France, and claimed that he alone had the right to give orders to the people of France. Once the landings had taken place these difficulties did not diminish, and the Joint Chiefs during their stay in England had a taste of these complications when de Gaulle undertook to change the regulations about the use of United States currency in France by American troops. The joint chiefs sent for General Koenig, who, as the commander of the French forces of the interior, was serving as a direct subordinate of Eisenhower's in the Allied organization, and asked him what the difficulty was. It appeared that Koenig could not see de Gaulle's point either. As Eisenhower was troubled about the correct manner of managing civilian affairs in France until a proper organization could be set up, he asked the Joint Chiefs what to do, and they proposed that he at once send a message to the President, suggesting that if de Gaulle would not cooperate properly, another Frenchman be designated to manage French civilian affairs, and de Gaulle be ignored, entirely. The Joint Chiefs did not stay to hear the answer from the President, but later that evening they received word that he had concurred.[5]

The CFLN enjoyed all of the success that de Gaulle had hoped for, with the resistance groups generally accepting its authority. Even Roosevelt had to agree that the CFLN was the accepted government of liberated areas of France, and when de Gaulle visited Washington in July, he received a warm reception. Official recognition of the CFLN's role did not follow from the United States until 23 October, and shortly afterwards the United Kingdom also recognized it. No doubt more important for de Gaulle was the liberation of Paris on 26 August 1944, which the other Allies left to French troops. After his rapturous welcome by the citizens of Paris, de Gaulle served as the president of France until January 1946, and, of course, again from 1958 to 1969. His first term of office was consequent upon the war, occupation and liberation, but his second term paradoxically was caused by civil war in Algeria and the need to take firm decisions to grant independence despite violent opposition from French settlers.

De Gaulle may have been anathema to both Churchill and Roosevelt, but he ensured that France continued in the war even after defeat, surrender and occupation. He provided a focus for those Frenchmen opposed to the Vichy regime, and looked ahead to the day of liberation, laying plans that in the end served the country well and relieved the other allies of what could have been a troublesome task and a distraction from the main aim, that of defeating the Axis powers.

Notes
1 and 2   Imperial War Museum, Accession No 19940.
3, 4 and 5 *Fleet Admiral King*, King, Fleet Admiral Ernest J., USN, and Whitehill, Walter Muir, Eyre & Spottiswoode, London, 1953

CHAPTER THIRTEEN

Madagascar

T he collapse of France and Italy's intervention in the Second World War had changed the situation in the Mediterranean, which was soon in danger of fulfilling Mussolini's boast and becoming *Mare Nostrum*, 'Our Sea'. The change didn't happen overnight. Indeed, during late 1940, not only did the convoys to Malta and Alexandria continue to get through, but just before Christmas, the commander-in-chief of the Mediterranean Fleet, Admiral Sir Andrew 'ABC' Cunningham, felt so confident that he took his flagship, the modernized Jutland battleship HMS *Warspite*, into the Grand Harbour in Malta.

It could even be argued that in late 1940, this was one theatre of war in which the British were winning. The Italian fleet had three of its six battleships put out of action in the Fleet Air Arm's daring attack on Taranto, which had also seen other ships damaged and a seaplane base and oil storage depot destroyed. The British Army was holding its own in North Africa.

Certainly, the reversal of fortunes in the Mediterranean did not occur overnight. Had Italy entered the war and immediately sent her battle fleet and air force to pound Malta into submission, which is what the Germans had expected, the entire war could have taken a different turn. It would also have been less likely that German forces would have had to become involved in the Balkans, delaying the start of Operation Barbarossa, the invasion of the Soviet Union, so that German forces would not have been overtaken on the Russian steppes by winter, for which they were ill-prepared. On the other hand, even if everything had gone to plan in the Soviet Union, when the autumn rains and then the harsh cold of the winter forced the Germans to stop their advance on Moscow, they had already outrun and over-extended their logistics chain. This was a penalty of being heavily dependent upon horses for their transport, and while the retreating Soviet forces had sabotaged the railway system, it was also the case that the Russian railways operated on a broader gauge from those in most of Western Europe.

Logistics and concentration of force were indeed what this stage of the war was to be about. First, the German dismay and even anger that the Italians had half of their six battleships, a force three times in number of that of the German navy, put out of action in a single night, meant that a crack Luftwaffe unit, *Fliegerkorps X*, with considerable anti-shipping experience, was sent to Sicily, just eighty miles from Malta. Second, the splitting of the British forces in North Africa to aid Greece, meant that not only was first Greece and then Crete lost to the Allies, but fortunes were completely reversed in North Africa. With Vichy territory to the west in Morocco, Algeria and Tunisia, the Axis powers in Libya and then able to invade Egypt, and German and Italian forces in Italy, Yugoslavia, Albania and Greece, the Mediterranean soon became impassable for Allied shipping.

Instead of the Mediterranean and the Suez Canal remaining the short cut between the United Kingdom and the Middle East, India and Australia, the Mediterranean was closed and the Suez Canal became the back door into Egypt. The long haul from the British Isles, across the Bay of Biscay within reach of German U-boats and aircraft based on occupied France, and then down into the South Atlantic, round the Cape of Good Hope and into the Indian Ocean, then northwards through the Red Sea and into the Suez Canal, is generally estimated, with the diversion for shipping on the other routes that had used the canal, to have required the Allies to provide an extra million tons of merchant shipping. The vulnerability of the convoys in the Bay of Biscay was the most obvious weakness of this extended route, but it was not the only one. The French island colony of Madagascar was strategically placed to cut this lifeline, and indeed, offered whoever occupied it the possibility of domination of the Indian Ocean, or at least the western half of it.

MAGIC AND MADAGASCAR

A tropical island off the coast of Mozambique in what was then Portuguese East Africa, Madagascar is more than a thousand miles, 1,610 km, long, and had been a French protectorate since 1886, although it had been colonized by Africans some 2,000 years earlier, and then by Arabs in the twelfth century.

In the desperate fighting of the Battle of France, some 34,000 Malagasy soldiers had been dispatched to France, which had been quick to gather in the manpower resources of its empire to save the country from the German threat. When France surrendered, the island's governor initially supported General Charles de Gaulle and the emerging Free French forces, continuing the fight against the Axis powers. The attacks on the French fleet at Mers-el-Kebir and Oran, and then at Dakar, in July 1940, transformed the situation immediately. The governor resigned and was replaced by a representative of the Vichy regime.

The Vichy armed forces actually based in Madagascar were relatively small and in themselves posed no major threat to the Allied convoys. This changed in 1942. While much has been written about the United Kingdom's 'Ultra' intelligence which decoded German communications from early in the war, less has been written about 'Magic', which originated as a codeword for deciphered Japanese diplomatic communications and was later used to describe all Japanese military communications during the Second World War. One reason for Magic's relative obscurity was that the name was eventually confined to diplomatic messages only and all of the deciphered Japanese military messages were classified 'Top Secret Ultra', which did at least confuse the Allies if not the enemy!

Madagascar was far enough away to be difficult for German and Italian forces to use as a base. The Italians would have had to run the gauntlet of the Straits of Gibraltar, the Germans would also have been at risk of attack from Gibraltar and the British Force H, even if they managed to use French bases and avoid either the English Channel or the run north of Scotland and then west of Ireland. Both nations would then have had the problem of forces based in British colonies in West Africa, and then finally South Africa itself, whose armed forces grew increasingly strong during the war years and whose bases were much used by major British warships. Perhaps more telling even than all of these problems for the Axis, was that they were increasingly short of fuel with which to support and maintain substantial surface fleets.

Nevertheless, Germany and Italy did have an ally in Japan. The Japanese connection might, perhaps, be in danger of being over-stated. There was in fact very little cooperation between the European end of the Axis and that of Japan. The Japanese did not benefit from German technical advances to any great extent, while the Germans did not benefit greatly from Japanese involvement in the war. In fact, the tripartite Axis alliance had got off to a difficult start as Germany had invaded Poland with a secret non-aggression treaty with the Soviet Union in place, while Japan and the USSR were at loggerheads over Manchuria. From the time the Soviet Union and Germany were at war, the Axis powers were just six months from war with the United States. By one of those contradictions that saw Germany first viewing the Soviet Union as a major enemy, then becoming if not quite an ally, at least a co-conspirator in the suppression of Poland, Japan also moved from antagonism with the USSR to a neutrality pact, signed in Moscow on 13 April 1941, just a little over two months before the launch of Operation Barbarossa. Even without such a pact, Japan did not have the resources to mount an attack on Siberia that might have eased the pressure on the German forces stuck outside Moscow and Stalingrad as she prepared herself for the attack on Pearl Harbor and her massive strike westwards into the Malay Peninsula and then the Netherlands East Indies. While Germany had followed its treaty obligation to Japan by declaring war on the United States in December 1941, this really was a case of admitting the inevitable, as German politicians and military strategists were convinced that war with the United States was a question of 'when' rather than 'if'.

If indeed Japan enjoyed some advantage from the relationship with Germany and Italy, it came from the fact that, despite her attack on the US Pacific Fleet at Pearl Harbor, priority was accorded by the Anglo-American alliance to the war against Germany. The massive effort by the Allies to supply the Soviet Union, even at the expense of supplying and equipping other theatres of war, including notably Malaya and Singapore, also helped Japan, while the USSR delayed declaring war on Japan until August 1945.

Nevertheless, the one thing that Germany could see Japan doing for the war in Europe was the conquest of Madagascar. The Germans started to press Japan to invade the island early in 1942, and by March this much had been picked up by the American Magic intelligence deciphers of Axis communications.

Taking Madagascar would have stretched Japanese forces to the limit, and indeed, in all probability, far beyond it. The rapid expansion of the Japanese empire between December 1941 and spring 1942 was in itself an astonishing achievement, with the distance between Singapore and Tokyo being similar to that between New York and Southampton. Ceylon, now Sri Lanka, was attacked between 5 and 9 April 1942, but this was the furthest west that Japanese forces got. It could be that the island's proximity to India meant that the Japanese felt that it would be a burden on their own stretched resources, while they had already been fought to a standstill on the border between Burma and India. On the other hand, Madagascar was more than 3,000 miles from the nearest Japanese-occupied territory in Sumatra, itself still further from Tokyo than Singapore.

In short, Germany was asking too much, and being

completely unrealistic about the Japanese strategic situation, ignoring the fact that Tokyo was suffering from the same shortages of trained manpower, industrial capacity, fuel, food and raw materials that themselves were already apparent in the German war effort, even at this early stage. The Japanese had struck west into the British and Dutch colonies with the same sense of desperation that had also driven the German attack on the Soviet Union and the quest for the agricultural output of the Ukraine and the oil of the Caucasus. Madagascar was within easy reach of British bases in East Africa, and the excellent port facilities and air stations of South Africa.

The Allies were not fully aware of the growing predicament of the Axis powers, although they did have some indication, but in early 1942, Japan and Germany had both acquired the reputation of being unstoppable. Any Japanese attempt to invade Madagascar had to be forestalled. What followed was the first British amphibious operation of the war.

In the demanding terms of Second World War invasions, the Madagascar affair was relatively small, and preparation was extraordinary quick.   The British chiefs of staff decided to invade the island and as a first step seize the naval base of Diego Suarez at the very north of the island. Major General Robert Sturges took two army brigade groups and No5 Commando, while a naval task force was commanded by Rear Admiral Neville Syfret, who had the benefit of Fleet Air Arm support from two of the Royal Navy's most modern aircraft carriers, *Indomitable* and *Illustrious*, with the latter back from her extensive repairs in the United States following her sufferings off Malta in early January 1941. Syfret flew his flag in the elderly battleship *Ramillies*, and was supported by two cruisers and eleven destroyers. This was not a force that could have survived fierce and well-armed resistance.

On 5 May, before dawn, the first troops went ashore, and with the defenders taken completely by surprise, met little resistance at first, although counter-attacks followed later in the day. The crew of a German ship, the *Warenfels*, attempted to scuttle the vessel, although without success as she was being refitted in the dry dock at the time, and the ship was salvaged and repaired by the Allies, An attack during the night of 6/7 May, with a diversionary raid on nearby Antsirane, on the opposite side of the bay from Diego Suarez, proved successful, but it was not until 8 May that the invasion force was securely established ashore with the French defenders at Diego Suarez and Antsirane having surrendered late on 7 May. Nevertheless, the Vichy governor refused to surrender and retreated with the forces left to him towards the south of the island.

The only counter-attack of any importance came much later, on 30 May, when a Japanese midget submarine struck at *Ramillies*, while she was in the harbour at Diego Suarez. This, and an unsuccessful attack on Allied warships in Sydney Harbour, on 31 May, were the two furthest flung ventures by the Japanese midget submarine force.

While the Allies had originally only planned to capture Diego Suarez and the surrounding area, the prime minister of South Africa, General Smuts, insisted that the other ports be captured as well, and further landings were made on the west coast of Madagascar at Majunga and, further south, at Morondava, on 10 September, and these were followed by landings at Tamatave on 18 September, and at Tulear and Fort Dauphin, in the south, on 29 September. These further landings used South African and East African troops. It was not until 5 November that an armistice was arranged between the Allies and the Vichy governor, largely because neither side had compelling superiority of forces, although the Allies did at least have supplies, and afterwards the island was handed to control by the Free French. The first high commissioner was General Paul Legentilhomme, but in May 1943, he handed over to a civilian governor-general.

In taking the island, the Allies not only removed a potential threat to their supply lines, they also gained air bases, albeit relatively primitive ones, and ports with dockyard facilities.

CHAPTER FOURTEEN

Syria

U nlike Madagascar, French Morocco, Algeria or Tunisia, Syria had not been colonized by the French during the period of European colonial expansion, but had instead been part of the Ottoman Empire, and with its collapse, became a French protectorate in 1920 under a League of Nations mandate after being occupied by British and French troops in 1918. A similar position arose with adjoining Lebanon, except that this country became independent in 1941. The British gained neighbouring Palestine also under a League of Nations Mandate from the Ottoman empire.

After the fall of France in June 1940, and in contrast to Madagascar, Lebanon and Syria's French administrators immediately aligned themselves with the Vichy regime, Later that year, in December, General Henri-Fernand Dentz became the Vichy High Commissioner in Syria. Dentz had previously been military governor of Paris. Like Madagascar, Syria was strategically placed to be at least of nuisance value to the Allies, and in fact the Germans were allowed by Dentz, on instructions from Vichy, to make use of Syrian airfields in May 1941, when they sent aircraft to support Rashid Ali's revolt against British forces in Iraq.

Given such cooperation between the Vichy forces in Syria and the Axis, the British were concerned that Syria could be used as a base for an offensive against the Suez Canal. This would have meant British forces fighting on two fronts, in the Western Desert and in Palestine or Egypt, apart from the obvious threat to their operations in Iraq, and later what is now Iran. The British could only react to such a provocative move, and on 8 June 1941, British, Australian, Indian and Free French troops invaded Syria, supported by aircraft based in Cyprus and Palestine. The overall force was commanded by Lieutenant-General Maitland Wilson, with General Paul Legentilhomme in command of the Free French contingent, which included a number of French Foreign Legion troops.

'The disastrous effect of the German control of Syria was obvious,' according to Cunningham. 'It would open the Nazi way to the south-east and isolate Turkey, making the Turks more responsive to German pressure. The threat to the Haifa fuel-oil supplies and even to Egypt would be dangerous.'[1]

In fact, while Ultra intelligence had clearly indicated that Vichy was cooperating over Iraq, German interest in using the country for an assault on the Suez Canal zone was considerably exaggerated. Nevertheless, after the Allied invasion, the Germans did allow their aircraft based in Greece and the Dodecanese islands to mount sorties in support of the Vichy forces, and Hitler himself allowed Vichy to send troops to re-inforce Dentz, mainly drawn from the substantial forces still available to Vichy in North Africa.

Planning the invasion fell to General Sir Archibald Wavell, but the forces that he could assemble were much smaller than those available to the defence.

The British and Free French expected little opposition to their invasion, and coupled this with a promise to grant inde-pendence to both Syria and the Lebanon. Dentz, however, showed no interest in a cease-fire, but instead, aware of the deli-cate relationship between the Vichy regime and Nazi Germany, was anxious to show that the Germans could count on his loyalty and steadfastness.

Dentz's resources included a mixed force of around 45,000 French colonial troops and locally raised forces, as well as four battalions of the French Foreign Legion, which effectively found its men fighting on both sides. While the French Foreign Legion was officered by French nationals, its other ranks were drawn from across much of the world, and especially Europe.

For the invasion, the Royal Navy was asked to provide support from the sea, but being under considerable pressure in the Mediterranean, it could provide nothing heavier than light cruisers, sending HMS *Ajax*, one of the victors of the Battle of the River Plate, and *Phoebe*, with an escort of four destroyers, *Jackal*, *Janus*, *Kandahar* and *Kimberley*, under the command of Vice-Admiral E. L. S. King, who had his headquarters at Haifa in Palestine, now Israel.

Fighter cover for the force was equally problematic. The Fleet Air Arm deployed Fairey Fulmars forward to Palestine, but the two-seat Fulmar was no match for a contemporary single-seat fighter. The aircraft had the same Rolls-Royce Merlin engine that powered the Supermarine Spitfire and Hawker Hurricane, but with the additional weight of the Fulmar, performance was not comparable with these aircraft. Naval strike aircraft were also deployed to Cyprus. Cunningham professed himself disappointed that the Fleet Air Arm Fulmars were no match for the French shore-based fighters, and shocked when on 9 June, three Fulmars were shot down and two more badly damaged. He supposed that the Fulmars were inferior because they were designed to operate from aircraft carriers, a notion held by many British naval officers at this stage of the war who found it hard to believe that high performance aircraft could operate from aircraft carriers, despite American and Japanese experience that showed that they could.

Some minor elements of the French fleet were also based in the area, in the harbour at Beirut. The ships included two 'flotilla leaders'* in Cunningham's words, in fact the Bison class *contre-*

---

* Cunningham's assumption that the larger 'super destroyers' or *contre-torpilleurs*, were flotilla leaders doubtless came from the British practice at the time of building two sizes of destroyer in most classes, with the larger ships being the flotilla leaders as the captain of the flotilla would have a small staff

torpilleurs Guepard and *Valmy*, a sloop, three submarines and a patrol vessel. The problem for Cunningham was whether the attack on Syria would affect the attitudes of the French force still in harbour at Alexandria, but Godfroy assured him that their agreement would be honoured. There was no way of knowing how the French naval commander at Beirut would respond.

The Royal Navy also provided transport for special forces personnel embarked at Port Said to Syria on the night of 7/8 June, with the idea that they would be deployed ashore to take and hold a bridge.

Fierce fighting ensued, with Dentz managing to create an effective force from his disparate troops, and major battles at the River Litani, and again at Kissoue, where inevitably, Frenchman fought Frenchman. On 19 June, a British battalion and two Indian battalions were cut off and then surrounded at Mezze, and forced to surrender. Free French and Australian troops finally entered Damascus on 21 July, with the French Foreign Legion units of both sides fighting each other in the streets. Damascus fell the following day, and the Allies were then reinforced by HABFORCE, a hastily-raised mixed force of British troops accompanied by units of the British-officered Arab Legion, which advanced from Iraq into Syria. The next objective was Palmyra, which was attacked by HABFORCE and the original British Empire and Free French force on 26 June, and which proved extremely difficult to take, with fierce fighting while the largely French Foreign Legion garrison managed to hold on for nine days. Meanwhile, in the only action fought at sea by the Vichy French, a French flotilla was defeated.

At sea, the doubts about the Vichy fleet were soon vindicated. On 9 June, *Phoebe* narrowly escaped being torpedoed by one of the French submarines. After the two British cruisers withdrew to Haifa to refuel, the two French *contre-torpilleurs* left port and

---

of his own over and above the ship's company, including such posts as the flotilla torpedo officer, torpedo gunnery officer, etc. In some cases, the extra personnel were accommodated by omitting one of the aft gun turrets, but generally, a leader was a slightly larger vessel.

attacked the *Janus*, which was on her own off Sidon. The French ships were almost light cruisers, although classified as 'super destroyers', and when a salvo of three shells struck the British ship, she was dead in the water with her bridge destroyed, her boiler-room out of action and the fire control system inoperative. Two more shells exploded in her as she lay stopped, and the other three British destroyers only just managed to arrive in time to drive off the French ships, which retired at full speed.

Retaliation came on 13 June, when Fairey Swordfish from Cyprus torpedoed a French merchantman in the harbour at Juneh, eight miles north of Beirut. Nevertheless, the small British naval force continued to suffer casualties, with the *Isis* and *Ilex* bombed and badly damaged while providing fire support for British army units ashore. When the Vichy French attempted to run arms into Syria, on 16 June, the Fleet Air Arm again sent Swordfish from Cyprus, sinking the French *contre-torpilleur Chevalier Paul* while she was between the island and the Syrian coast. Six days later, the *Vauquelin*, another *contre-torpilleur* was bombed and damaged during an aerial attack on the harbour at Beirut. The following day, 23 June, the *Guepard* put to sea and after dark engaged the two British cruisers in an indecisive action which nevertheless saw her damaged by a British 6-in shell. On 25 June, the Vichy submarine *Souffleur* was sunk by the destroyer *Parthian* while off Beirut. Then on 4 July, the Fleet Air Arm sank another merchantman off the Turkish coast.

It was clear that neither side had the overwhelming force necessary to force a conclusion, but this changed when General Sir William Slim also entered Syria by way of Iraq with his 10th Indian Division, enabling the Allies to isolate Dentz's forces, which were by this time falling back on Beirut, the Lebanese capital. The Royal Navy also found another two cruisers to double the number operating off the coasts of Syria and the Lebanon. It was not until 10 July, with Australian troops just five miles from Beirut, that Dentz sought an armistice, but it took four days of hard negotiating before this document, known as the Acre Convention, could be signed by the British and the

Vichy commanders, but the Free French steadfastly refused to be a party to the agreement.

The Free French objections to the Acre Convention were largely based on its generosity to the Vichy troops, who had fought well and were spared becoming prisoners of war. The Free French stance infuriated General de Gaulle, who 'became rather wild about it, and at one time wished to denounce the armistice' according to Cunningham, but in the recriminations and bargaining that followed, he was allowed to seek recruits for his forces from those of Vichy in Syria and the Lebanon, and eventually 6,000 joined him, although the majority of those who were left sought repatriation to France. Also able to return home were those Allied prisoners-of-war held in Syria.

Less fortunate than the forces he had commanded so ably was General Dentz. He was blamed for a number of infringements of the armistice, and interned briefly. When the war ended, he was condemned to death by a French military court that had found him guilty of high treason, but as with many others in a similar position, his sentence was commuted to life imprisonment, although he died before the end of the year.

While Lebanon received its independence after the Allied intervention, that of Syria did not follow until 1946.

Notes
1 *A Sailor's Odyssey*, Admiral (later Admiral of the Fleet) Sir Andrew Cunningham, RN, Hutchinson, London, 1951

CHAPTER FIFTEEN

Operation Torch

By November 1942, the tide had begun to turn irrevocably in the Allies' favour. They moved rapidly to the offensive and before dawn on 8 November, the first landings began in North Africa, using French Morocco and Algeria. This was to be a further bone of contention with the Free French, as the landings had been kept from them and their forces were not involved initially. This was doubtless due to concerns about de Gaulle being tempted to broadcast to his fellow countrymen in advance, but it also reflected British and American concerns about the security of the Free French organisation in London, which either inadvertently or because it held Vichy agents, did let information leak out.

One Frenchman who was very much in the picture was General Henri-Honore Giraud, who arrived at Gibraltar in a British submarine and was then flown into Algiers with General Mark Clark of the United States Army on 9 November, following the Anglo-American invasion fleet planning to take command of the Vichy forces in North Africa. Another Frenchman who was closer to the action than he would have liked from the political standpoint was none other than Admiral Darlan, the Vichy Minister for Marine and commander-in-chief of the Marine Nationale, who was visiting Algeria at the time.

Naturally, the Allies hoped for minimal or no resistance from the Vichy forces, but they were wise enough to appreciate that resistance was likely, with their experiences in Madagascar and Syria still fresh in the memory.

THE VICHY FLEET

The Vichy Navy did not take an active part in the Second World War in the sense that it did not see action, but that is not to say that it remained in port. After a spell on a naval transport, Arsene Le Poittevin had been posted aboard the torpedo boat *Simoun* (the name relates to a type of wind found in Africa), which at 1,300 tons displacement was more akin to a destroyer. He spent the period between the summer of 1940 and autumn 1942 escorting convoys between Oran or Mers-el-Kebir and Casablanca, and at first occasionally got as far as Dakar.

Convoys to ports in Vichy France or the French colonies were usually allowed to pass unmolested by the Allies, and this effectively meant just the British. A few months after the unfortunate events at Oran and Mers-el-Kebir, Le Poittevin started to lobby his fellow crew members to support de Gaulle and the Free French. He even went so far as to get leaflets printed. His duties as a wireless operator meant that he was able to pick up radio transmissions from London, including those by de Gaulle and others for the people of occupied Europe. On a number of occasions, he was warned by his officers that what he was doing was wrong and very dangerous.

'We were asked to declare our allegiance to Pétain and Vichy,' Poittevin recalled. 'The officers did so and encouraged us to do the same, but I could not.

'On one occasion, as we approached Gibraltar, I had many members of the crew ready to seize the ship. There was no intention of using violence. But as we got closer, my shipmates were afraid, and refused to act.'[1]

In fact, his persistent campaigning eventually resulted in Poittevin being arrested and spending a week in a naval cell.

'On one occasion, we were escorting a convoy and British warships approached us and called for us to follow them,' he remembers. 'Now men are funny. I wanted to fight the Germans, but I didn't want to do so at the point of a gun. I was pleased when my commanding officer told me to signal back "merde" (shit), and sat in my little cabin tapping out the Morse, tap, tap, tap . . .'[2]

The problem was, he often felt, was that life was too comfortable for many of the Vichy sailors.

'We had good food, everything was provided free, including not just food and a wine ration, but uniforms as well. Not only that, our pay had quadrupled, partly because we were stationed abroad, but also because they wanted to keep the sailors with the fleet. Of course, we had nothing to spend it on, except when we went ashore to bars, the cinema, or a café.'[3]

Shortly afterwards, he was transferred to another ship and went on convoy to Dakar. When in Dakar, he was detained aboard the ship while some of his like-minded shipmates went ashore. They planned to desert and make their way overland to Gabon, so his friends took food and also some of his clothes ashore with them. But, the venture was badly conceived, with men having to make their way through tropical jungle on foot, without training in jungle craft or proper clothing and footwear, and they were caught and jailed again.

TORCH

Overall control of the invasion, code-named Operation Torch, was divided between the two Allies, with Admiral Sir Andrew Cunningham, the former commander-in-chief of the British Mediterranean Fleet and First Sea Lord, as Allied Naval Commander, but with the American General, Dwight Eisenhower, as Supreme Commander.

The invasion took place with three waves landing at different points.

The Western Task Force, TF34, had sailed direct from the

United States with twenty-three transports to land Major-General Patton's 34,000 troops to the north and south of Casablanca, on the Atlantic coast of French Morocco. The supporting naval force included three American battleships, the light aircraft carrier USS *Ranger* and four escort carriers, seven cruisers and no fewer than thirty-eight destroyers.

The area around Tangier, Spanish Morocco, had to be avoided, so the Centre Task Force landed at Oran in Algeria. This had come direct from the south of England with two escort carriers, three cruisers and thirteen destroyers, which protected twenty-eight transports and nineteen landing craft, putting ashore 39,000 men under the command of Major-General Frendall.

The Eastern Task Force included the two oldest British aircraft carriers, HMS *Furious* and *Argus*, with three cruisers and sixteen destroyers, protecting sixteen transports and seventeen landing craft which put a mixed force of 33,000 British and American troops ashore near Algiers under the command of Major-General Ryder.

No seaborne invasion has been spread over such a long stretch of coastline, especially bearing in mind the gap between the landings near Casablanca and those in the Mediterranean. Good communications were essential, and the naval commander of the Centre Task Force, Commodore Troubridge, had a signals team in the former armed merchant, or auxiliary, cruiser *Large*. The signals team used a dozen radio wave bands and more than a hundred signals specialists. All preparations had been in some haste, and later, the officer in charge of the signals section, Robert Phillimore recalled that: 'The bunk house for staff officers at the back of the bridge was so unfinished that we had to protect ourselves from the weather with umbrellas.'[4]

The landings in Algeria started at around 01.00 at Oran, and then soon afterwards at Algiers, while those on the Atlantic coast of French Morocco followed at around 04.30. At first, there was almost complete surprise. Aboard the US ships, many of the aircrew were very inexperienced, and during the passage from the United States, there had been concern about accidents and possible damage to the USS *Ranger*. Aboard one of the escort carriers, the *Santee*, there were just five experienced pilots, and during the action that followed, she lost twenty-one of her thirty-one aircraft, almost all because of accidents and just one, 'possibly', to enemy action.

ALGIERS

Because of the element of surprise, there was little opposition as the troops landed at Algiers. The landings were not easy, however, as unexpectedly strong currents made handling the unwieldy landing craft difficult and the crews had not been trained as well as would be the case on later operations. Some units were landed in the wrong places, and others became mixed up. It was fortunate that there was no serious counter-attack during the landings.

It was from the Vichy naval forces that the most determined initial resistance came. Naval personnel manned most of the shore batteries around the ports, and when two British destroyers, *Broke* and *Malcolm*, steamed into the harbour at Algiers carrying US troops with the difficult task of preventing the harbour installations from being sabotaged, and also to attempt to seize French ships before they could be scuttled, they both came under heavy fire. *Malcolm* received several hits in her boiler rooms just before she entered the port and was forced to withdraw. *Broke* made four attempts to enter, and on her fourth attempt, charged the harbour boom at high speed and 'broke through' at 05.20, managing to land the three companies of US troops aboard on a jetty, so that they could seize the port's power station and oil storage depot.

A period of relative calm seems to have followed, for it was not until about 08.00 that the French re-opened fire, with further guns coming into action so that by 09.15, the *Broke* was in a difficult situation and was forced to withdraw leaving 250 US troops behind, who were soon rounded up by the Vichy forces and became prisoners-of-war. She left not a moment too soon, being hit several times and suffering heavy damage. She was soon crippled and on leaving the port was taken in tow by another destroyer, *Zetland*, which had been bombarding coastal batteries, but the *Broke* sank the following day as the weather worsened.

The aerodrome at Maison Blanche to the east of Algiers was taken by Allied troops around 08.30, and by 10.00, RAF Hawker Hurricane fighters from Gibraltar had landed and were soon ready for operations. Inland, the Fleet Air Arm's Grumman Martlets (the Royal Navy's name for the Wildcat until names were standardized later), forced the airfield at Blida, some twenty miles from Algiers, to surrender at 08.30, and RAF Supermarine Spitfires flew in from Gibraltar shortly afterwards, even before Allied troops occupied the airfield before noon.

Despite these early successes, all of them representing significant strategic gains, French resistance stiffened as the morning wore on. The Fleet Air Arm and the guns of the fleet had to bomb and shell the shore batteries around Cape Matifu before these were taken at around 16.30. Worsening weather showed just how fortunate the invasion forces had been in their timing, with the unloading of supplies badly delayed by heavy waves crashing on to the beaches, while around forty-five landing craft were destroyed.

Amongst the Fleet Air Arm aircraft involved in the operation were twelve Supermarine Seafires operating from the veteran aircraft carrier *Furious*. Their take-off was some time before dawn, and for many of the pilots, it was their first night take-off from an aircraft carrier. Lieutenant (later Captain) George Baldwin remembered the operation well.

We thought that we had taken the French air force by surprise as we caught their bombers on the ground, and this was just before the sun came up over the horizon. It was just light enough to see targets for strafing and we went in among those French bombers rather over-confidently. I certainly made three strafing runs, which was later a forbidden . . . tactic . . . it became doctrine that you only ever made one run on a strafing attack because the danger rose so rapidly after the first run. I was sure that I had done very heavy damage to three bombers.

After pulling out of the . . . attack, I was horrified to see a French Dewoitine fighter coming straight at me head on at about a thousand feet. I managed to evade him and turn in behind him, and give two bursts of machine-gun fire, because all my cannon ammunition had been used in the strafing. Saw hits and his undercarriage fell down.

I then decided it was time to get home as quickly as possible . . . but just as I was making my way back to the coast, I saw a second Dewoitine at right angles to me on my port side. And as I saw him, I saw machine gun fire coming underneath me, and this was followed instantly . . . by a huge explosion in the fuselage behind my seat, and I expected the aircraft to go out of control, but curiously nothing seemed to happen at all . . .[5]

It was perhaps fortunate that Baldwin, just twenty-one years old, was already an experienced naval test pilot having flown with the Naval Air Fighting Development Unit at Yeovilton in Somerset. He tested the controls of his aircraft cautiously, but everything seemed to work. Only when he came within radio hailing distance of *Furious* did he discover that his radio wasn't working. The next discovery was that his aircraft's pneumatic system had also suffered damage. He flew past the ship, signalling that he would have to land without using flaps. It was with some relief that he discovered that his undercarriage was still working, and he made the hazardous fast approach and landed without flaps, but succeeded in putting the aircraft down safely on the flight deck.

As soon as I was down, a large crowd of sailors and other pilots surrounded the aircraft, and as I climbed out, I could see why. There was a huge hole about two feet in diameter on the port side of the fuselage directly behind my seat, and the whole of the rear fuselage was full of acid where the accumulator had been blown apart, and the radio was in pieces. The control wires to the rudder had been completely severed except for one wire, so I had been very lucky indeed.[6]

That Baldwin had been very lucky could not be in doubt. In addition to the explosion when the accumulator had blown up, the fuselage behind his seat had been peppered with shrapnel, and yet he was unhurt. While the Seafire was often criticized by pilots for its tendency to bounce when making a carrier landing, and to pitch forward on its nose, some describing its as being too genteel for the 'rough trade' of carrier work, the armour plating behind the cockpits of the Seafire and its land-based cousin, the Spitfire, had saved many a pilot. Later, Baldwin worked out that, since he had been flying at more than 300 mph, the Dewoitine's machine-gun burst had missed him in the cockpit by around a 400th of a second.

Other pilots were not quite so lucky, including Baldwin's squadron commanding officer, Lieutenant Fraser Harris. He was the only member of his squadron to be shot down, but in this case by anti-aircraft fire, which few of the other pilots had noticed over the target. He managed to bale out safely, and was immediately taken prisoner by the Vichy French. He was taken to the office of a French general while his captors worried over what to do with him. When they eventually surrendered, he was back aboard *Furious* with his squadron two days later, having enjoyed one of the shortest spells on record as a prisoner of war.

'At about 5 p.m., Vice-Admiral Burrough (in command of the Eastern Task Force) had a message from Major-General C.W. Ryder, in command of the troops on shore, which was passed on to us at Gibraltar,' recalled Cunningham. '"Darlan wishes to negotiate immediately. He will not deal with any Frenchman . . . Resistance of Navy in isolated batteries has been severe. Resistance of Army has been token."'[7]

The first occupying troops entered Algiers at 21.00, and an appointment was made for Gen Ryder to meet Darlan at 10.00 the following day, 9 November. Nevertheless, German resistance continued, and when Burrough took his flagship, *Bulolo*,

into the harbour at dawn the next day, she was attacked twice by
Junkers Ju88s, and her engine-room telegraphs were put out of
action, so that when she arrived alongside the jetty, she
ploughed into shallow water which brought the ship to an
abrupt stop, but not without first displacing some masonry in a
stone wall that lay ahead of her. That apart, a warm welcome
was given by the large crowds assembled around the harbour.

A follow-up landing at Bougie, a hundred miles east of
Algiers, had been planned for 9 November, but the bad weather
forced this to be delayed until 11 November. By this time, there
was no opposition as Allied troops scrambled ashore at dawn.
Elsewhere, some other landings were still impossible due to the
bad weather, even on 11 November.

Even so, aircraft continued to attack the ships, and on 11
November, the British monitor, HMS *Roberts*, was hit and set on
fire, and a transport, the *Cathay*, was set on fire and damaged so
badly that she later sank, with a similar fate awaiting another
transport, the *Awatea*, and, on 12 November, the *Karanja*. That
day also saw the auxiliary AA ship, *Tynwald*, sunk.

On 12 November, another unopposed landing took place at
Bone, 225 miles east of Algiers, but the two destroyers that
landed the troops were dive-bombed throughout the day,
although unharmed.

ORAN

While the landing craft all reached the correct beaches at Oran
and their troops encountered no resistance as they landed, the
Royal Navy fared worse. Two destroyers, HMS *Hartland* and
Walney carrying troops once again prepared to prevent sabotage
in the port, but as they steamed in at full speed, their
commanding officers used loud-hailers to demand that the
French forces ashore should surrender, losing all element of
surprise. The consequence was that they came under heavy fire
from the port batteries and both ships went down with heavy
losses amongst their crew members. The Vichy French then

undertook an extensive programme of sabotage, sinking the floating docks and many ships, before the Allies could take the port.

The Vichy Navy was once again shown to be prepared to prove itself. Three French destroyers and a submarine chaser left Oran to attack the landing fleet, but soon found themselves facing the cruiser *Aurora* and British destroyers, the crews of all of these ships having considerable battle experience by this time, unlike the French at Oran who had enjoyed a peaceful war since June 1940. The British ships sank a French destroyer and the submarine chaser, another destroyer was driven ashore, while the remaining ship was hit, and then turned and raced back to Oran.

The British destroyer *Achates* entered the harbour, found the French Diane class submarine *Argonaute* (600 tons surface displacement) there, and sank her by gunfire.

The battleship *Rodney*, from Force H, provided heavy gunfire support to suppress fire from coastal batteries, while the Fleet Air Arm attacked the airfields at La Senia and Tarafaoui, as well as maintaining fighter patrols over the fleet and the invasion beaches, with these sorties putting around 80 per cent of the French aircraft out of action, and providing tactical reconnaissance. The need for these actions was soon proven, for when the French air stations were taken, it was found that the bombers were already bombed up and ready to attack, while seaplanes at a base at Arzeu were armed with torpedoes and ready for take-off.

Despite the fierce resistance at and around Oran, by the evening of 8 November, the USAAF had fighters based at Tarafaoui.

DARLAN AND THE ARMISTICE

Operation Torch, the Allied landings in North Africa, had been far from a walkover, but the campaign looked as if it was drawing to a close after just two days of fighting. Neither the

British nor the Americans wished to prolong the fighting with forces which they believed should really be on their side. Not all of the French saw it this way. Some were actively pro-German, while others believed that they owed their loyalty to Vichy and that their territory had been invaded. Just to make matters more complicated, there was the feeling amongst others that the British had betrayed them through leaving France to her own devices at Dunkirk. Needless to say, amongst many the attack on the French fleet in its bases in North Africa and at Dakar was something that they found hard to forgive.

Most of the Allied representatives, including Generals Clark and Giraud, turned up at the Hotel St George in Algiers on the morning of 10 November at 10.00, as planned. The one exception was Cunningham, who had sent his chief-of-staff, Commodore Dick, whom he felt would be more useful because of his excellent French. They had had an uncertain night, believing at one stage that Darlan was planning to go back on his word and arrest them. The previous evening had also brought a disappointment. Hopes that General Giraud would be able to persuade his fellow countrymen to follow him were soon dashed, with even friendly French officers reluctant to take orders from him.

The French also fielded a strong representation. The delegation was led by Admiral Darlan with two other admirals, Battet and Fenaud, as well as Generals Juin and Mendigal. For a constructive conference, the setting was far from ideal. The Allied negotiators were unarmed, while almost all of the Vichy officers in the hotel were armed, and French naval guards were inside protecting the hotel and its occupants. Outside the hotel was surrounded by armed American troops. Cunningham described the atmosphere as 'electric'.

On offer from the Allies was an armistice that would cover the whole of North Africa, although obviously Darlan couldn't deliver German or Italian forces. In any event, Darlan refused to sign anything without the authority of Vichy. He got up to leave, but was forestalled by Clark saying that he must take his own measures, and getting up to leave with the rest of the Allied delegation following. According to Cunningham, the Allies were planning to organize the arrest of all the French officers present, which was likely to be contested bloodily by the armed men present in the building, when Admiral Battet took an American officer by the arm and asked for five minutes grace.

When the Allies returned five minutes later, it was to hear Darlan announce that he would order all French forces in North Africa, including Morocco and Tunisia as well as Algeria, to cease fighting at once. He then signed the orders, which were dispatched by air, while the commanders of Vichy French forces were telephoned as well.

Giraud then sought a conference with Darlan, who refused initially, but eventually relented so that they met that afternoon. Clark also had a further discussion with Darlan, asking him to order the ships at Toulon to proceed to North Africa, but Darlan hesitated, simply telling the American general that he had ordered the fleet to be prepared to sail at short notice if the Germans should enter the *zone libre*, and that under no circumstances would the fleet be allowed to fall into German hands.

On receiving the official Vichy response to his actions, Darlan was preparing to cancel his cease-fire orders, which prompted Clark to tell him that he would not be allowed to do so. Darlan's reaction was that he would have to be made prisoner, to which Clark agreed. Arrest effectively meant house arrest for Darlan in Admiral Fenaud's official residence. Satisfied by assurances that General Juin would not revoke the cease-fire, Clark once again tried to get Darlan to order the ships at Toulon to leave for Algiers, but Darlan pointed out, quite reasonably, that his orders would no longer be obeyed, although he would issue a plea to the fleet.

While Juin and Giraud were still attempting to broker a compromise, intelligence arrived that the Germans were preparing to enter Vichy France. This broke the deadlock with Darlan, who announced that if this could be verified, he would regard himself as free of any moral obligations to the Vichy government. In fact, the German occupation of Vichy France resolved many difficulties for the Allies, as it was now clear to the French just who the enemy was, but there was some delay in

Darlan receiving verification of the news. Nevertheless, eventually Darlan's house arrest was lifted, with the initial reason being that Clark felt it lowered the admiral's status and made negotiations difficult.

While efforts were made to get Darlan to order the French warships to proceed to Gibraltar to refuel and then cross the Atlantic to the United States, Giraud and Juin were being urged to get Admiral Esteva in Tunis to declare for the Allies. Meanwhile, Darlan signalled Admiral de la Borde, commander-in-chief at Toulon:

> The protest sent by the Marshal (meaning Pétain) to Marshal Von Runstedt shows that there is no agreement between him and the German General for the occupation of France. The armistice is broken. We have our liberty of action. The Marshal being no longer able to make free decisions, we can, while remaining personally loyal to him, make decisions which are most favourable to French interests. I have always maintained that the Fleet would remain French or perish. The occupation of the Southern Coast makes it impossible for the Naval forces to remain in Metropolitan France. I invite the Commander-in-Chief to direct them towards West Africa. The American commander declares that our forces will not encounter any obstacles from Allied Naval Forces.
> Admiral of the Fleet, François Darlan.

Nevertheless, in conversation with Commodore Dick, who told him of the arrangements to cover the French fleet as it moved towards Gibraltar, Darlan replied that the British were being optimistic, as the fleet would not sail.

TORCH AND VICHY

After Operation Torch, the relationship between the Germans and the Vichy regime underwent a marked change. Vichy leaders had been at great pains following French surrender to ingratiate themselves with the Germans and ensure as equal a relationship with the Germans as possible, but the Germans had made it clear that they were the victors. When the Allies invaded North Africa, the Vichy forces there fought for a couple of days before surrendering themselves and their equipment to the Allies. This was a case of realism on the part of the Vichy leaders actually in North Africa, fighting for no particular cause and without any chance of reinforcements or supplies of munitions and other war materiel, with the alternative of joining the Free French forces as an attractive alternative prospect. By contrast, the Axis forces in North Africa had been routed only four days earlier by General Montgomery's Eighth Army at El Alamein.

Vichy trust was not misplaced, with few, if any, taken as prisoners of war for more than a few days, while their leader was made high commissioner of the French possessions in North Africa.

This gesture by the Allies, calculated to reassure the French, and win 'hearts and minds' and act as a balm on French sensibilities following the actions against the French fleet at Oran and Dakar, only heightened the fears of the Germans, even more than the decision to surrender in North Africa had of itself sent shock waves through the Nazi leadership. The Germans were well aware that the most senior Vichy officer in Algiers was none other than Admiral Françoise Darlan, a committed Anglophobe, and commander-in-chief of the Vichy French armed forces and, although out of favour, still officially successor to Marshal Pétain.

In vain the Vichy government attempted to persuade the Germans that Darlan's actions in arranging a cease-fire were illegal. One biographer of Darlan (G. Mikes), maintained that Darlan had 'betrayed the Germans, he betrayed Pétain, he betrayed France.' If Vichy forces could be turned by the Allies so quickly, then the Vichy regime occupying the southern part of France could not be trusted. Despite Germany's heavy commitments on the Eastern Front, Hitler ordered the occupation of Vichy France on 11 November, sending large numbers of troops into the area. After difficult negotiations with the Vichy authorities, Hitler then ordered the seizure of the French fleet at Toulon on 19 November. At this time, French warships in Toulon numbered around eighty with a total tonnage of 200,000, around a third of the 1940 tonnage, and included the battleship *Provence*, 22,500 tons, and the two modern battlecruisers *Dunkerque* and *Strasbourg*. It was not until 27 November that German forces actually moved against the dockyard to seize the vessels, encountering armed resistance from French forces that allowed five submarines to escape, and, even more important, gave the French crews aboard the warships time to scuttle them.

Whether these warships could have been used by the Germans remains a moot point to this day. Increasingly, the German navy had come to concentrate on submarine warfare with its major fleet units confined safely to port. Manpower and fuel would both have been problems, while the operation of non-standard calibre guns would have been dependent on the extent of the munitions stockpiled by the French before the surrender in 1940. At this stage of the war, attracting sufficient French naval personnel prepared to throw in their lot with the Germans would have been difficult.

The question also arises: just what use would these ships have been to the Germans? An elderly battleship and two battlecruisers would have been vulnerable to increasingly confident Allied air power in the Mediterranean. Malta was still vulnerable, but with the arrival of the convoy Operation Pedestal in August, the siege of the Maltese islands had begun to be lifted. British submarines had also played their part in the war in the Mediterranean, and at times had severed the lifeline between Italy and the Axis forces in North Africa, contributing to the victory in the Desert War. The French submarines would have stood a better chance of joining the U-boats and continuing the submarine war against the Allies, but these too would have been vulnerable to Allied air and naval forces.

The Italians, by contrast, had neglected the battlecruiser and instead had favoured a combination of battleships, and heavy and light cruisers, as well as destroyers. In 1940, they had many more submarines than the Germans. Like the Germans, they planned aircraft carriers, but inter-service rivalry meant that the air force, or Regia Aeronautica, was determined to retain control of all service aviation. Yet, the Italians had also failed to make use of their surface fleet. There had been two set piece battles with the Royal Navy, at Punto Stilo and Matapan, as well as a number of smaller actions, often including the defence of Axis convoys. Hitler wanted the Italians to use their six battleships, three of which were old, but modernized, to shell Malta on Italy's entry into the war, but instead these had been caught in port five months later and three of them were put out of action by the Royal Navy's Fleet Air Arm in the brilliantly conceived and gallantly executed attack on Taranto. The operation had been Pearl Harbor on a smaller scale, and the loss of life had only been so low because none of the ships had a magazine blow up – but it had been close.

Clark's dealing with Darlan were not popular with the two Allied governments, who felt that their obligations to de Gaulle had been compromised. The blame eventually fell upon Eisenhower as Supreme Commander-in-Chief, who reputedly was in despair over the reaction by the politicians, who seemed to ignore the realities of the war.

Notes

1, 2 and 3 IWM Accession No 19864
4 *Daily Telegraph*, 2 March 1997
5 and 6 Imperial War Museum Sound Archive Accession No 12038
7 *A Sailor's Odyssey*, Admiral (later Admiral of the Fleet) Sir Andrew Cunningham, RN, Hutchinson, London, 1951

CHAPTER SIXTEEN

Scuttle!

Darlan's decision to order a cease-fire in North Africa placed the Vichy leader, Marshal Pétain, in an impossible situation. Pétain immediately countermanded Darlan's order and declared his action illegal, but too late. The Germans realized just how vulnerable they were if other Vichy officers were to take a similar line as soon as Allied forces approached, and within days had occupied the Vichy *zone libre* with some help from Italian forces. Darlan had left secret orders for one of the commanders of the Vichy French forces, Lieutenant-General Jean-Marie de Lattre de Tassigny, to resist any German attempt to seize Vichy, and for his actions, de Lattre was imprisoned by the Vichy regime. Otherwise, the Germans met little resistance, and moved to disband the 100,000-strong army that had been permitted Vichy.

Occupying Vichy did not simply give the Germans additional territory, it brought with it a tremendous dowry in that the largest part of the French fleet was stationed at Toulon. There were some eighty ships there, a force which on its own was larger than most of the world's navies. Indeed, in terms of the number of major surface units, it came close to matching Germany's own, although by this time the German U-boat fleet had overtaken the French submarine fleet in terms of numbers.

Toulon was the French fleet's main port, and the dockyard itself was well over a mile-and-a-half long and half-a-mile deep.

At Toulon, two other French admirals were in command. Admiral de la Borde commanded the larger warships that pre-war would have constituted the Atlantic and Mediterranean Squadrons. He had been ordered by Darlan to move his ships to Dakar, where they would have been out of reach of the Germans and for the time-being at least, difficult for the Allies to take over as well. When he received Darlan's order, de la Borde's response had been brief, and to the point: 'Merde!'[1] Admiral Marquis was the port admiral, but he flew his flag in the elderly battleship *Provence*.

Under de la Borde's command were the two powerful battle-cruisers, *Strasbourg* and *Dunkerque*, both 26,500 tons, although the latter had been badly damaged in her encounter with Force H at Mers-el-Kebir. He also had three obsolescent heavy cruisers, two light cruisers, ten large 'super' destroyers of the *contre-torpilleur* type as well as three smaller destroyers. In addition to *Provence*, Marquis also had the *Commandant Teste*, 10,000 tons seaplane tender, two destroyers, four torpedo boats and ten submarines. In addition to these ships, which seem to have been fully or nearly fully manned, there were another two cruisers, eight *contre-torpilleur* destroyers, six smaller destroyers and ten submarines that had actually been decommissioned under the armistice terms and which simply had skeleton crews aboard. Apart from these, there were also minesweepers and other minor naval vessels and auxiliaries.

This was a prize worth having.

The major fleet units, including the destroyers but not the submarines, were steam-powered, which meant that steam had to be raised before they could leave port. Since it could take eight hours to raise steam, once the Germans were at the gates of the dockyard, flight was not an option.

It soon became clear that the Germans were occupying all military and naval installations, and that Toulon could not be far down the list. On 27 November, the personnel at Toulon received the briefest possible warning of what was intended, with German troops and tanks advancing on the port, followed by German naval personnel who were obviously expected to take over the ships.

As in most naval bases, the larger ships were lying alongside the outermost piers with others lying alongside them, while five ships were sitting in the large dry docks, including *Dunkerque*.

The Germans had intended to take the dockyards and the ships by surprise, using a pincer movement with one group travelling along the road from Nice while another three groups, including the crack *Das Reich* division seized the Toulon peninsula and the town. While the dockyard had defensive positions, including gun batteries outside the dockyard area, there were just two gateways and a high wall to be passed as well. When Marquis was captured at 04.30, aroused from his sleep by an advance guard of German troops, his staff had time to send a warning signal to de la Borde, although at first he refused to believe that the Germans would attack the base. Nevertheless, he had the presence of mind to immediately order all commanding officers to raise steam on their ships, even though this would take several hours, and to be on their guard to prevent the Germans boarding any vessel. Then the order to scuttle was re-issued, and then repeated as the Germans attempted to enter the dockyard area, but encountered fierce resistance from Vichy forces, who had also been alerted by a dispatch rider sent by a gendarmerie outpost. In the confusion, five submarines, *Venus*, *Casablanca*, *Marsouin*, *Iris* and *Glorieux* with their diesel engines providing power almost immediately, managed to slip away and out to sea. The ease with which they did this, their crews manning their deck armament, suggests that the whole procedure had already been rehearsed. Nevertheless, their escape wasn't easy. They were bombed, strafed and depth charged by the Luftwaffe, leaving *Venus* so damaged that she had to be scuttled, while *Iris*, also damaged, was taken by her commanding officer and crew to Spain, where they spent the rest of the war in internment. Nevertheless, the other three boats reached North Africa.

After a German bulldozer forced its way through the main gates, the act of scuttling those ships that could not flee was started. Through the main gate at 05.00, the Germans took another hour to reach the first of the ships, and when they reached the piers alongside which the *Strasbourg* had been moored, they found that she was already drifting away after her crew had cast of all lines to the shore. Admiral de la Borde was aboard his flagship, and to discourage him from taking the ship to sea, which would have been impossible, a German tank fired an 88mm shell into 'B' turret, fatally wounding a gunnery officer. The crew responded, but with machine guns and other light weapons. The officer in command of the German troops demanded that de la Borde return his ship to the pier and hand her over to his forces, but de la Borde replied that scuttling had already started, with her sea cocks opened and the ship settling slowly in the water. Further communication was prevented by the first of a series of loud explosions ripping through the ship. In addition to setting explosive charges, the crew were also setting about wrecking the ship's machinery with hand grenades and oxy-acetylene cutters. There wasn't enough depth of water for the ship to sink completely, but instead she settled on the bed of the port, leaving her distinctive superstructure sticking out of the water.

Nearby, the crew of the heavy cruiser *Algerie*, 13,900 tons, also had opened her sea cocks and her main armament had been destroyed by explosives. This did not prevent a German officer from declaring to Admiral Lacroix that he had come to seize the ship, only to be informed by a bemused Lacroix that he was too late. A brief stand-off then occurred as the German said that he would come aboard the *Algerie* if the ship would not blow up, to be countered by Lacroix's declaration that the ship would indeed be blown up if the German boarded. Added emphasis came to the exchange a couple of minutes later when one of the two after twin 8-in turrets blew up. The ship continued to burn for the next two days during which occasional explosions could be heard as her ammunition went up. This was far from a record, as the light cruiser *Marseillaise*, which had settled at an angle, took more than a week to burn herself out. Another cruiser, the *Colbert*, was boarded by a German party, but when they saw fuses being set and one of her officers setting fire to his float-plane, they left promptly, but only just in time before her magazine blew the ship apart. The German party that had set foot aboard another cruiser, the *Dupleix*, also had a narrow escape when she blew up.

Scuttling on its own often causes little damage, and ships scuttled in shallow port waters can be re-floated and salvaged, which was one reason why so much emphasis was given to setting off the magazines and ready use ammunition, not to mention the attacks by grenade and oxy-acetylene cutters. This point was brought home later when another cruiser, a sister ship of the *Marseillaise*, *La Galissonniere*, was scuttled, but then re-floated and taken by the Italian navy, although returned to the French in 1944.

In the confusion, the elderly battleship *Provence* was one ship that was nearly taken by the Germans, as her commanding officer hesitated when he was given the message that the Vichy premier, Pierre Laval, had ordered that there were to be no 'incidents'. Nevertheless, while he sent an officer to seek clarification, his crew, seeing the other ships sinking and blowing up, opened the sea cocks and the ship began to settle in the water even while the Germans argued with her CO on the bridge.

Nevertheless, it was clear that there were to be victims amongst the French ships. A ship in dry dock cannot be scuttled, and it is usual, for the safety of dockyard workers, for ships entering dry dock to be de-stored. The battlecruiser *Dunkerque*, sister ship of the *Strasbourg* and pride of the pre-war French navy, was in dry dock and rather than being refitted and returned to service, she suffered the ignominy of being scrapped by a large gang of Italian workers imported for the purpose, so that she could be sent to Italy in pieces as part of a scrap metal drive intended to rebuild Italy's dwindling stocks of war materials. The decision to scrap the ship was caused not so much by the damage inflicted two years earlier by the Royal

Navy, but by the damage inflicted on her armament and turbines in the brief period between the warning being given and the Germans finding their way to the ship.

Out of the eight *contre-torpilleur* destroyers, three, *Lion*, *Tigre* and *Panthère* were being refitted and their skeleton crews did not have enough time to sabotage them effectively, so these survived to pass to Italy along with the smaller destroyer *Trombe*.

Despite having lost his ship, de la Borde was left aboard the *Strasbourg* when she settled on the bottom of the harbour. He refused to go ashore, remaining aboard and accusing the Germans of breaching the terms of the armistice in attempting to seize the French fleet. Incredibly, the first indication that French naval units in North Africa had of the events at Toulon were when they picked up Pétain's signal to de la Borde: 'I learn at this instant that your ship is sinking. I order you to leave it without delay.' Meanwhile, the Germans had left de la Borde, reasoning that in theory he had gone down with his ship. Certainly, he was no longer a threat.

Not all of the submarines had managed to escape, and the four that were left behind at Toulon were scuttled at their moorings.

In the aftermath of the battle of Toulon and the attempted seizure of the fleet, everyone on the base, including the ships' crews, were interned, effectively becoming prisoners of war. The Vichy authorities argued that their actions were in accordance with the terms of the armistice, and for once won the argument with the Germans. The internees were all released, and the naval personnel spent the rest of their war on full pay from the Vichy authorities!

ALEXANDRIA

The German attempt to grab the fleet at Toulon and Darlan's orders led Cunningham to expect Godfroy at Alexandria to re-activate his fleet, and join the Allies. 'They have no excuse for remaining inert,' he wrote home on 1 December 1942. 'Except perhaps that so many Frenchmen at the present time appear to have lost all their spirit. Doubtless it will revive; but at present the will to fight for their country is completely absent.'[2]

Notes
1 Shit!
2 *A Sailor's Odyssey*, Admiral (later Admiral of the Fleet) Sir Andrew Cunningham, RN, Hutchinson, London, 1951

CHAPTER SEVENTEEN

The French Fleet at War

While the survivor and beneficiary of the surrender of Vichy French forces in North Africa following the Allied landings, Darlan's future was uncertain. The Gaullists planned to charge Darlan with treason once France was liberated. There was also a faction amongst the British and Americans that would have had Darlan move to the United States while his son had medical treatment, as a political answer to the problem over who should now lead the French forces. The Allies favoured General Giraud, who had made a spectacular escape from prison, but Darlan was popular with the substantial French community in North Africa – more popular than Giraud.

Later, Admiral Esteva was court marshalled for treason at the end of the war. He was, after Operation Torch, responsible for Tunisia, and when the Germans invaded that French colony, the US General Clark asked Darlan to order Esteva to resist – but Darlan's response was that, since he had been sacked as head of the French navy, he was not sure whether anyone would obey his orders. Nevertheless, he did try. He did write to both Esteva and de la Borde. His letters had no effect either in Tunis or in Toulon. Esteva maintained that he was keen to act, but could not get the commander of the French ground forces to follow him. A further order, two days later, insisting that the Germans and the

211

Italians were the enemy had little effect, and when Darlan telephoned to follow up the order, Esteva answered with a German
officer at his side.

Darlan was not to share the same fate as the other senior
French officers who had sided with Vichy – prosecution for
treason with a death sentence that was eventually commuted to
life imprisonment, which in turn in many cases meant serving
no more than five years.

Even today, opinions remain divided over whether Darlan's
assassin, the young Fernand Bonnier de la Chapelle, was an
agent of the Axis powers, an unbalanced Gaullist or whether, as
Britain's Admiral Cunningham, commander-in-chief of the
Mediterranean Fleet at the outbreak of war and later First Sea
Lord, put it: 'many hands were in it,' and continued with: 'it was
of no service to the Allied cause.' Gaullist involvement there
may have been, with de Gaulle in his memoirs referring to a
'policy resolved to liquidate a "temporary expedient" after
having utilized it.'

Darlan had not made himself popular with the Gaullists, and
on one occasion refused to meet an envoy from General de
Gaulle. Roosevelt had coined the term 'temporary expedient' to
describe Darlan, and it seems that the Allies elevated him after
the cease-fire in North Africa simply to gain and retain control
of the Vichy forces.

Darlan himself was under no illusion about the Allies attitude
towards him, indicating that he expected to be thrown away like
a 'lemon' once the Americans had finished 'squeezing it'.

On 22 December 1942, Darlan arrived at his High Commission
offices in an old Moorish palace, accompanied by his chief-of-
staff, Captain Hourcade. As he passed through an ante-chamber,
with Hourcade in front, a shot rang out and Hourcade turned to
see Darlan slumped on the floor. Hourcade attempted to grab
the gunman, and was shot in the neck and thigh before the
assassin, de la Chapelle, jumped through an open window in an
attempt to escape. He was caught almost immediately by a Spahi
cavalryman.

Darlan was declared dead on arrival when he reached

hospital. His assassin was tried for murder and executed by a firing squad. He was just twenty years old.

The assassination was the start of accusations flying between all of the parties involved in North Africa. Henry Stimson, the US Secretary of State for War, was convinced that those behind the murder must be either pro-Axis or pro-Vichy elements amongst the French community. The French Deuxième Bureau (Secret Service) in North Africa, investigated and declared that the main suspects were Gaullist, with one Gaullist, Andre Achiary, blaming the Abbé Cordier and the Assistant Secretary of State for Political Affairs at the High Commission, Henri d'Astier de la Vigerie. The commissioner of police, Garidacci, was also arrested for withholding a confession by the assassin, naming his accomplices, and replacing this with a false confession stating that he had acted alone.

Certainly, de la Chapelle made further statements while being held awaiting trial, naming prominent Gaullists and others who said that 'Darlan must disappear'.

The connection with the Abbé Cordier had started when de la Chapelle had admitted planning to kill Darlan in a confession, and that subsequently, Cordier had provided him with plans of the High Commission premises, and also enabled him to obtain a handgun and ammunition.

THE FRENCH FLEET SWITCHES TO THE ALLIES

Despite the cease-fire, the breaking of the armistice by the Germans, and the growing number of French service personnel fighting on the Allied side in the Free French forces, it was not for some six months, until 17 May 1943, that Admiral Godfroy, who had remained in Alexandria, decided to join the Allies. Two days earlier, he had received a letter from General Giraud, asking him to join the 'Naval Forces of Africa', reassuring him that such action would be beneficial to France. Godfroy signalled his intentions to Vichy, and in return was ordered by Laval to scuttle his ships.

After the stand-off at Alexandria had been resolved, many of Godfroy's men had been repatriated to France. Fortunately, the shortfall was made good with sailors from the bases in Algeria. Godfroy then took his Force X, which included the battleship *Lorraine*, the cruisers *Duquesne*, *Tourville*, *Suffren* and *Duguay-Trouin*, through the Suez Canal and on the lengthy and roundabout route to Dakar via Cape Town. Quite why, given the change in the balance of power in the Mediterranean, he did not take the direct route is not clear, but Sicily had still to be invaded and there were extensive minefields off Malta. The destroyers *Basque*, *Fortune* and *Forbin*, with the submarine *Protée*, did take the direct route to Algeria.

If Godfroy was expecting a warm welcome on reaching Dakar, he was to be bitterly disappointed. On arrival, he was immediately relieved of his command, and spent several months ashore, once again in enforced idleness. In the end, he actually read about his compulsory retirement in a newspaper, and learned from the same source that it was a 'disciplinary measure'.

RETURNING TO ACTIVE SERVICE

With the troublesome personalities out of the way, it was time to set the fleet and its crews to the task of returning to service and an active participation in the war on the Allied side. Despite the scuttling at Toulon, and other wartime losses, the contribution to the Allied cause was still formidable. All in all, at Dakar, Mers-el-Kebir and Oran, the French had around 250,000 tons of naval vessels, which of course was much higher than the Washington Naval Treaty limit of 175,000 tons, which the treaty navies had been forced to ignore as the arms race prior to the outbreak of the Second World War had got under way.

The French Committee for National Liberation, CFLN, formed by de Gaulle and Giraud on 3 June 1943, at first held out hope that a genuine rapprochement had been achieved, but as the earlier chapter on de Gaulle and the Free French shows, harmony did not last long and Giraud was to become another of those French officers destined to be sidelined. The differences between de Gaulle and Giraud owed much to a clash of personalities, rivalry, vanity on both their parts, and a desire to lead. What happened to many other French officers was little more than a settling of old scores.

Rather than attempt to rebuild relationships and work towards victory and liberation, before long the Committee began to re-open old wounds. It established a 'Committee of Epuration' (purification), and began to interfere with the decisions being taken by the French naval command.

One of the first victims of the Committee was Admiral Michelier, who was unpopular with Giraud and also with the Americans, who resented his strong opposition to the landings at Casablanca. No doubt the Americans were happy when he was 'epurated'. His successor, Vice-Admiral Collinet, who had been at Dakar, did not last long either before he too was 'epurated'. In his case, his sin was asking for a seat on the Committee, which was dominated by the generals, and who seemed to be fighting yet another internal French battle, in this case to ensure that the navy once again became a subordinate service.

Charges such as these interfered with the efficient functioning of the fleet and while none of the officers was executed or even imprisoned, events had the taste of Stalin's show trials, something which would have horrified the senior officers concerned.

The fleet included the battleships *Lorraine* and *Richelieu* as well as the uncompleted *Jean Bart*, the elderly aircraft carrier *Béarn*, three heavy cruisers, seven light cruisers, an auxiliary cruisers, five of the *contre-torpilleur* 'super' destroyers that were so close to the concept of a light cruiser, six destroyers and seven corvettes, two sloops, and nineteen submarines. These were the major fleet units, but there were another eighty-four smaller vessels, such as minesweepers, coastal defence vessels and river craft. Missing from the list was the *corsair* submarine *Surcouf*, which had been lost in mysterious circumstances in the Caribbean, believed torpedoed by another submarine. Her aircraft hangar and large size could have made her ideal for the submarine 'milk runs' from Gibraltar to Malta that had contributed so much to allowing the island to remain in the war.

This substantial fleet was refitted, necessary after almost three years of idleness and neglect, with boilers and hulls needing attention in the dockyards. More than this, the fleet was re-equipped so that it met the naval standards expected in 1943. The ships were equipped with radar and ASDIC, while anti-aircraft armament was increased substantially, reflecting the Allied experience of warfare at sea. Not all of the work could be done in the dockyards of French Africa, and many ships received substantial refitting and modernization in the dock-yards of the United States, including the *Richelieu*, as well as a number of cruisers and destroyers. As increasing numbers of Frenchmen came forward for service at sea, the Allies even started transferring ships to the new Marine Nationale. Some of the ships were actually being handed back having been taken by the Royal Navy, but the British also added a Hunt class destroyer, which was renamed *La Combattante*, by the French, six frigates and three submarines, plus a captured Italian boat, a number of corvettes and other smaller warships and auxiliaries, making seventy-six naval vessels in all. The United States Navy provided 228 naval vessels, including six destroyers and forty landing craft. As German and Italian forces were forced further northwards, after the Italian surrender left that country's armed forces divided just as those of France had been, the French re-covered the *contre-torpilleur Tigre* and the *Trombe*.

The most immediate task for the French warships as they returned to service was in convoy escort duty, around Africa, in the Mediterranean and, of course, across the North Atlantic.

Nevertheless, all was not well. The American press didn't help, describing the battleship *Richelieu* as part of the 'French Nazi Fleet'. There were also attempts by Gaullists to attract naval personnel away to join the Gaullist cause, ready for the liberation of France. It took the intervention of the British First Sea Lord, Admiral Cunningham, and Frank Knox, Secretary of the United States Navy, to curb the Gaullist tactics. Even so, in the French African colonies, the Gaullists were busy making further mischief, with Vice-Admiral Derrien, the former commanding officer at Bizerte, charged with treason and not scuttling the ships under his command. His trial was handled by senior army officers rather than naval officers, as should have been the case. He was left to languish in an old Foreign Legion prison, became seriously ill, and died a few days after his release. Needless to say, despite the charges against him and his treatment, he was buried with full military honours.

The *Richelieu* completed her modernization in the Brooklyn Navy Yard and returned across the Atlantic to join the Home Fleet in its forward base at Scapa Flow in Orkney.

In another group of islands, the French Antilles, there were also a number of French warships. The islands were run by Admiral Robert, a professional sailor who also filled the role of High Commissioner. He had to contend with Vichy, Gaullist and Communist factions, and when he received 300 tons of gold that had arrived there in 1940, he resisted Vichy orders to scuttle the ship holding the gold after the cease-fire in North Africa. Nevertheless, it took another eight months before a new administrator for the islands arrived aboard the *Terrible*. What should have been one of the most important units of the French fleet was in the Antilles, this was the elderly aircraft carrier, *Bearn*. She was sent to New Orleans for refitting there, but because of her age, her new role was once again to become an aircraft transport. The training cruiser *Jeanne d'Arc*, was refitted in Puerto Rico and then sent to help cover the Allied landings in Corsica, which in turn preceded the landings in the South of France. Less fortunate was the other cruiser in the Antilles, the *Emile Bertin*, whose refit and modernization took so long that she only returned to service shortly before the end of the war in Europe.

Sufficient ships were available for the Marine Nationale to play a part in the Normandy landings, including the light cruisers *Montcalm* and *Georges Leygues*, which supported the battleship USS *Arkansas* in shelling German positions and covering the landing of US troops, and the former British destroyer *La Combattante*, which helped cover landings by British troops, eight frigates and corvettes, as well as motor torpedo boats and minesweepers. This was an important morale booster for the fleet, and a psychological boost for the French themselves. Amidst this action, the old First World War battleship *Courbet* suffered the ignominious fate of being towed from Southampton and sunk with other ships to provide a breakwater at Ouistreham.

After the Allied landings in the South of France, it fell to the light cruiser *Montcalm* to liberate the important port of Marseilles, not far from the major base at Toulon. Unlike Normandy, where few French troops had been involved other than those in specialised units, the landings in the South of France, Operation Anvil, included substantial French ground forces. Led by the battleship *Lorraine*, three French cruisers and three *contre-torpilleur* destroyers operated alongside British and American naval forces in bombarding enemy positions. In contrast to the Atlantic Wall, the massive fortifications built by the Germans along the Channel coast, there had been neither the time, the money or the manpower to create a similar defensive line along the Mediterranean coast, and indeed, it would have had to be much longer given the increasing capability of Allied amphibious forces. Part of the fortifications that were in place, however, were the guns from the old battleship *Provence*, salvaged after she had been scuttled, the *Lorraine* became involved in an artillery duel with these guns.

While Free French forces attacked Toulon from inland and from the eastern coastal route, French naval vessels were amongst those bombarding the port's shore batteries. In return, the Germans attempted to scuttle *Strasbourg* and *La Galissonnière* to block the southern channel into the port, but USAAF North American Mitchell bombers sank the ships first, along with three German U-boats. Fierce fighting continued in and around Toulon, however, and while the town was entered on 25 August 1944, fighting continued for another three days.

Other ships also worked with the British, covering the landings in the Dodecanese. The submarines sank eight Axis ships during forty-five patrols, but lost one of their number, the *Protée*.

The *Richelieu* probably had the most distinguished service

record of the new Marine Nationale, joining the British Eastern Fleet which had returned to the war against Japanese forces in the Far East. Close anti-aircraft cover was provided by *Richelieu* for the aircraft carriers HMS *Illustrious* and the USS *Saratoga* during the first Anglo-American air raids on Sabang. Later, she returned for a refit at Gibraltar, and then returned to the Far East in April 1945, operating with the battleship HMS *Queen Elizabeth* in bombarding Sumatra and the Andaman Islands, off the coast of Malaya. Preparing to attack a Japanese cruiser, her prey was snatched from her by British destroyers in a torpedo attack, depriving the French navy of its one chance in the Second World War of a sea battle between opposing warships. Given the disparity in their armaments, the *Richelieu* could have been expected to win. She was in port at the British base at Trincomalee in Ceylon (now Sri Lanka) when news came of the Japanese surrender.

Like navies of many of the European colonial powers, the Marine Nationale maintained flotillas of small gunboats for river and coastal patrols in its tropical colonies. When the Japanese moved to occupy French Indo–China, just two of these gunboats, the *Frezouls* and the *Crayssac*, managed to escape from Haiphong (in what is now Vietnam), reaching the coast of China. They then spent a miserable war paying ransom to the Chinese Nationalist army and to local pirates, before returning after the surrender of Japan to help in the French reoccupation of Indo-China.

There can be little doubt that the return of the fleet to the Allies was a considerable boost to Allied sea power. Unlike the Dutch and the Canadians, who had been able to use their wartime efforts to create carrier-borne naval air power, the Marine Nationale had to wait until the war in Europe was over before it received its second carrier, on loan from the Royal Navy, so that carrier air power could become an integral part of the French fleet once again.

APPENDIX I

The French Fleet in 1940

A rmament shows torpedo tubes as submerged or above the water, otherwise all torpedo tubes are deck-mounted. The number of tubes is given followed by whether these are twin or triple tubes, so that 6 X 3 torpedo tubes means six triple tubes.

Battleships

Jean Bart, Richelieu
1939 / 1940
35,000 tons; LOA: 800 ft; 30 knots.
Armament: 8 X 15-in; 12 3.9-in AA; 4 aircraft, two catapults.

Lorraine
1916
22,200 tons; LOA: 545 ft; 22 knots.
Armament: 8 X 13.5-in; 14 X 5.5-in; 5 X AA; 1 aircraft and catapult.

221

Bretagne, Provence
1915, but rebuilt 1919/1920 and again 1933–1935.
As above but with 10 X 13.5-in, no aircraft.
Note: when reconstructed in 1934/35, *Lorraine* had her
midships twin 13.5-in turret replaced by aircraft and catapult.

Courbet, Ocean, Paris
1913/1914, but rebuilt 1928/1929
22,200 tons; LOA: 550 ft; 20 knots.
Armament: 12 X 12-in; 22 X 5.5-in; 10 X AA; 12 submerged
torpedo tubes.

Battlecruisers

Dunkerque, Strasbourg
1936, 1940
26,500 tons; LOA: 702 ft; 30 knots.
Armament: 8 X 13-in; 16 X 5.1-in; 8 X AA; 2 aircraft and 1
catapult.

Cruisers

Algérie
1934
10,000 tons; LOA: 617 ft; 31 knots.
Armament: 8 X 8-in; 12 X 3.9-in AA; 6 X 3 torpedo tubes; 3
aircraft and catapult.

Colbert, Dupleix, Foch, Suffren
1928–1931
9,900 tons; LOA: 644 ft; 32.25 knots.
Armament: 8 X 8-in; 8 X 3-in AA; 6 X 3 torpedo tubes; 3 aircraft
and catapult.

Duquesne, Tourville
1928
10,000 tons; LOA: 627 ft; 33 knots.
Armament: 8 X 8-in; 8 X 3-in AA; 6 X 3 torpedo tubes; 3 aircraft and catapult.

Georges Leygues, Gloire, Jean de Vienne, La Galissonière, Marseillaise, Montcalm
1935–1937
7,600 tons; LOA: 565/588 ft; 32 knots.
Armament: 9 X 6-in; 8 X 3.5-in AA, plus 8 small AA; 4 X 2 torpedo tubes; 4 aircraft and catapult.

Emile Bertin
1934
5,900 tons; LOA: 580 ft; 34 knots.
Armament: 9 X 6-in; 4 X 3.5-in AA; 6 X 3 torpedo tubes; 1 aircraft and catapult.

Pluton (minelaying cruiser)
1931
4,800 tons; LOA: 500 ft; 30 knots.
Armament: 4 X 5.5-in; 4 X 3-in AA; 6 X 3 torpedo tubes; mines.

Duguay-Trouin, Lamotte-Picquet, Primauguet
1926
7,300 tons; LOA: 595 ft; 34 knots.
Armament: 8 X 6.1-in; 4 X 3-in AA; 12 X 3 torpedo tubes; 1 aircraft and catapult.

Jeanne d'Arc (training cruiser)
1931
6,500 tons; LOA: 558 ft; 25 knots.
Armament: 8 X 6.1-in; 4 X 3-in AA; 2 torpedo tubes; 2 aircraft and catapult.

Aircraft Carrier

Béarn
1927
22,000 tons; LOA: 600 ft; 21 knots.
Armament: 8 X 6.1-in; 6 X 3.9-in AA plus 8 smaller; 4 above waterline torpedo tubes; 40 aircraft.

Seaplane Tender

Commandant Teste
1931
10,000 tons; LOA: 560 ft; 20 knots.
Armament: 12 X 3.9-in AA; 25 aircraft and 4 catapults

Large Destroyers or *Contre-Torpilleurs* ('Torpedo-Boat-Catchers')

MOGADOR CLASS
Desaix, Mogador, Hoche, Kléber, Volta, Marceau
1937–1939
2,900 tons; LOA: 450 ft; 38 knots.
Armament: 8 X 5.5-in; 10 X 2 torpedo tubes.

FANTASQUE CLASS
L'Audacieux, L'Fantasque, L'Indomptable, Le Malin, Le Terrible, Le Triomphant
1935–1936
2,600 tons; LOA: 435 ft; 43 knots (*Le Terrible* is supposed to have set a record of 45.25 knots).
Armament: 5 X 5.5-in; 9 X 3 torpedo tubes.

BISON CLASS
Bison, Guepard, Lion, Valmy, Vauban, Verdun
1929–1931
2,400 tons; LOA: 430 ft; 36 knots.
Armament: 5 X 5.5-in; 6 X 3 torpedo tubes.

AIGLE CLASS
Aigle, Albatros, Cassard, Epervier, Gerfaut, Kersaint, Le Chevalier, Paul, Maillé-Brézé, Milan, Tartu, Vauquelin, Vatour
1931–1934
2,400 tons; LOA: 425 ft; 36 knots.
Armament: 5 X 5.5-in; 6 or 7 torpedo tubes.

CHACAL CLASS
Chacal, Jaguar, Léopard, Lynx, Panthère, Tigre
1926/1927
2,100 tons; LOA: 416 ft; 35 knots.
Armament: 5 X 5.1-in; 8 AA guns; 6 X 3 torpedo tubes.

Destroyers

CASQUE CLASS
Adventurier, Casque, Epee, Fleuret, Intrepide, Lansequenet, Le Corsair, Le Filibustier, Le Hardi, Mameluck, Opinaitre, Temeraire
1938–1939
1,800 tons; LOA: 400ft; 36 knots.
Armament: 6 X 5.1-in; 7 X 2 torpedo tubes.

ADROIT-CLASS (SOMETIMES CLASSED AS *TORPILLEURS*, OR 'TORPEDO-BOATS')
Basque, Bordelais, Boulonnais, Brestois, Forbin, Foudroyant, Fougueux, Frondeur, L'Adroit, L'Alycon, La Palme, La Railleuse, Le Fortune, Le Mars
1927–1929
1,400 tons; LOA: 330 ft; 32 knots.
Armament: 4 X 5.1-in; 6 X 3 torpedo tubes

Simoun class (sometimes classed as *torpilleurs*, or 'torpedo-boats')
Bourrasque, Cyclone, Mistral, Orage, Ouragan, Simoun, Sirocco, Tempête, Tornade, Tramontane, Trombe, Typhon
1924/1925
1,300 tons; LOA: 347 ft; 33 knots.
Armament: 4 X 5.1-in; 2 X AA guns; 6 X 3 torpedo tubes

Torpedo Boats

Enseigne, Gabolde
1924
800 tons; LOA: 270 ft; 33 knots.
Armament: 3 X 3.9-in; 1 X 3-in AA; 4 X 2 torpedo tubes.

Enseigne Roux
1915
800 tons; LOA: 290 ft; 30 knots.
Armament: 2 X 3.9-in; 1 X 3-in AA; 4 X 2 torpedo tubes.

L'Agile class
L'Agile, L'Alsacien, Le Breton, Le Fier, L'Estrerenant, Le Corse, Le Farouche, Le Niçoise, Le Normand, Le Parisien, Le Provencal, Le Saiettongeais, Le Savoyard, Le Tunisien
1938–1940
1,000 tons; LOA: 300 ft; 34 knots.
Armament: 4 X 3.9-in; 4 torpedo tubes.

Baliste-class
Baliste, Bombarde, Bouclier, Branlebas, L'Incomprise, L'Iphigenie, La Bayonnaise, La Cordelière, La Flore, La Melpomene, La Pomone, La Pursuivante
1935–1937
600 tons; LOA: 265 ft; 34 knots.
Armament: 2 X 3.9-in; 4 torpedo tubes.

Submarines

Displacement tonnages have the surface displacement followed by submerged displacement, with surface speed followed by maximum submerged speed, although this would usually be a dash of one or at the most two hours, with patrol speed being much lower, at around 4 or 5 knots.

Surcouf ('Corsair' submarine)
1931
2,900/4,300 tons; LOA: 360 ft; 18/10 knots.
Armament: 2 X 8-in; 2 AA; 10 torpedo tubes; 1 aircraft.

La Praya, Roland, Morillot
1939/1940
1,100/1,610 tons; LOA: 280 ft; 23/9knots.
Armament: 11 torpedo tubes.

REDOUBTABLE CLASS
Acteon, Acheron, Achille, Agosta, Ajax, Archimede, Argo, Beveziers, Casablanca, Fresnel, Henri, Poincare, L'Espoir, Le Centaure, Le Conquerant, La Glorieux, Le Heros, Le Tonnant, Monge, Ouessant, Pascal, Pasteur, Pegase, Persee, Phenix, Poncelet, Protee, Redoubtable, Sfax, Sidi-Ferruch
1928–1938
1,400/2,100 tons; LOA: 302ft ; 20/10 knots.
Armament: 1 X 3.9-in; 2 AA; 11 torpedo tubes.

SAPHIR CLASS
Daimant, Nautilus, Perle, Rubis, Saphir, Turquoise
1928–1935
700/900 tons; LOA: 220 ft; 12/9 knots.
Armament: 1 X 3-in; 5 torpedo tubes; 32 mines.

REQUIN CLASS
Caiman, Dauphin, Espadon, Marsouin, Morse, Narval, Phoque, Requin, Souffleur
1924–1926, reconstructed 1938–1940
1,000/1,400 tons; LOA: 258 ft; 16/10 knots.
Armament: 1 X 3.9-in; 10 torpedo tubes.

René Audry (Originally completed by Germany as *U-119* in 1918)
1918
1,000/1,500 tons; LOA: 268 ft; 13/9 knots.
Armament: 1 X 5.9-in; 4 torpedo tubes; 40 mines.

AURORE CLASS
Aurore, L'Africaine, La Bayadere, La Creole, La Favorite
1938–1940
800/1,100 tons; LOA: 268 ft; 13/9knots.
Armament: 1 X 3.9-in; 9 torpedo tubes.

DIANE CLASS
Amazone, Amphitrite, Antiope, Aréthuse, Argonaute, Atalante, Ceres, Diane, Iris, Junon, Meduse, Minerve, La Psyche, La Sultane, La Sybille, La Vestale, Ondine, Oréade, Orion, Orphée, Pallas, Venus
1930–1937
600/800 tons; LOA: 200 ft; 14/9 knots.
Armament: 1 X 3-in AA; 7–9 torpedo tubes.

SIRENE CLASS
Ariadne, Calypso, Circe, Danae, Doris, Eurydice, Galatee, Naiade, Nymphe, Sirene, Thetis
1925–1927
550/780 tons; LOA: 200 ft; 14/7 knots.
Armament: 1 X 3.9-in; 7 torpedo tubes.

Minelayers

Castor
Originally completed in 1916 by Swan Hunter as ice-breaker for Russia.
3,150 tons; LOA: 250 ft; 14 knots.
Armament: 4 X 3.9-in; 370 mines.

Pollux
Originally completed in 1915 by Swan Hunter as ice-breaker for Russia.
2,500 tons; LOA: 211ft; 14 knots.
Armament: 4 X 3.9-in; 240 mines.

Netlayer

Le Gladiateur
1934
2,300 tons; LOA: 370 ft; 18 knots.
Armament: 4 X 3.5-in.

Sloops (*Avisos*)

CHARNER CLASS
*Admiral, Charner, Beautemps-Beaupré, Bougainville,
D'Entrecasteaux, D'Iberville, Dumont, D'Urville, Le Perouse,
Rigault de Genouilly, Savorgnan de Brazza Ville, D'Ys*
1931–1934
2,000 tons; LOA: 370 ft; 18 knots; diesel-powered.
Armament: 3 X 5.5-in; 4 AA.

ELAN CLASS
Amiral, Senez, Annamite, Bambarra, Bengali, Chamous, Chevreuil,
Commandant, Bory, Commandant, Delage, Commandant, Duboc,
Commandate, Rivière, Cormoran, Elan, Ensiene, Ballande, Gazelle,
Goeland, Ibis, L'Impetueuse, La Boudeuse, La Batailleuse,
La Capricieuse, La Curieuse, La Furieuse, La Gracieuse, La Joyeuse,
La Moquese, La Surprise, La Trompeuse, Matelot, Leblanc, Mouette,
Pelican, Regeot de la Touche
1935–1940
620–650 tons; LOA: 240 ft; 20 knots.
Armament: 2 X 3.9-in AA.

Anti-Submarine Craft/Submarine-Chasers
ARRAS CLASS
Amiens, Arras, Bapaume, Belfort, Coucy, Calais, Epinal, Laffaux,
Les Eparges, Nancy, Reims, Revigny, Tahure, Vauquois
1918/1919
640 tons; LOA: 250 ft; 17 knots.
Armament: 2 X 5.5-in; 1 X 3-in AA; depth charges.

AISNE CLASS
Aisne, Marne, Meuse, Oise, Somme, Yser
1917
600 tons; LOA: 220ft; 20.5 knots.
Armament: 4 X 3.9-in.

Conquerante
1917
400 tons; LOA: 220 ft; 17 knots.
Armament: 2 X 3.9-in; depth charges.

DILIGENTE CLASS
Diligente, Engageante, Luronne, Surveillante
1916/1917
300 tons; LOA: 200ft; 15 knots.
Armament: 2 X 3.9-in; depth charges.

AUDACIEUSE CLASS
Audacieuse, Batailleuse, Dedaigneuse, Etourdi, Gracieuse,
Impetueuse, Tapageuse
1916/1917
265 tons; LOA: 180 tons; 15 knots.
Armament: 2 X 3.9-in; depth charges.

Minesweepers

Ch, 1, Ch2, Ch3, Ch4
1935
150 tons; 20 knots.
Armament: 1 X 3-in.

Submarine Depot Ship

Jules Verne
1932
5,700 tons; LOA: 380 ft; 16 knots.
Armament: 4 X 3.5-in AA.

Comparison of British and French Naval Officers' Ranks

The following table needs some brief explanation. The comparisons are those officially accepted, but during the Second World War British frigates, and even destroyers, were often commanded by officers holding the rank of lieu-tenant-commander. Just as comparisons between our own services sometimes shows differences in responsibility or ranks for which there is no equivalent in another service, there are some differences here, in particular for the lack of a comparable rank for the two grades of lieutenant in the French navy. Midshipmen are included although, of course, these were not officially officers.

French	British
Admiral of the Fleet	Admiral of the Fleet
Admiral	Admiral
Vice-Admiral	Vice-Admiral
Contre-Admiral	Rear Admiral
Capitaine de Vaisseau	Captain
Capitaine de Frégate	Commander
Capitaine de Corvette	Lieutenant-Commander
Lieutenant de Vaisseau	Lieutenant
Enseigne	No equivalent*
Enseigne 2nd Class	Sub-Lieutenant
Aspirant	Midshipmen

* Equates to Lieutenant (Junior Grade) in the United States Navy.

Bibliography

Auphin, Amiral and Mordal, Jacques , *The French Navy in World War II*, US Naval Institute.

Baldensperger, Denis, *Mers-el-Kebir*, Rouf, Paris, 1967.

Cunningham, Admiral (later Admiral of the Fleet) Sir Andrew, RN, *A Sailor's Odyssey*, Hutchinson, London, 1951

Dear, I.C.B., *The Oxford Companion to the Second World War*, Oxford University Press, Oxford & New York, 1995.

Heckstall-Smith, A, *The Fleet That Faced Both Ways*, Blond, 1963.

King, Fleet Admiral Ernest J., USN, and Whitehill, Walter Muir, *Fleet Admiral King, A Naval Record*, Eyre & Spottiswood, London, 1953.

Roskill, Captain S.W., RN, *The Naval War 1939–1945*, Collins, London, 1960.

The War at Sea, 1939–1945, Vols I-III, HMSO, London, 1976.

Talbot-Booth, Lt-Cdr E.C., RNR, *All The World's Fighting Fleets*, Sampson Low, London , 1939.

Tompkins, Peter, *The Murder of Admiral Darlan*, Weidenfeld & Nicholson, London,

Tute, Warren, *The Deadly Stroke*, William Collins, London, 1973.

Vader, John, *The Fleet Without a Friend*, New English Library, London, 1971.

Varillon, Pierre, *Mers-el-Kebir*, Amiot-Dumont, Paris, 1949.

Index

NOTE: French warships are given only where they appear in the text, with a complete list of the fleet in 1940 provided by class in Appendix I, page 221.

Abrial, Adm, 93, 110;
Abyssinia, 19/20;
Achiary, Andre, 213;
Acre Convention, 187;
Admiralty, British, 47, 70, 101, 114/115, 133/134, 141, 147;
Admiralty, French, 115, 133, 142;
Adriatic, 1, 23;
Advanced Air Striking Force, AASF, 74–91;
Aeronavale, 144;
Afrika Korps, 166;
Aichi D3A1; 53;
Airliners, 15;
Albania, 23/24
Alexandria, 105, 107, 128–135, 139/140, 144, 185, 209/210, 213/214;
Algeria, 136–144, 173, 182, 188–203;
Algiers, 107, 136, 167, 188, 192–196, 198;
Alsace, 5, 38, 95/96;
Andalsnes, 69–71;
Andrea Doria-class, 55;
Anglo-German Naval Agreement, 1935, 44, 47;
Anschluss, 22;
Antsirane, 181;
Arab Legion, 185;
Arctic convoys, 53;

Ardennes, 84, 87;
Armee de l'Air, 37, 88, 107;
Armistice, 95–118;
Athenia, 66;
Atlantic Squadron, French, 34;
Australia/Australian forces, 19, 185;
Austria, 21/22, 127
Austro-Hungary, 19, 2, 23;
Awatea, 196;
Axis Forces/Treaty, 20, 22, 35, 144/145, 183, 201/202, 212;

Balkan Wars, 55;
Bakans, 176;
Baldwin, Lt (later Capt) George, RN, 193–195;
Battet, Adm, 198/199;
Baudouin, Paul, 100;
Bayeux, 172;
Belgian Army, 80;
Belgium, 4/5, 72, 74–77, 80;
Belorussia, 30;
Bergen, 68;
Bir hakeim, 165;
Bison-class, 184;
Bizerte, 35, 107, 217;
Blackburn Skua, 66;
Blida, 193;
blitzkrieg, 81;
Blomberg, General, 12;
Bolshevism, 7;
Bomber Command, RAF, 75, 91;
Bone, 196;
Bordeaux, 43, 152;

Bothnia, Gulf of, 70;
Bougie, 196;
Brazzaville, 162;
Brazzaville Declaration, 158;
Brest, 104, 108, 110/111;
Bristol Blenheim, 75;
British Army, 75–91, 175;
British Broadcasting Corporation, BBC, 153;
British Expeditionary Force, BEF, 75–91;
Brittany, 106, 141, 154;
Burrough, Vice-Adm, 195;

Cambodia, 159/160;
Campbell, Sir Ronald, 100/101;
Cape of Good Hope, 176;
Cape Town, 146, 214;
Casablanca, 35, 106, 116, 132, 147, 191, 215;
Casablanca Conference, 168;
Cathay, 196;
Catroux, Gen Georges, 159–161, 163;
Cavagnari, Adm Domenico, 58;
Centre Task Force, 191;
Chad, 157;
Chamberlain, Neville, 25/26;
Channel Dash, 108/109;
Cherbourg, 42, 91, 93–95, 106, 110, 141, 145, 154;
Chiang Kai-Shek, 18, 160/161;
China, 16–18, 20;
Churchill, Winston, 70, 89, 92/93, 95, 143, 147, 150, 152–154, 158, 168/169, 173;
Clark, Gen Mark, 188, 198/199, 211;
Coastal Command, RAF, 89–91;
Collinet, Vice-Adm, 215;
Commissaires de la Republique, 172;
Communism, 25;
Condor Legion, 21;
Congo, 157;
Constantine, 136;
contre-torpilleur, 36/37, 39/40, 94, 117, 138, 147, 184–186,205, 215/216;
Cordier, Abbe, 213;
corsair submarine, 40, 62, 215;
Council of Defence, 158;
Cross of Lorraine, 150–174;
Cunningham, Adm (later Adm of the Fleet) Sir Andrew 'ABC', RN, 27, 30, 56/57, 76, 107, 132–135, 140, 144, 175, 183–185,190, 195, 198/199, 209, 212, 217;
Cyprus, 183/184, 186;
Czechoslovakia, 22/23;

Dakar, 35, 105, 110, 132, 144–149, 157/158, 189/190, 198, 214;

Damascus, 185;
Danzig, 25, 27;
Darlan, Adm Jean Francois, 93, 100–103, 113/114, 120, 122, 125, 133, 140, 167/168, 188, 195, 198–201, 204/205, 209, 211–213;
d'Astier de la Vigerie,Henri, 213;
de Gaulle, Brig Gen (later Maj Gen) Charles, 43, 122, 124, 127, 146–148, 150–174, 177, 187–189, 212, 215;
de Hautecloque, Capt Viscount Pjilippe, 146, 157;
de la Borde, Adm, 113, 200, 205–209, 211;
de la Chappelle, Fernand Bonnier, 212/213;
de Lattre de Tassigny, Lt-Gen Jean-Marie, 171, 204;
de Pozamparc, Capt Yves Urvoy, 93;
Deat, Marcel, 121, 127;
debt, international, 9, 12, 14;
Decoux, Vice-Adm Jean, 160/161;
Deladier, 151;
Democraatic Alliance, 151;
Denmark, 68;
Dentz, Gen Henri-Frenand, 182, 185–187;
Derrien, Vice-Adm, 217;
Desert Air Force, 166;
Deutsches Luft Hansa, 15;
Deuxième Bureau, 213;
Dewoitine fighters, 194/195;
Dick, Cdre, RN, 198;
Diego Suarez, 180/181;
Dodecanese, 19, 60;
Doenitz, Adm (later Grosseradmiral) Karl, 48–50;
Dornier, 15;
Dornier Do 18, 66;
Dover, 93–95;
Dowding, ACM Sir Hugh, RAF, 89;
Dunkirk, 89–91, 93–95, 106, 110/111, 141, 145, 154;
Dutch Army, 81–84;
Dutch naval forces, 93;

E-boats, 54, 89;
East Africa, 19;
Eastern Task Force, 191, 195;
Eben Emael, 80, 83;
Eboue, Felix, 157;
Eden, Anthony, 168;
Eighth Army, British, 170, 201;
Eisenhower, Gen Dwight, 190;
Entente Cordiale, 1–5;
Eritrea, 19;
Esmonde, Lt-Cdr Eugene, RN, 109;
Esteva, Adm, 200, 211/212;

Estonia, 31;
evacuation, 89–95, 106;

Fairey Battle, 29, 75, 88/89;
Fairey Fulmar, 184;
Fairey Swordfish, 91, 109, 142, 186;
Fall Gelb, 75, 86–91;
Falmouth, 93;
Fantasque-class, 117;
Farouk, King of Egypt, 131/132;
Fenaud, Adm, 198/199;
'Fighting French', 163;
First World War, 3–6, 8/9, 15, 19, 38, 44, 48, 53–55, 74/75, 79, 83, 88, 95, 97, 101, 103, 114, 131, 150;
Fleet Air Arm, 54, 69, 71, 89, 91, 109, 175, 180, 186, 193,197;
Fliegerkorps X, 176;
Force H, 139–144, 147, 178, 197, 205;
Force X, 214;
Fort Dauphin, 181;
Fourniere, Capt de Fregate, 94;
franc-tireur, 101, 146, 169;
France, Battle of, 74–91;
Franco-Prussian War, 3, 38;
Franco, General, 21/22, 126;
Free French, 145–149, 152, 154 et al;
Free Polish, 69, 72, 85, 90, 93, 111;
French Army, 79–91;
French Cameroons, 157;
French Committee for National Liberation, CFLN, 159, 168/169, 172/173, 214;
French Foreign Legion, 72, 160, 183, 185;
French Indo-China, 159–161, 219;
French Morocco, 170, 182, 188–203;
French Navy, see Marine Nationale;
French Revolution, 7;
Frendall, Maj-Gen, 191;

Gabon, 157/158, 190;
Gauthier, Jean-Pierre, 41/42, 143, 147/148;
Gazala Line, 166;
Geneva Conference on Disarmament, 1932, 9, 12, 14;
Geneva Convention, 101;
Genoa, 59;
Gensoul, Adm Marcel, 140
George VI, HM King, 162/163
German Navy, 32, 36/37, 40, 44–53, 105/106, 128/129;
German-Soviet Treaty of Friendship, Co-operation and demarcation, 30;
Germany, 9 et al
Gestapo, 167;

Gibraltar, 35, 130, 138–147, 167, 178, 188/189,193, 195;
Giraud, Gen Henri-Honore, 167–169, 188, 198–200, 211, 213–215;
glider attack, 83;
Gloster Gladiator, 71, 75;
Godfroy, Vice-Adm, 107, 132–135, 185, 209, 213/214;
Goebbels, Joseph, 13;
Goering, Reichsmarschall Herman, 52, 110, 120;
Goemboes, Julius, 14;
gold reserves, French, 114;
Griffiths, Lt-Cdr, RN, 116;
Grumman Martlet/Wildcat, 193;

HABFORCE, 185;
Handley Page Hampden, 29, 86;
Harris, Lt Fraser, 195;
Hatston, 69;
Hawaii, 18;
Hawker Hurricane, 71, 73, 75, 88, 184;
Hitler, Adolph, 10–14, 20–23, 25/26, 31, 34, 44, 48–50, 65, 99, 103, 109, 119/120, 124, 150, 183, 201/202;
Holland, Capt, RN, 141/142
Home Fleet, British, 34;
Hong Kong, 19;
Horn of Africa, 19;
Hourcade, Capt, 212
Hungary, 23;
Huntziger, Gen, 99;

Imperial German Navy, 4;
Imperial Japanese Army, 16;
Inter-Allied War Council, 29, 76;
internment (French naval personnel), 116/117;
Iran, 183;
Iraq, 131, 182;
Italian Navy, 37, 55–60, 138;
Italian Somaliland, 19;
Italy, 19–21, 23/24, 34/35, 39, 47, 74, 115, 132, 141, 175, 177/178, 208;

Japan, 9, 15–20, 35/36, 46/47, 50, 74, 159–161, 177–180;
Japanese Naval Air Force, 53;
Juin, Gen Alphonse, 170/171, 198–200;
Junkers Ju52, 15, 21, 83/84;
Junkers Ju87 Stuka, 52/53, 88, 94;
Jutland, Battle of, 44, 175;

Karanja, 196;
Kessler, Contre-Adm Jean, 102;
King, Vice-Adm, E.L.S., RN, 184;

King, Adm (later Fleet Adm) Ernest, USN, 162/163, 168/169, 172/173;
Kirkwall, 70;
Koenig, Maj-Gen (later Lt-Gen) Marie-Pierre, 165, 173;
Kriegsmarine, see German Navy;
Kristiansand, 68;
Kupi, Col Abas, 24;
Kwantung Army, 16/17;

L'Orient, 42/43;
La Spezia, 59;
Lacroix, Adm, 207;
Landriau, Adm Marcel, 94;
Laos, 159/160;
Lausanne Conference on International Debt, 1932, 9;
Laval, Pierre, 97, 119–121, 125–127;
Le Bigot, Adm, 110;
Le Poittevin, Arsene, 42/43, 143, 189/190;
League of Nations, 14, 19/20, 182;
Lebanon, 137, 159, 161, 182, 186/187;
Lebensraum, 9, 12, 16;
Leclerc, Maj (later Lt-Gen) Philippe, 146, 156/157;
Legentilhomme, Gen Paul, 181,183;
Lepanto, Battle of, 55;
Lesjeshogen, 71;
liaison officers, 78, 117;
Libya, 165;
Liddell-Hart, Basil, 150;
Lillehammer, 70;
Lorraine, 5, 38, 95/96;
Luftwaffe, 32, 45, 71, 77, 84, 89, 93/94, 108/109, 113, 176;
Luxembourg, 85, 95;

M-class, 40;
McIntosh, F/O, RAF, 88;
Madagascar, 101, 129, 147, 159, 162, 175–182;
Magic, 177–180;
Maginot Line, 72, 74, 76, 80, 86, 90, 151;
Mahir, Ali, 131/132;
Maison Blanche, 193;
Majunga, 181;
Malaya, 19, 159, 179;
Malta, 35, 130, 138, 175/176, 180, 202, 214;
Manchukuo, 17;
Manchuria, 161/17, 50, 178;
manpower, 36, 41–43;
Marine Nationale, 34 et al
Marquis, Adm, 205;
Marshall, Gen George, 163;
Martin, Capt de Fregate Paul, 116;
Martinique, 114;
Mass Observation, 23;

Matapan, Battle of, 203;
Mediterranean, 19, 34/35, 130, 139, 175;
Mediterranean Fleet, British; 19, 34/35, 130, 139, 190;
Mediterranean Squadron, French, 34, 130;
Meknes, 117;
Mendigal, Gen, 198
Merchant Navy, 79;
Mers-el-Kebir, 35, 38, 105, 107, 132, 137/138, 140, 142/143, 177, 189, 205, 214;
Mesopotamia, 131;
Messerschmitt Bf 109, 52/53, 63, 71;
Michelier, Adm, 215;
Middle East, 15;
Milice, 125;
Montevideo, 67;
Montgomery, Gen (later Field Marshal) Bernard, 201;
Morondava, 181;
Mukden, 16;
Munich Agreement, 22/23, 31, 87;
Musilier, Vice-Adm Emile, 163/164;
Mussolini, Benito, 19, 21/22, 34, 56, 97, 99, 175;

Namsos, 70;
Nanking, 18;
Narvik, 68–73;
Narvik, Battle of, 69;
National Socialism, 7, 10, 13, 22, 26;
Nazi Party, 82, 110, 183;
Nazi-Soviet Pact, 26;
Netherlands, 72, 76–84, 96/97, see also 'Dutch';
New Zealand, 19;
No5 Commando, 180;
No.825 Naval Air Squadron, 109;
North, Adm Sir Dudley, RN, 147;
North Atlantic Treaty Organization, NATO, 61;
North Africa, 136, 188–203, but see also Algiers, Casablanca, Dakar, Oran, Mers-el-Kebir
North American Mitchell, 218;
North Cape, Battle of, 53;
Norway, 53, 67–73, 76, 118. 151;
North China Incident, 18;

O'Connor, Capt Rory RN, 134;
Odend'hal, Adm, 114/115;
Olliver, Marcel, 155/156
Operations: Barbarossa, 176, 178;
Catapult, 115–118; Pedestal, 202;
Torch, 166/167, 188–203;
Oran, 35, 105, 107, 132–134, 136–138, 140, 142, 177, 189, 191, 196/197, 214;

Order of Liberation, 158;
Oslo, 68;
Ottoman Empire, 182;

Pacific Fleet, US, 18;
Palestine, 182, 184;
panzer units, 28, 43, 82/83, 90, 109;
Panzerschiffe, 39, 51/52, 62, 66/67, 105/106;
paratroops, 83/84;
Patton, Maj-Gen, 191;
Pearl Harbor, 18, 179;
Peking, 17;
Peninsular & Oriental Steam Navigation Co, P&O, 66;
Petain, Marshal Henri Philippe, 97/98, 103, 119–127. 152/153, 189, 200/201, 204, 209;
Phillimore, Robert, 191;
Plan Z, 40, 48–50, 105, 107, 128;
Plymouth, 106, 114–118;
Poland, 12, 14, 23, 25–33, 65, 87;
Polish Air Force, 28;
Polish Corridor, 25;
Polish Navy, 31;
Port Arthur, 16;
Port Said, 185;
Portsmouth, 105/106, 114–118;
Prussia, 25;
Pu-Yi, Emperor; 17;
Punto Stilo, Battle of, 203;
PZL P-37, 28;

Queen Elizabeth-class, 38;

Raeder, Grosseradmiral, 44, 48/49, 51;
Ramsay, Adm Sir Bertram, 94, 139;
Rawalpindi, 66;
Rearmament, 12;
Regia Aeronautica, 36;
Regia Navale, see Italian Navy.
Reichsmarine, 47;
reparations, 9, 12, 14;
Reynaud, Paul, 4, 96–98, 103, 151–153, 155;
Rhineland, demilitarization/re-occupation, 9, 14, 20;
Riccardi, Adm, 57;
River Plate, Battle of, 52, 66;
Robert, Adm, 217;
Rockley, L/S Joseph, 142.
Ronarc'h, Capt de Vaisseau Pierre, 111–113;
Roosevelt, President Franklin, 155, 161, 168/169, 174;

Rotterdam, 83;
Royal Air Force, 15, 29, 43, 70, 71, 73, 86–92, 107–109, 129, 153;
Royal Egyptian Navy, 131;
Royal Naval Reserve, RNR, 79;
Royal Naval Volunteer Reserve, RNVR, 79;
Royal Navy, 3/4, 34, 44, 46, 48, 53/54, 61, 66, 68–73, 77–79, 108, 115–118, 184–186, 196, 203;
Russia, 16, 25;
Russian Civil War, 5–8, 25;
Russian Revolution, 6/7;
Russo-Japanese War, 16;
Ryder, Maj-Gen, 191, 195;

Saarland, 29;
St Cyr,170;
St Nazaire, 95, 111–113;
St Pierre et Miquelon, 164;
Scapa Flow, 66, 73;
Selassie, Haile, 20;
Senegal, 144;
Shanghai, 18;
Sicily, 176;
Siluro a Lenta, 59;
Simoun-class, 93;
Simpson-Jones, Sub-Lt Peter, RNVR, 114/115, 117;
Singapore, 19, 159, 179;
Sino-Japanese War, 18;
Smuts, Gen Jan, 181;
Somerville, Vice-Adm Sir James, RN, 139–143, 147;
South Africa, 181;
South Manchurian Railway, 16;
Soviet Union, 8, 16/17, 26, 29/30, 48, 50, 74, 82, 176,178;
Spanish Civil War, 20/21, 67, 124;
Spanish government, 98;
Spanish Morocco, 191;
Special Operations Executive, SOE, 171;
Sprague, Lt-Cdr, RN, 116;
Stalin, Joseph, 26, 30, 155;
Stavanger, 68;
Stimson, Henry, 213;
Sturges, Maj-Gen Robert, 180;
Sudetenland, 23;
submarines, 37, 48, 50, 66, 89, 105–109, 176, 202;
Suez Canal, 19/20, 129/130, 135, 176, 214;
Supermarina, 57;
Supermarine Seafire/Spitfire, 86, 109, 184, 193, 195;
surrender, French, 91–118, 154;
Sweden, 31;

Switzerland, 74, 124;
Syfret, Rear Adm Robert, 180;
Syria, 103/104, 132, 159, 161, 163, 182–187;

Tallin, 31;
Tamatave, 181;
Tangier, 191;
Taranto, 59/60, 175;
Thailand, 160;
Toulon, 35, 104, 107, 144, 146/147, 200, 202, 204–209, 218;
Town-class, 47;
Trieste, 59;
Triple Entente, 4;
Tronheim, 68–70, 72;
Troubridge, Cdre, RN, 1911;
Tulear, 181;
Tunisia, 182;
Turkey, 103, 131;
Type VII U-boat, 50;

Ukraine, 30;
Ultra, 177/178;
United States, 18;
United States Army Air Force, USAAF, 32, 197, 218;
United States Navy, 32, 46, 48;
Uruguay, 67;

Velchrezelt, 83, 88;
Verdun, 97;
Versailles, Treaty of; 7–9, 14, 20/21, 38, 44/45;
Vichy France, 35, 102, 104–127, 144–148, 152, 154 et al;
Vickers Wellington, 29, 86;
Victoria Cross, 109;
Viet Minh, 161;
Vietnam, 159;
Von Rundstedt, Marshal, 200;
Vroenhoven, 83, 88;

Waffen SS, 82;
Walcheren, 93;
Warenfels, 180;
Warships:
   British: HMS Acasta, 73; Achates, 197;
   Achilles, 66; Ajax, 66, 184; Ardent, 73;
   Argus, 89, 191; Ark Royal, 47, 51, 66,
   141/142; Aurora, 197; Broke,
   192/193; Bulolo, 195; Cossack, 67;
   Courageous, 51, 66, 73; Devonshire,
   114; Dreadnought, 3; Exeter, 66/67;
   Furious, 53, 191, 193–195; Glorious,
   51, 73; Graph, 63; Hartland, 196;
   Hermes, 46, 145; Hood, 109, 142/143;
   Indomitable, 180; Illustrious, 51, 63,

180, 219; Jackal, 184; Janus, 184, 186;
Kandahar, 184; Kimberley, 184; Large,
191; Malcolm, 192; Nelson, 39;
Neptune, 134; Parthian, 186; Phoebe,
184/185; Prince of Wales, 55; Queen
Elizabeth, 219; Ramillies, 180; Roberts,
196; Rodney, 39, 197; Royal Oak, 66;
Tynwald, 196; Vanquisher, 113;
Walney, 196; Warspite, 53, 69, 71;
Zetland, 193;
French: Algérie, 39, 207; Alsace, 38;
Argonaute, 197; Audacioux, 147/148;
Basque, 214; Béarn, 35, 37, 47, 105,
215, 217; Bison, 72; Bouclier, 93;
Bourrasque, 94; Bretagne, 38, 62, 142;
Casablanca, 206; Casque, 41, 143, 147;
Chevalier Paul, 186; Colbert, 208;
Commandant Teste, 205; Condorcet,
38; Courbet, 38, 62, 94, 114; Crayssac,
219; Cyclone, 93; Duguay-Trouin,
214; Dunkerque, 39,61, 106, 129, 138,
142, 202, 205/206, 208; Dupleix, 208;
Dusquesne, 135, 214; El Djezair, 71;
El Kantara, 71; El Mansour, 71; Emile
Bertin, 39, 71, 114, 217; Emile
Deschamps, 95; Forbin, 214; Fortune,
214; Frezouls, 219; Georges-Leygues,
147, 217; Glorieux, 206; Guepard,
185/186; Hardi, 113; Iris, 206; Jean
Bart, 38, 61, 106, 111–113, 215; Jean
d'Arc, 217; Joffre, 40, 105;
L'Audacieux, 40; L'Illustre, 63;
L'Indomptable, 40; La Combattante,
216, 218; La Galissonnière, 208, 218;
Le Fantasque, 40; Le Malin, 40; Le
Terrible, 40; Le Triomphant, 40, 117;
Lion, 209; Lorraine, 38, 62, 214, 215,
218; Maillé-Brézé, 72; Marseillaise,
207/208; Marsouin, 206; Mistral, 94,
116; Mogador, 39; Montcalm, 71,
217/218; Ocean, 38, 62; Orage, 93;
Oriole, 94; Painleve, 40, 105; Panthère,
209; Paris, 38, 62, 94, 114, 116;
Parthian, 186; Protee, 214, 219;
Provence, 38, 62, 202, 205, 208, 218;
Richelieu, 38, 61, 106, 145, 148,
215/216, 219; Sidi Ferruch, 148;
Simoun, 189; Souffleur, 186;
Strasbourg, 39,61, 106, 129, 138, 143,
202, 205, 207–209, 218; Suffren, 214;
Surcouf, 40, 62, 115/116, 215;
Terrible, 217; Tigre, 209, 216; Trombe,
209, 216; Tourville, 214; Valmy, 185;
Venus, 206; Volta, 39;
German: Admiral Graf Spee, 52,
66/67,109; Admiral Hipper, 62;
Altmark, 67; Bismarck, 50/51, 53,

105; *Blucher*, 68; *Deutschland*, 67, 109; *Gneisenau*, 15, 39, 52, 62, 66, 73, 105, 108, 129; *Graf Zeppelin*, 52; *Lutzow*, 67; *Prinz Eugen*, 62, 108/109; *Scharnhorst*, 15, 39, 52, 62, 66, 73,105, 108, 129; *Tirpitz*, 50/51, 105; *U-570*, 63;

Italian: *Andrea Doria*, 61; *Caio Duilo*, 55, 61; *Conte di Cavour*, 55, 57; *Guilio Cesara*, 57; *Littorio*, 55;

United States: USS *Arkansas*, 217; *Langley*, 46; *Ranger*, 191; *Santee*, 192; *Saratoga*, 219;

Washington Naval Treaty, 1922, 9, 34/35, 39, 45–47, 53, 55, 214;

Wavell, Gen Sir Archibald, 183;

Wehrmacht, 13;

Western Approaches, 66;

Western Task Force, TF34, 190;

Westland Lysander, 75;

Weygand, Gen, 96, 170/171;

White Russians, 7;

Wilson, Lt-Gen Maitland, 183;

Wilson, President Woodrow, 20;

Zog, King, 24;